The United Arab Emirates

About the Book and Author

The United Arab Emirates: Unity in Fragmentation
Ali Mohammed Khalifa

This first comprehensive book on the United Arab Emirates discusses the background, emergence, and development of the UAE as an integrative venture. Dr. Khalifa asserts that the UAE came into existence because pertinent political elites perceived that the emirates as individual entities were unable to assume the responsibilities of statehood in a highly complicated world, weakened as they were by over a century of dependence on a foreign power. He concludes that the UAE as a federation of ministates will hold together as long as major regional powers judge such an amalgamation to be in their respective national interests or, at least, not incompatible with those interests.

Ali Mohammed Khalifa, an administrative officer in the Department of Foreign Procurement, Ministry of Defense and Aviation, Saudi Arabia, received his Ph.D. in political science from the University of California at Santa Barbara. He has been a visiting lecturer at the Military Academy in Riyadh, Saudi Arabia.

The United Arab Emirates: Unity in Fragmentation

Ali Mohammed Khalifa

ξ

Westview Press • Boulder, Colorado

Croom Helm • London, England

This volume is included in
Westview's Special Studies on the Middle East

Copyright © 1979 by Westview Press, Inc.

Published in 1979 in the United States of America by
  Westview Press, Inc.
  5500 Central Avenue
  Boulder, Colorado 80301
  Frederick A. Praeger, Publisher

Published in 1979 in Great Britain by
  Croom Helm Ltd.
  2-10 St. John's Road
  London, S.W. 11

Library of Congress Catalog Card No. 79-4385
ISBN (U.S.): 0-89158-394-7
ISBN (U.K.): 0-7099-0111-9

Printed and bound in the United States of America

To my wife, Monira, who knows how to combine,
with remarkable skill and diplomacy, her two roles
as a dedicated mother and a devoted wife

Contents

Tables and Figures

Figures

Preface

Britain's 1968 decision to terminate its official colonial presence east of Suez as of 1971 prompted the small emirates on the Coast of Oman in the oil-rich Arabian-Persian Gulf to start the search for a form of partnership that would help them cope with a postcolonial era. Following three years of difficult negotiations, Abu Dhabi, Dubai, Sharigah (Sharjah), Ajman, Umm al-Guiwain, and Fujairah established the United Arab Emirates (UAE) as a federal entity on December 2, 1971. The seventh emirate, Ras al-Khaimah, joined the union two months later. Whether in content or context, this federation differs significantly from any modern federal venture anywhere.

This study is an attempt to trace the background, consummation, and development of the UAE as a federal entity in a primarily tribal culture. Tribalism, paternalism, territorial disputes among member states, and the immigrant phenomenon are approached as influences tending to hinder integration efforts. The quest for survival of the status quo, rising standards of living, the existence of a core unit, gradualism, the sense of mission, geographical contiguity, and cultural commonality are elaborated on as primarily integrative factors. This study also attempts to identify and discuss the political dynamics that shape the vital region in which the union has emerged, the role played by major regional actors in this emergence, and the significance of this part of the Middle East in the perception of foreign policymakers of the two superpowers.

Over the last few years, particularly since the energy crisis of 1973-1974, there has been a spate of scholarly works on the gulf region in both Arabic and English. I have relied heavily on these sources as well as on the various documents, mainly in Arabic, that pertain to the union structure and development. In addition, surveys and extensive interviews with selected members of federal and local governments at various levels, as well as with prominent members of the intelligentsia and the private sector, were conducted in the spring of 1977 during a two-month visit to the area. Questions in these interviews revolved around the internal political and economic dynamics of the union, sources of perceived threats to its integrity, and its prospects in the direction of either stagnation or development.

In consideration of the relatively short time since the union came into being, conclusions reached in this study must be viewed on a most tentative basis. Time and further research are needed in order to attest to their final validity. This is only a beginning.

This study would not have been at all possible without the understanding and approval of H.R.H. Prince Sultan bin Abdul-Aziz, minister of defense; H.R.H. Prince Turki bin Abdul-Aziz, deputy minister of defense; His Excellency General Othman al-Humaid, Chief of the general staff; and Col. (Dr.) Ahmed al-Malik, director, Department of Foreign Procurement. To all of them, I would like to express my gratitude.

Included in my scholarship was a two-month research tour to the gulf and the Arabian Peninsula during March and April of 1977. To mention here all of those who helped is absolutely beyond the scope of this page. However, I would like to thank H.R.H. Prince Saud al-Faisal, the Saudi foreign minister, and His Excellency Ahmed al-Suwaidi, the UAE foreign minister, for their timely response to my written questions regarding the foreign policies and relations of their respective governments. And for making my short stay in the gulf more fruitful and pleasant, I especially thank Messrs. Abdullah al-Shudukhi, Husain Abdullah, Mutlaq al-Ghufaili, Fawaz al-Kudsi, Khalid Safarini, and Abdullah Abu Izzah, all in the UAE, Abdullah al-Olayyan, Qatar, and Mohammed al-Romaih, in Bahrain.

In the course of this study, I have worked closely with Professors Wolfram Hanrieder, Stanley Anderson, Henry Turner, and George Haddad. They have remarkable abilities for inspiring self-confidence in their students. I am truly indebted to them for this no less than their diligent academic guidance.

I must hasten to say, however, that responsibility for errors of fact and/or interpretation is solely mine.

1
Introduction

One of the most remarkable postwar changes in the international arena has been the proliferation of sovereign nation-states following the liquidation of the Western colonial system, which, in varying degrees, dominated world politics for centuries. Whether this phenomenon is a stabilizing or destabilizing factor in international relations has been, and still is, debatable. In view of the delicate and highly abstract nature of the issue, it will be difficult to establish even a notion of minimum consensus. After all, there has often been, to say the least, a delicate balance between the national goals of self-determination and continued self-assertiveness on the part of the nation-state, on the one hand, and an international imperative, both moral and legal, for world peace and stability, on the other. It is not the purpose of this brief study to deal with such questions.[1]

What this study purports to do is to deal with another, though less encompassing, trend that might have gained ground, inter alia, as a consequence of the atomization of the political world into smaller entities that often crosscut cultural and ethnic communities. This trend is integration—integration in a specified cultural, geographical, political, and economic setting.

Integration as a Conceptual Field:
Current Definitions and Applications

The emergence of the European Coal and Steel Community (ECSC) in 1950 and the formation of the European Economic Community (EEC) seven years later have represented two greatly significant steps along the arduous path toward the total unification of Western European economies. Accompanying this trend toward supranation-

ality, and of no less significance, has been the increase in scholarly
interest in the concept of integration on national, regional, and
international levels. Conceptualizing integration as a dependent
variable, analysts have often searched for the causes that lead peoples to
unite, deriving, in some cases, from historical integrative occurrences
what they consider to be the missing links in the causal chain.[2]

One safe observation based on the Western European integrative
experience since 1950 is probably the fact that theorizing efforts have
often trailed supranational institutional development rather than the
converse. Obviously, there is nothing unusual about such a sequence
except that where it has occurred the theoretical assumptions,
hypotheses, measurement and verification tools, and derived conclusions have tended to be socially, politically, and economically more
geared to and conditioned by the Western European regional setting.
Thus, their applicability to integrative endeavors in other regions
should be approached with a sizable dose of caution. Before we turn to a
discussion of the unique features of the political system whose
integration is the subject matter of this inquiry, a brief look into some of
the approaches to the study of integration, both historical and modern,
might help illuminate the extent of their relevance to our case.

There are probably as many definitions of integration as there are
students. Two prominent and pioneering scholars of this approach to
the study of international relations defined the concept separately as
follows:

1. The attainment, within a territory, of a "sense of community"
   and of institutions and practices strong enough and widespread
   enough to assure, for a "long" time, dependable expectations of
   "peaceful change" among its population[3]
2. The process whereby political actors in several distinct national
   settings are persuaded to shift their loyalties, expectations and
   political activities toward a new centre, whose institutions
   possess or demand jurisdiction over the preexisting national
   states[4]

Both definitions involve the expansion of the spheres of both allegiance
and jurisdiction so as to transcend the preexisting national boundaries
of community members. Both have equally influenced later theoretical
developments in the area of regionalism.

On the basis of a study of ten historical integrative and disintegrative
areas, Deutsch and his Princeton associates identify two forms of
international integration.[5] On the one hand, there was the so-called

amalgamated security community whereby formal mergers had taken place between two or more previously independent units with the development of supreme central institutions that had the jurisdiction to make binding decisions within the union. A "pluralistic security community," on the other hand, had fallen short of legal merger and had opted instead for a mere closer cooperation among its essentially autonomous member states.[6] Given their loose structure, and provided their raison d'être was the preservation of peace, pluralistic security communities, the authors observe, were easier both to attain and later to preserve than the more formal amalgamations.[7]

The low level of mass political participation during the historical segments in which the authors' communities came into being apparently heightened the significance of roles played by elites in the formation of international unions. The convergence of expectations, the flow of rewards, and the compatibility of self-images on the part of key elites are held to have been crucial not only in the development of integration but in its preservation as well. Part of this elitist conception is the import accorded to core areas. "These core areas," according to the Princeton group, "were larger, stronger, more advanced political units around which integration developed."[8] The superiority of these units' political and administrative systems, their educational institutions, and the strength of their economies enabled them to assume leadership roles in their respective regions. Although Prussia played an elitist core role in the process of German unification in the last century, the present international system is replete with examples of unit leaders born outside and inside regional groupings. The United States obviously plays this role in any form of Atlantic partnership, in the Organization of American States, and in its relations with the European Economic Community. Britain has also played a similar role in the development of federations such as those of Nigeria and the West Indies and still does so today in the European Free Trade Area.[9]

Another major approach to the study of regional integration is the so-called neofunctionalism. The "functional" view of the development of unions among previously autonomous units finds its clearest expression in Haas's theoretical works on European integration.[10] Although concepts and conclusions of this approach tend to confirm and complement most of those contributed by earlier studies,[11] the functionalists' preoccupation with the inevitability, given certain conditions, of the politicization of economic integration has been a source of weakness in their theory. This automaticity of linkage between the two spheres of economics and politics, i.e., the spillover effect, has been expressed by Haas and Schmitter in the following terms: -

Integration can be conceived as involving the gradual politicization of the
actors' purposes which were initially considered "technical" or "noncon-
troversial." Politicization implies that the actors, in response to
miscalculations or disappointment with respect to the initial purposes,
agree to widen the spectrum of means considered appropriate to attain
them. This tends to increase the controversial component, i.e., those
additional fields of action which require political choices, concerning
how much national autonomy to delegate to the union. Politicization
implies that the actors seek to resolve their problems so as to upgrade
common interests and, in the process, delegate more authority to the
center. It constitutes one of the properties of integration—the intervening
variable between economic and political union—along with the
development of new expectations and loyalties on the part of organized
interests in the member nations.[12]

This continuum view of the linkage between economics and politics
provides the basis for the authors' conceptual framework, which they
construct around three sets of pattern variables. The background
variables consist of the size of participating units, the rates of
transactions around these units, the degree of pluralism within each
potential member, and the extent to which elites' self-images and
expectations are complementary. Variables at the time of economic
union are said to be the degree of shared government purposes and the
range of powers delegated to the union. Finally, process variables consist
of the style of decision making after the union is formed, the rates of
transactions, and the extent of government adaptability in crisis
situations. These nine observable variables might be empirically
measured along a high-mixed-low scale in almost any case of economic
integration.[13] The authors hypothesize that the higher the mark on the
scale for an economic union, the more likely its gradual politicization.
And since it is only in the case of Western European integration that "the
element of automaticity . . . is provided by the internal logic of
industrialism, pluralism, and democracy," a search for "functional
equivalents" in other cultural settings is necessary in order to
compensate for the lack of such attributes.[14] Indeed, *functional
equivalent* appears to be a catch-all phrase signifying those cultural and
environmental attributes characteristic of a certain transitional region
under the broad headings of leadership style, perception of threats from
the outside, sense of nationalism, and the like, as they affect the relation
between politics and economics, and as they play a central role in the
perception of policymakers from one state to the other within the region
and from that region toward the outside world.

In contrast to the heavy emphasis on levels in the course of integration schemes in the two approaches we have noted so far, Joseph Nye bases his conceptual framework on the "disaggregation" of the concept of integration into empirically measurable component parts. In Nye's terms, the concept of integration can be broken down into economic integration (formation of a transnational economy), social integration (formation of a transnational society), and political integration (formation of a transnational political interdependence).[15] Further disaggregations of each of these major component parts, along with operationalization methods, are provided. Disaggregation, according to the author, "will tend to force us to make more qualified, and more readily falsified, generalizations with the *ceteris paribus* clauses filled in, so to speak, and thus pave the way for more meaningful comparative analysis than that provided by the general schemes used so far."[16]

Of the three types of integration disaggregated by the author, political integration is by far the most relevant to this study. In this particular segment of his framework, Nye distinguishes four variables: institutional (jurisdictional and bureaucratic); policy interactional; attitudinal; and the security community elaborated by Deutsch and his associates.[17]

The concept of institutional integration revolves around measuring the bureaucratic and jurisdictional strengths of the central institutions in a union of political units. For instance, a researcher may choose to identify both size and growth of budgets and administrative staff of these institutions relative to those of member countries. Additional questions would be: To what extent are these central institutions autonomous? To what extent are they supranational; i.e., how binding are their decisions on all members? What is the scope of legal powers assigned to these institutions, and to what extent is it fulfilled in practice? Is the scope of jurisdiction expanding, stagnating, or narrowing? And so on.

An important subtype of the concept of political integration, according to Nye's approach, is the extent to which regional community participants enact public policy as a group. To test the degree of community in this area, the author suggests the use of three indicators. These are (1) the scope, or the number of public policy sectors treated in common; (2) the extent, or how much of a sector is treated in common; and (3) the salience, or how vital or important the commonly treated sectors are.[18] The second variable is not concerned with "the legal or institutional type of decision . . . [rather with] how much of the process of arriving at the decisions in a field is subject to group interaction as against completely independent action."[19]

The third component of the concept of political integration, in Nye's scheme, is the measurement of elite and mass attitudes toward the union in question. Most theorists in this field agree that it takes more than just the establishment of central institutions for a successful integration to be attained and sustained. A sense of "common identity and mutual obligation" should develop. Whether this sense of loyalty can be accomplished through strong central institutions—the federalists' view—or through gradual processes of interaction—the neofunctionalists' view—remains to be reconciled, though such reconciliation may well prove highly difficult. The point here is that of measurement. For this, various devices can be utilized, such as interviews with significant elites, content analyses of policy statements and journalistic commentaries, public opinion polls (an elusive device, notwithstanding), and so forth. Although these might be oriented so as to also measure the intensity of attitudes toward a union, gaps between attitudes and actual behavior, especially on the elite level, should be observed with caution.

The security community as a component of the concept of political integration is one of the oldest and most difficult to operationalize.[20] It centers on the degree of reliability of "expectation of nonviolent reactions" among community partners. Scales for this particular concept can be constructed based on occurrences of hostile incidents between member states, provided, of course, that reliable accounts of such incidents, if and when they occur, can easily be obtained.

In this section, we have underscored some of the most salient concepts generated by three approaches to the study of international integration: Deutsch and his associates' essential requirements for successful historical unions; Haas and Schmitter's background, union, and process variables; and the more horizontally disaggregated and comparatively oriented scheme elaborated by Nye. Against this array of concepts, we next elucidate the ways in which our subject of inquiry, the United Arab Emirates (UAE), is unique and inquire into the extent of this uniqueness.

The Unique Features of the United Arab Emirates (UAE) as an Integrative Case

For nearly a decade following the advent of the European Coal and Steel Community (ECSC), Western Europe provided the focal point for regional integration studies. Emulation of the European experience in other regional settings, however, has stimulated many perceptive students of the field to apply more or less the same principles, concepts, and approaches to the nascent regional groupings, in some cases with no adequate consideration of cultural variables endogenous to the regions within which such groupings emerge.[21]

But, above all, what sort of lesson has the European experience taught its students? The most precise answer to such a question, in the view of this writer, has been provided by Haas and Schmitter:

> Economic integration proceeds most readily and produces political consequence most speedily whenever there exists a considerable pre-integration network of trade, travel and *intellectual communication*. It [the case of Western Europe] suggests further that the political implications of economic interdependence become speedily apparent whenever and wherever the countries in question possess an *open elite structure*, a pattern of *industrial pluralism* in which each functionally specific group in one country easily establishes common values and articulates common interests with its opposite number across the frontier. Finally, a pattern of regional—rather than national—loyalties develops in proportion to the capacity of *articulate citizens to participate in policy formulation and to demand benefits* which can be linked to the policy of integration.[22]

If these are the background conditions necessary for the emergence and maintenance of unions, can the fact that most of the integrative ventures in the developing world have failed so far to "spill over," or even to "take off," be attributed to the absence of these factors? To answer in the affirmative might seem attractive in the sense that most of the developing regions are still dominated by nonpluralistic and highly stratified social structures, low levels of interest-group consciousness and political participation, and a heightened sense of parochialism and national exclusiveness. However, even in Western Europe, where the converse is generally true, the spontaneous linkage between economic integration and political union, i.e., the spillover from economics to politics, after twenty years of EEC existence, still lies in the future, if ever, now that its prospect has been weakened by the expansion of the community into nine members. It is conceivable, at least, that in all these unions, particularly insofar as economic aspects are linked to politics, there are more local, regional, and global variables than the neofunctionalist approach is prepared to accommodate.

The United Arab Emirates, or Dawlat al-Emarat al-Arabiyyah al-Muttahidah (hereinafter UAE), came into being on December 2, 1971, following more than three years of negotiations. The union[23] consists of the seven Arab shaikhdoms, formerly known in Western literature as the Trucial States. These are Abu Dhabi, Dubai, Sharigah (Sharjah), Ras al-Khaimah, Fujairah, Ajman, and Umm al-Guiwain. As will be emphasized later, the seven member emirates of the federation vary widely in terms of their territorial size as well as in the human and material resources they command.

Of all the regional integrative undertakings since the Second World War, whether in Africa, Central and Latin America, or in Northern Europe, the UAE contrasts most sharply with the European Economic Community (EEC). The remainder of this section is an attempt to elucidate the major factors in this contrast.

We can approach the factors that make the UAE a unique case of integration, by almost any standard, from two broad perspectives. The first perspective is the background of the union, encompassing those major factors/variables that emanate from the cultural setting or the particular experience of the region in which the union was later to take shape. These include (1) the sociopolitical milieu; (2) the historical experience; (3) the economic structure and underdevelopment; and (4) the participating units' variation in both size and capabilities. The other perspective, on the other hand, deals with the salient characteristics of the union itself at the time of its inception, which, to a great extent, can be considered a reflection of the preunion situation. These character- istics are (1) the elitist nature of the federation; (2) its development around a core area; (3) its security orientation; and (4) the political nature of its existence. We now turn to a brief discussion of each of these eight factors.

The Preunion Perspective

1. *Sociopolitical Milieu.* Until recently, the societies of the lower gulf had lived a predominantly traditional-tribal life. Islam and tribal customs, which in many respects predate Islam but were modified by it, provided the body of rules—tribal law—that governed the life of every individual in both its religious and secular aspects.[24] Political authority was invested in a tribal paramount chief who, though theoretically bound by no limits except as dictated by the Kuran, the Moslem holy book, had to incorporate in practice principles of consultation (*shura*) and coordination with tribal elders, religious leaders, and subchiefs without whose participation intra- and intertribal balance could hardly be achieved. This tribal pattern was further characterized by a tendency to form tribal coalitions in times of external dangers; however, these coalitions rapidly shifted according to the vicissitudes of tribal relations. Indeed, it seems that the best guarantee against the liquidation of a paramount tribe's authority was its continued ability to maintain its overall strength or, in other words, the skill of its chiefs to conceal its weaknesses.

In addition, individual loyalty was primarily lodged in the tribe, and the concept of territoriality in a modern sense came to be recognized, in the terms of one student of the region, only "when the British gave the name of 'state' to the sum of political influence that one of the undersigning sheiks could muster among the tribes."[25] Furthermore, political authority in this tribal setting was highly personalistic; it was, and for the most part still is, patrimonial in the sense that "the sovereign is located at the center of the political system [where] he is surrounded by advisors, ministers, military leaders, personal secretaries, and confidants . . . [who all share an] unquestioned personal loyalty to the leader."[26]

The relative affluence brought about by the discovery and exploitation of oil in the early 1960s has undoubtedly shaken the tribal structure (though by no means brought about its demise) through geographical and, to a lesser extent, social mobility, increased literacy, improved means of communication, contact with the outside world on an unprecedented scale, and so forth. These societies are now undergoing a rapid socioeconomic change with all the strains and stresses that this phenomenon might entail. This process, along with the nonplurality of the social structure and the low level of political participation and consciousness, helps to create the region's unique situation.

2. *Historical Experience.* The seven tribal shaikhdoms had, prior to their independence and federation in 1971, undergone a long history of British protection dating back to the first half of the nineteenth century (see Chaper 2). Though fundamentally of an imperial nature, the British control in the lower gulf differed in many respects from that exercised in Africa or in the Caribbean. Great Britain, for the duration of its protective status in the region, had taken over the two crucial areas of foreign affairs and defense with little or no interference in the tribal structure and pattern of rule except in cases when these might have intruded upon the fairly consistent effort to keep internecine tribal hostilities to a minimum. This resulted in a great measure of autonomy for the individual emirates; but it also contributed to the delay in political and economic development.

3. *Economic Structure and Underdevelopment.* Unlike the case of Western Europe, the lower gulf societies have predominantly nonindustrialized, single-resource economies whose strengths depend heavily on markets beyond their immediate surroundings. This is particularly true of the three oil-producing shaikhdoms of Abu Dhabi, Dubai, and Sharigah. These three units, though the richest and largest among the seven, can hardly claim to consume domestically over 1 percent of the oil they produce. In addition to their relatively low level of technological know-how and entrepreneurial spirit, none of the seven participating

units has been able to seriously count on any agricultural potential of noted significance. Thus, notwithstanding entrepôt trade preeminence of some of the emirates (notably Dubai) over others, the nature and structure of their economies seem to suggest that the extent to which economic integration takes place depends more on deliberate and planned action by the federal authority, rather than the gradual, smooth, and functional pattern characteristic of the highly indus-trialized economies of Western Europe.

4. Variation in Size and Capabilities. The seven emirates vary widely in both territorial expanse and means of power in a way perhaps un-paralleled in the case of any contemporary regional union. In terms of size the emirates range from Abu Dhabi's 26,000 to Ajman's 100 square miles. As to human resources, again Abu Dhabi, with its 235,662 inhabitants, is the most populous among the group, and Umm al-Guiwain is the least with its 16,879 inhabitants.[27] But it is really in national income, thanks to accidents of geology, that the variation is the sharpest. Again, Abu Dhabi, with a total revenue of over U.S. $4.6 billion (1976), commanded more than the other six combined. And even among these, income disparity is as great, reflecting variations in resources and commercial skills.

Main Characteristics of the Union Formation

1. Elitism. The catalytic role of a state in the formation of unions and/or associations of other, less powerful units, without actually joining such a venture, has been increasingly recognized as an important feature of regionalism.[28] In addition to the overwhelmingly superior material and diplomatic resources of such an elite-outsider, its task has often been facilitated by its perceived sense of neutrality, selflessness, and impartiality in bringing together otherwise disparate units. In the course of the UAE formation, Great Britain assumed such an elitist role in nearly the same manner that it previously played in the cases of the Nigerian Foundation, the East African Common Market, and the Federation of the West Indies. Similarly, regional actors, such as Saudi Arabia and Kuwait, out of their conviction that such a union would be a factor for stability, played important supportive roles throughout the assiduous years of negotiations.

2. Development around a Core. The overwhelming superiority of Abu Dhabi in both territorial size and material resources has enabled this unit to provide a core area for the development of the union. Indeed, it might not be an overstatement to assert that this emirate has the means to subsidize the federation with all the socioeconomic and political implications that might be involved. A discussion of whether this core orientation will be accompanied in the long run by a gradual shift in loyalties from the peripheries to the core, along with a development of common identity and regional consciousness, will be deferred until later chapters.

3. Security Orientation. For nearly 150 years before 1971, the seven shaikhdoms had been dependent on British prowess for their external security. When the British Labour government announced in 1968 its intention to relinquish the protectorate status in the gulf as of 3 years later, the question of security of these prospectively independent entities, particularly in light of territorial problems in the region (see Chapter 7), came to assume first priority. In fact, the overriding matter of survival might have charged the union with a sense of urgency seldom matched elsewhere. Moreover, the sense of security that has been obtained now that the union is a reality is probably more psychological than material when we realize, for instance, that the size of the native population of the new entity is only a little larger than the size of the armed forces of, say, Iran across the waters of the gulf. Nevertheless, it must be emphasized here that it was the perception on the part of those concerned that unity was more likely to discourage external ambitions than disunity, at least from an internationally legalistic and moralistic perspective.

4. Political Nature. The federation of the seven Arab emirates is primarily a political union brought about by the deliberate action of political elites. Its politicization has thus been abrupt, not gradual. The Western European conception of spillover is alien to this federal experiment. In fact, if there is any spillover at all, it runs in an opposite direction; that is, a spillover from politics to economics exists in the form of planning for economic development by relevant political elites and the more balanced distribution of wealth and economic growth.

Furthermore, to the extent that the union is elitist, core and security oriented, it might be considered a historical union by modern means. Although an external military threat was not considered an essential condition in the development of Deutsch and his coauthors' historical unions,[29] it was of overriding importance in the emergence of the UAE, even though its sources have not been clearly identified. Put differently, the union came to life in an atmosphere approaching what Haas and Schmitter have called a "creative crisis."[30]

From another angle, the federation cannot be considered one of nations, but of tribes within a much larger sphere—Arab nationalism.[31] Loyalty within the nascent union will somehow stay divided for some time. Its passage from the tribe to the federation will not only have to await the passage of time but also will duly require the persistent inculcation of federal symbols and principles into the minds of all citizens through a consciously dedicated system of education.

The Approach Utilized in This Study

In the last section, I have attempted to identify eight main factors in the background and in the formation of the UAE insofar as these factors contribute to the uniqueness of the federation vis-à-vis other integrative endeavors, whether in Western Europe, Latin and Central America, or Africa. In short, I hope it has become clear that when we talk of this gulf union, we are in essence referring to a significantly different cultural context.

Having this observation in mind, and by arraying these eight factors against the three approaches identified in the first section, we swiftly discover that none of these approaches can perfectly qualify, by itself, as a scheme for analysis here. To be more specific, only the first four of the nine conditions found by Deutsch and his associates as vital to the attainment and sustenance of unions can be said to have been significantly present at the time the emirates' federation was formed.[32] By the same token, the Haas-Schmitter approach, in view of the fact that it is based primarily on economic, not political, integration in one region, i.e., Western Europe, espouses some concepts and variables that are of little relevance to our case; most notable, as suggested earlier, are the two concepts of spillover and pluralism. Finally, the political component of Nye's framework seems at first hand plausible. However, this is only a part of his scheme, and even here some of the variables are more or less difficult to operationalize.

Does this mean we discount the utility of these approaches to the understanding of our integrative case? The answer is in the negative, otherwise we would not have taken the trouble of summarizing them here. The approach I propose to employ borrows from each. It is simply an eclectic one. This approach draws from Deutsch's historical study its emphasis on the role played by both political elites and core areas, as well as the security emphasis in the emergence of many political unions. It also borrows from the Haas-Schmitter framework those variables that are seen most relevant, such as size variation, complementarity of elite images and expectations, scope of federal powers, style of decision making, and the degree of adaptability of the central administration.

Moreover, much of the institutional, policy-interactional and, to a lesser extent, attitudinal emphases of this study, as subsequent chapters will show, owe a great deal to the framework constructed by Nye.

At this juncture, I would like to stop and define those concepts that I consider pivotal in the conduct of this study. For our purposes, the concept of *integration* refers to *the voluntary amalgamation of two or more separate, or potentially separate, political entities, some or all of which, due to factors peculiar to their own local and regional environments, might otherwise lack the means of viability on their own.* Needless to say, this definition, like many definitions, is designed to fit a certain case. Here, it characterizes the federation set up by the emirates of the lower gulf.

First of all, our definition of integration stresses action from above, i.e., at the apex of power. It leaves matters such as the transfer of loyalty, the development of common identity, and the like, as measuring rods to be utilized in the subsequent determination of the extent to which the integrative process is working. Secondly, this definition also emphasizes the voluntary nature of integration. Mergers that are effected either by the use of military force, the threat to use such force, or by withholding vital benefits are considered coercive and therefore excluded from this definition. In the course of the UAE formation, one emirate, Ras al-Khaimah, chose not to join the union until two months after its inception. In addition, the two shaikhdoms of Qatar and Bahrain both took part in the negotiations that led to the union, but finally opted for independence. The third aspect of our definition is that integration is viewed as an open-ended process with no teleological implications except insofar as it can be empirically shown to have contributed to the welfare of the societies it aggregates.[33]

Two additional concepts need to be clarified. On the one hand, *disintegrative factors* refer to those characteristics of a sociopolitical and economic nature that are inherent in the domestic environment of the union. These factors tend to affect the development of this experiment negatively due to the incompatibility between them and the nature of federalism in general. *Integrative factors,* on the other hand, are those contextual characteristics, inanimate or volitional, that tend by their very nature to yield supportive inputs either during the union's emergent phase or its later development.

To help our understanding of this integrative venture, several important questions are raised revolving around the concepts we have just defined. The main task of this study is to attempt to pursue such questions in their relevant perspectives in order to derive conclusions about federalism in an essentially tribal context. For instance, what are the circumstances under which the UAE emerged in light of the shaikhdoms' long history of de facto British protection? To what extent is integration elite inspired and forged; and to what extent, if any, is it mass inspired? What is the role of the federal institutional structure in the integrative process, and to what extent does this process seem to be succeeding on all major domestic institutional fronts? What is the significance of the existence of a core within the union? What are the disintegrative and integrative factors on the local scene, and how do they operate to hinder or enhance the union? What are the major political dynamics of the region in which the UAE is an actor? What types of variables might shape the behavior of the two superpowers vis-à-vis the region in view of its strategic and economic significance? What general observations can this study render in terms of the union's present situation and future viability in light of locally, regionally, and globally generated supports and stresses?

The UAE is a fairly new experiment in federation building. The circumstances of its emergence and development over the first five years of its existence, as well as its interaction with the gulf's principal powers, suggest several propositions of a highly tentative nature. These propositions are:

1-1. The UAE came into existence mainly as a result of the perception by pertinent political elites of an external military threat posed by the regional and/or global environments following the 1968 British decision to abrogate the protective treaties as of late 1971.

1-2. The less the number of the member units of a prospective federation, the better the chances for its realization and, then, growth.

1-3. The more capabilities a core unit in a federation has, the greater the acceleration of integration among these units.

1-3-1. Given the various constraints of the environment in which the UAE emerged, economic rewards at the disposal of the core unit are more likely to contribute to integration of the federating units than that core's military capabilities.

1-4. The more varied and developed the means of communication among member states in a federation, the greater are the chances for integration to develop among the same units.

1-5. The UAE as a federation of ministates will hold, and hence be categorized as successful, as long as major regional powers perceive such an amalgamative venture to be in their respective national interests or, at least, not incompatible with those interests.

  1-6. Major Western industrialized nations, including Britain, the former protecting power, perceive that the need for stability in the gulf region is greatly enhanced by the fact that this region supplies a highly significant portion of the West's petroleum demand and controls the world's largest known reserves of this vital energy resource.

The approach utilized in this study is contextually oriented. The first two parts deal with the domestic context of the federation. Thus, Chapter 2 presents a brief account of the British involvement in the gulf region over nearly one and a half centuries, including the British-initiated efforts of the 1950s at cooperation among the Coast of Oman's emirates. This chapter also traces the lengthy negotiations that started in 1968 and finally led to the consummation of the union in 1971. Chapter 3 deals with the federal institutional structure on the central and local levels based upon the union's Provisional Constitution. Chapter 4, on the other hand, discusses the union over the first five years of its existence with special emphasis on institutional integration and development. Chapters 5 and 6 deal with the local disintegrative and integrative aspects of the union, respectively. Tribalism, territorial disputes, political paternalism, and immigration are discussed insofar as they seem to contribute negatively to the process of integration. On the other hand, survival, sense of mission, improved standards of life, gradualism, the existence of an overwhelming core, geographical contiguity, and cultural commonality are viewed here as integrative factors and discussed accordingly.

The regional and international contexts provide the stage for the material discussed in Part 3. Chapter 7 deals with the regional and global dynamics that shape the area within which the federation exists. Thus, dimensions of political hegemony, territorial disputes, collective security, and radicalism are discussed. In addition, this chapter provides a brief look into the factors shaping the two superpowers' relations with the gulf region in general. Although material in the body of this study may tend to support or refute the initial propositions stipulated above, a discussion of such propositions and the likelihood of their verifiability has to await the concluding chapter.

Part One
The Union as an
Amalgamative Undertaking

2
Foundations and Emergence
of the Union

The federation that came into being on December 2, 1971, among six of the seven present UAE member states was more than just an expedient reaction to the British withdrawal from east of Suez. This union's background includes more than a century and a half of British involvement, nearly a generation of antecedent integrative—or more correctly, cooperative—ventures, and over three years of generally genuine and arduous negotiations. This chapter is devoted to a brief description of each of these background periods.

British Involvement in the Gulf Region

Long before the advent of the oil era, the sea-lanes around the Arabian Peninsula had been the target for ambitious maritime European powers whose main concern was the promotion of mercantile and strategic interests. The first European influence to appear in the region along these lines was that of the Portuguese in the early 1500s. However, a century later, this sea power's already evanescent era came to an end when in 1622 a combined flotilla of British and Persian forces captured the Portuguese stronghold at Hormuz on the Persian side of the gulf. For one and a half centuries afterwards, British, French, and Dutch mercantile interests competed, and on occasion cooperated, in the gulf area through the construction of trading centers (factories) at Basrah, Bushire, and Bandar Abbas. The consolidation of the British East India Company's control of the Indian subcontinent in the latter half of the eighteenth century, in the aftermath of the Seven Years' War, coupled with an obviously increasing hostility in this tripartite competitive situation, led by 1770 to the whittling away of both Dutch and French influences in the gulf region. This left Britain as the sole outside power, one whose presence was to be felt for the next two centuries.[1]

Napoleon's occupation of Egypt and his subsequent threat to invade India, coupled with the rise of the Wahhabis in Central Arabia, are two probably unrelated developments at the turn of the eighteenth century that enhanced the strategic value of the gulf in the eyes of the British, and thereby inaugurated an era in which politics came to be recognized as a factor no less important than commerce in British relations with that part of the world.[2] Indeed, as early as the 1800s, British colonial planners seem to have recognized predominance in the gulf as an essential ingredient in the strategy of defense of the newly established empire in India. For this reason, and to forestall Napoleonic ambitions, the East India Company launched a series of political contacts with local gulf authorities that led to the conclusion in 1798 of a Treaty of Friendship with the sultan of Oman.[3]

The first two decades of the nineteenth century witnessed increasing threats to maritime shipping in the gulf through acts of piracy, local rivalries, and lawlessness. Successive expeditions were sent to the area by the British government of India, in cooperation with Omanis, in order to neutralize the naval power of al-Gawasim, rulers of Ras al-Khaimah.[4] This goal was finally achieved when a combined British-Omani expeditionary force defeated the latter at Ras al-Khaimah in 1820.

The defeat of al-Gawasim on the Coast of Oman ushered in an era of relative maritime tranquillity through a treaty appropriately labeled the "General Treaty for the Cessation of Plunder and Piracy by Land and Sea." This 1820 treaty is significant mainly for two reasons: (1) it touched upon the most vital issues that had hitherto disturbed peace in the waters of the gulf; and (2) it was probably the first engagement to yield what was certainly a legal obligation on the part of the shaikhs of the Coast of Oman. In addition to the cessation of plunder and piracy by land and sea, and the mechanisms of its implementation and supervision, as detailed in the first eight provisions, Article 9 of this agreement considered "the carrying off of slaves, men, women, or children from the coasts of Africa or elsewhere, and transporting them in vessels" a form of plunder and piracy that all parties to the treaty undertook to avoid.[5] In order to administer this treaty effectively, the British developed a system of "maritime control" by stationing a naval squadron at Basidu on Qishim island in the Strait of Hormuz.

Tribal strife on land and at sea, however, remained outside the 1820 treaty, and such acts of violence continued to disrupt the livelihood of inhabitants on the peninsular gulf coast. Conscious of the scarcity of natural resources in the area, and with British encouragement and support, the powerful Gasimi ruler of Sharigah and Ras al-Khaimah, Sultan bin Saqr, succeeded in 1835 in convincing several other shaikhs astride the Coast of Oman to agree on the prohibition of hostilities during the pearling season for one year. This system of initially seasonal peace was so popular that it was renewed annually until in 1843 hostilities were prohibited for a period of ten years.

The Perpetual Maritime Truce of 1853, on whose basis the epithet "Pirate Coast" gave way to the more appropriate, though prosaic, reference "Trucial Coast," represented a significant step in the pacification and general stability in the waters of the gulf. According to this treaty, the shaikhs agreed to a "complete cessation of hostilities at sea" between them, their dependent subjects, and successors forever. It was also agreed, according to Article 3 of the treaty, that the British government would take over the responsibility of supervising the observance of this engagement by all parties and that, in case of a breach, the injured party would not retaliate before first informing the British resident, who immediately would "take the necessary steps for obtaining reparation for the injuries inflicted" provided that a definite proof of breach was in fact available.[6]

Other regulatory agreements between the British government and the rulers of the Trucial States ensued. In this category, one finds, for instance, the further suppression of the slave trade, the protection of telegraphic facilities, and the return of absconding debtors. But as the nineteenth century drew to a close, other powers, notably the two empires of Germany and Russia, had revealed, directly or indirectly, their own ambitions to attain positions of preeminence in the gulf.[7] Perceiving this development as a threat to its century-old dominance in the area, Britain imposed upon the rulers what later came to be recognized as the Exclusive Agreements of 1892. Each ruler of the Trucial States, and other neighboring shaikhdoms as well, was pledged not to "enter into any agreement or correspondence with any power other than the British Government," not to grant residence to the agent of any other government without the prior approval of the British, and under no circumstances to "cede, sell, mortgage or otherwise give for occupation any part of [his] territory, save to the British Government."[8] These three commandments in effect gave the British sole control over the two vital areas of defense and foreign relations of the various emirates.

By the beginning of the twentieth century, it became obvious that Britain's interest in the gulf concerned not only the promotion of its trade, the suppression of slavery, and the security of the sea routes to India, but also its supremacy and monopoly of control in the area over both local and outside powers. The determination of the British authorities to maintain such a position was expressed by Lord

Cranborne, undersecretary for foreign affairs, before the House of Lords in 1902: "Our rights [in the gulf] and our position of ascendancy, we cannot abandon . . . our ascendancy is not merely a question of theory, but a question of fact. Our position of supremacy is assured by the existence of our maritime supremacy."[9] One year later, Lord Curzon, in his capacity as the British viceroy in India, toured the gulf and revealed before an assembly of Trucial States rulers his country's perception of its status in the area in the following terms:

> We found strife and we have created order. . . . We opened these seas to the ships of all nations and enabled their flags to fly in peace. We have not seized or held your territory. . . . We are not now going to throw away this century of costly and triumphant enterprise; we shall not wipe out the most unselfish page in history. The peace of these waters must still be maintained; your independence will continue to be upheld; and the influence of the British Government must remain supreme.[10]

The discovery of oil on the Persian side of the gulf during the first decade of this century introduced yet another dimension in Britain's relations with the littoral states on both sides of this vital waterway. To safeguard its oil investments and also its overall supremacy in the gulf,[11] Britain introduced to the shaikhs yet another exclusive agreement that came into effect in 1922. A typical text of such an undertaking on the part of the rulers read as follows:

> let it not be hidden from you that I write this letter with my free will and give undertaking to your Honour [the political resident] that if it is hoped than an oil mine will be found in my territory I will not give a concession for it to foreigners except to the person appointed by the High British Government.[12]

The General Treaty of 1820 and, particularly, the Perpetual Maritime Truce of a later date, had inescapably given Britain the supervisory role of a policeman with whom engagements were to be upheld. For this purpose, Britain had established, in addition to its occasionally visible naval patrols, a system of political control in the gulf that was subordinate to the government of India. The highest British authority in this context was exercised by the political resident who resided in Bushire on the Iranian side but moved in 1946 to Bahrain. The political resident was assisted in maintaining the British presence by political agents and officers assigned to the various shaikhdoms. In regard to the Trucial States, before 1946 a political officer resided only during the cold months of the year in Sharigah Town. From that date on, however, officers were appointed on a permanent basis, and in 1953 the post was upgraded to a full political agency and was moved to Dubai in view of its rising commercial preeminence. Abu Dhabi, following the discovery of oil in its territory in the late 1950s, was assigned a political officer of its own. This office was later revised to the status of a political agency. When India became independent in 1947, the British establishment in the gulf came under the jurisdiction of the Foreign Office in London.[13]

For the entire duration of British involvement in the gulf, which ended officially in 1971, the various treaties, agreements, and engagements had provided the legal basis upon which this foreign power's behavior in the region was justified. But unlike British imperial ventures elsewhere, the relation here between the foreign dominant power and its clients on the peninsular gulf littoral was of a truly special nature. For the most part, Britain viewed its interests as essentially in the sea and hence adopted, more or less, a hands-off policy toward tribal shaikhdoms on land. Indeed, "the states were allowed to fight each other at will, provided there was no breach of the Maritime Truce."[14] In view of the self-interested British imperial doctrine, there was in fact nothing on land to attract the attention of an enterprising power. The climate was, and still is, harsh, and the resources, before the discovery and exploitation of oil, were meager. Even the long-established fact of protection, under which the various shaikhdoms had practically existed, was not legally recognized until 1949 by an Order in Council for the purposes of the British Nationality Act of the preceding year.[15]

To sum up, Britain's presence in the Arabian-Persian Gulf was initiated by private mercantile interests as early as the opening decades of the seventeenth century. The consolidation of British hegemony over India late in the eighteenth century naturally led to a concomitant rise in the strategic value of sea approaches leading to that newly established empire in the East. Not the least among such routes was the gulf. Through a number of treaties and engagements with local tribal shaikhs, starting with the General Treaty of 1820 and ending with the Exclusive Agreements for oil prospecting and exploitation a century later (whose acceptance by local rulers had not always been voluntary), Britain was able to establish with a sense of legality a monopoly of control in the area for one and a half centuries, to the disappointment of the various contending outside powers. In its relations with the local atomistic entities, Britain kept its involvement in domestic affairs, at least officially, to a minimum and was mostly concerned with the maintenance of the status quo despite the fact that one of the most salient, but obnoxious, features of such a status quo had been the many cases of protracted tribal disorder on land and, in some instances, on the sea.[16]

Following the fall of the British Empire in India in 1947, the strategic value of the gulf as a sea approach, which Britain had hitherto often magnified and used as a logical reason for its continued supremacy, decreased. However, two other factors, one economic, the other political, had by this time attained a high degree of significance sufficient to provide Britain with incentives for an extended and further consolidated presence despite the rising fervor of Arab nationalism. This presence was to continue for over two decades until the Labour government of Prime Minister Wilson declared in 1968 its intention to disengage from east of Suez in 1971.[17] On the economic side, there were the huge petroleum investments in the gulf by British interests as well as numerous other Western concerns. On the political side, there had been the onset of the cold war, with the accompanying perception of a monolithic Communist menace that would lose no time in rooting out Western interests if such interests were inadequately defended. These two factors also helped to change the style of British policy toward the Trucial States in favor of a greater degree of involvement in local matters, particularly those pertaining to administration and development. Changes in these two areas can be looked at as a prologue to the ensuing federation of the discrete entities; hence, their brief discussion is in order.

Antecedent Efforts at Cooperation

The gradual shift in British gulf policy from an exclusive emphasis, at least formally,[18] on the conduct of the Trucial States' foreign and defense relations to more interest in their internal affairs has had, on the positive side, the benevolent effect of breeding some instruments of interstate cooperation despite a long history of tribal strife and animosities.[19] Two important institutions that emerged in the early 1950s under British initiative and supervision are worthy of special note. These are the Trucial Oman Levies (later the Trucial Oman Scouts) and the Trucial States Council. Both organizations were brought to life by a foreign power, but they also inaugurated an era of more stability and cooperation in an area that had long suffered from the absense of both.

The Trucial Oman Scouts (TOS)

Having decided to play a greater role in the intricate internal arena of Trucial Oman, the British authorities opted in 1951 for the formation of a land force, the Trucial Oman Levies (TOL), that could, now that gunboat diplomacy was far less effective, give more weight to decisions taken by the political agent in internal matters. More specifically, the initial task conceived and given to this desert force was the maintenance of intra- and interstate peace and security, including the protection of oil survey parties against incidents of desert marauding.[20]

The TOL established its headquarters in Sharigah with an initial strength of one British major, two Jordanian officers and thirty-two lower ranks, all on secondment from the renowned Jordanian Arab Legion. Attracting recruits from all the Trucial States irrespective of size, the levies grew gradually until in 1955 they comprised a total strength of three rifle squadrons of some 500 men. Further expansion of this organization ensued, and by 1957 its task had been reformulated to center on "defending the Trucial States against external aggression, as well as maintaining internal security."[21] It was also renamed the Trucial Oman Scouts (TOS).

During the 1950s, the TOS was further enlarged and the pattern of its officer recruitment changed to more reliance on Arab personnel. The scouts' total human strength of 1,324 (December 1964) comprised five rifle companies, fire support units, transport and maintenance units, signal and medical groups, a training depot, and a boys' squadron and school. The total cost of the force amounted to £2 million annually.[22]

For the entire two decades of its existence under British jurisdiction, the TOS acted as a peacekeeping force throughout Trucial Oman, particularly in territorial disputes arising from further granting of oil concessions by different rulers. But the scouts also saw action in foreign territories. The two cases in point are the TOS involvement in the Buraimi territorial dispute between Saudi Arabia and Abu Dhabi in 1955,[23] and their participation in combat against insurgents in al-Jabal al-Akhdhar (the Green Mountain) in Oman who were trying to secede from the sultanate in 1957. By the time they were turned over to the incipient federal authorities early in 1972, the 1,700 well-trained scouts represented so solid a formation as to provide the cornerstone for a union army (UDF) that subsequently contributed to a smoother integration of the otherwise disparate defense forces of the member states by the mid-1970s.

The Trucial States Council (TSC)

Another major development along the road to federation of the seven emirates was the establishment of the Trucial States Council (TSC) under British supervision and leadership in 1952. Presided over by the British political agent, the council was composed of the rulers of the seven Trucial States. The TSC had no written regulatory documents of any kind and, more importantly, was allowed only to provide recommendations on matters of common concern. In other words, the council was a mere consultative body.

For a period of two decades prior to the federation, the TSC helped to draw these tiny entities closer together to a greater degree than any other British innovation in the area. What makes this assertion plausible is not the volume of legislative output the council was capable of producing, for it had little power. Instead, what counts here is the fact that this body was used as a platform for the exchange of ideas that, in turn, contributed over the years to the formulation of common approaches to tackling common problems. It is precisely the fact that a shaikh could spring out of his tribal niche to meet his counterpart, in a noncombat atmosphere and on an equal basis, that is of relevance here inasmuch as it contributed to the creation of the habit of peaceful dialoguing.

Discussions in the council, which met twice annually for most of the years since its establishment, revolved around common issues facing the seven states in general. Among such issues were problems of economic development; total abolition of slave smuggling and sale; traffic regulations; citizenship and jurisdictional matters; travel documents; locust control; education and public health, and the administration of programs by other regional states in these two fields; and regulations relating to the preservation of game in Trucial Oman.

In 1958, the council moved a step forward in the way of organization when three committees for agriculture, education, and public health were formed. Six years later, a Deliberative Committee comprising two delegates from each state was set up. The main function of this committee was to examine and prepare proposals for the council.

But it was not until the mid-1960s that a new life was infused into the council by, first, transferring the chairmanship of this body from the British political agent to whomever the rulers might elect among themselves for a specified period of time,[24] and, second, by the establishment of a Development Office and a Development Fund, both to function under the aegis of the council. It was also at that time that the TSC, with its newly created, and adequately staffed, secretariat, moved to premises of its own.[25] An Arab legal expert, Ahmed Bitar, was appointed as the council's secretary-general.

The establishment of the Development Fund indeed represented a significant step inasmuch as it reflected the rulers' genuine desire to extend their cooperation to concrete and practical issues of economic development and welfare. Once established, the fund received £1 million as a British grant over three and a half years, £250,000 from the ruler of

Qatar, and £40,000 from the ruler of Bahrain. But it was the contribution of Abu Dhabi, which by 1970 exceeded a total of £7 million, that represented the major segment (over 80 percent) of the Development Fund's revenues.[26] Before it was incorporated into the appropriate federal ministries early in 1972, the Development Office had covered much ground in areas such as road construction, telecommunication development, technical education, improvement of health facilities, low-income housing, utilities, and urban infrastructure.

In sum, both the common defense force and the TSC may not have represented a genuine and solid integrative undertaking that could at the end produce a unitary political structure for the entire coast of Oman. In fact, there were no such intentions in the first place. One interpretation of the circumstances surrounding the establishment of these two organizations, for instance, is that the British were attempting at the time either to consolidate their control in the face of a rising tide of Arab nationalism elsewhere in the Middle East or to escape the blame for being there so long and doing so little toward socioeconomic development. But the overriding fact remains that, in the wake of the creation of these two bodies, a system of communications developed on both authoritative and social levels. Rulers could and did, for the first time in the history of their relations, exchange ideas as a group on a face-to-face basis. This helped over the years in the emergence of some sort of consensus in the tackling of problems of common concern.

Also of some importance along the path toward integration of Trucial Oman has been its treatment by outsiders as one geographical and social entity irrespective of the territorial boundaries separating the various emirates. Kuwaiti activities in the fields of education and health, the British system of jurisdiction and political control, and the various UN development ventures all tended to impose upon the area, despite its centrifugal tendencies, a sense of uniformity, which later proved to be one of the catalysts in the process of bringing these emirates together. But it took over three years of negotiations to realize such togetherness, and then only formally. The following section deals briefly with those years.

The Arduous Path to Federation

The stretch of time between Britain's announcement early in 1968 of its intention to terminate its official treaty obligations with all Trucial States, in addition to Qatar and Bahrain, and the actual fulfillment of this promise late in 1971 indeed represented a critical period for the entire gulf littoral. Diplomatic activities during this period revolved around attempts to steer the emergent political structure in the direction of more political stability, which was seen not only as mandatory for the preservation of the status quo in the individual states, but also as extremely vital for the security and tranquillity of the entire gulf region.

The efforts of over three years of negotiations on different levels won the characterization of both success and failure, depending on the level of expectation an observer entertained. For those analysts, with perhaps an extra dose of ambition, who joyfully observed the nine gulf states (the seven Trucial States plus Qatar and Bahrain) declare their federation early in 1968, but saw their number dwindle to six as the months went by, the whole endeavor was doomed. But for others, who had in mind the characteristically turbulent background of the several ministates and the fact that efforts at federation following the demise of Pax Britannica— whether in central Africa, the Caribbean, Malaysia, or South Arabia— had all ended in failure, the emergence of a union of seven instead of the original nine was a great accomplishment.[27]

The first reaction to the British announcement of its intended disengagement came in the form of an agreement, February 18, 1968, between Shaikh Zayed bin Sultan al-Nuhayyan, ruler of Abu Dhabi, and Rashid bin Said al-Maktum, ruler of Dubai. According to this bilateral agreement, the two rulers decided to establish a federation of the two emirates encompassing the areas of foreign affairs, defense and internal security, public services, and citizenship and immigration. But of no less significance is Article 4 of this agreement, in which the two rulers extended an invitation, first, to their counterparts in Trucial Oman to "discuss and participate in this agreement," and, second, to the rulers of Qatar and Bahrain to discuss the future of the area in order to reach a united stand in this regard.[28]

The response of the other seven rulers was in fact prompt, and all nine heads of the Trucial States, in addition to Qatar and Bahrain, met in Dubai on February 25, 1968, in order to map out the future of their respective states after the British withdrawal (see Figure 2-1). Following three days of deliberations, the rulers signed a Federation Agreement that was to go into effect approximately one month later.

The new federal entity, as the agreement spells out, was to be known as "The Union of Arab Emirates." Its highest authority was to reside in a Supreme Council of the nine rulers. Voting in this highest organ was to be based on the principle of unanimity, and, hence, each ruler, in a manner not unlike the Trucial System, was to be considered primus inter pares. The drafters of the Federation Agreement assigned to the Supreme Council the tasks of drafting a "complete and permanent" constitution for the union. In addition, the council was to enact federal

29

FIGURE 2-1:

THE NINE GULF STATES--IN SEARCH OF PARTNERSHIP

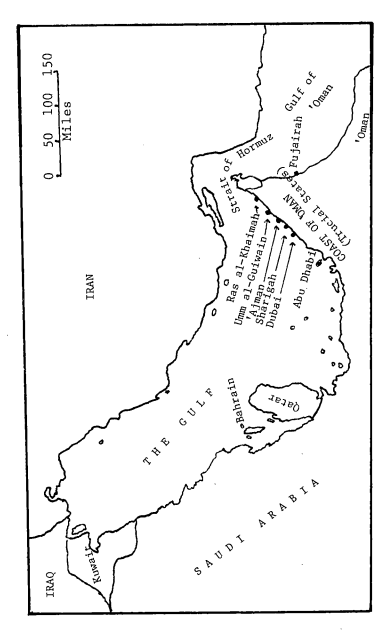

laws in the areas of foreign and defense affairs as well as economic and cultural matters (Article 4). Although Article 6 of the agreement assigned the task of approving and issuing the federal budget to the Supreme Council, it fell short of specifying the share of each member state in federal revenues.

Executive authority of the federation was vested in a Federal Council. However, its composition and organization and the scope of its responsibilities were to be defined later by law. The agreement also called for the establishment of a Federal Supreme Court to adjudicate in matters on the federal level. But again, the agreement was silent on the organization and jurisdiction of such a body. In the vital area of defense, Article 12 of the agreement invited the contracting parties to cooperate in strengthening their military capabilities in order to be able to defend their territories in case of aggression against all or any of the member states. The integration of the motley defense forces of the emirates into a federal defense force was not contemplated at that early stage.[29]

The 1968 Federation Agreement had brought under one umbrella nine gulf littoral states that varied greatly not only in size and levels of development but also in the influence and affluence each one of them could muster. This probably goes a long way in explaining the extreme generality in which the document was written. Once the rulers began to put the terms into practice, however, a chain of stumbling blocks stood in the way that finally led to the collapse of the union in October of the following year. The most obvious stumbling block of all, indeed the most serious, was the principle of unanimity adopted in Article 4 of the agreement. When negotiations started in earnest, each ruler soon discovered that it was within his power to veto decisions reached by the rest of the council's members should such decisions fail to meet his emirate's highest expectations.

From the date the Federation Agreement was signed, February 27, 1968, until late October of the following year, the Supreme Council held four successive meetings in an attempt to translate the terms of that document into a concrete and meaningful political reality.[30] The council's first meeting was held in Abu Dhabi on July 6, 1968. Early patterns of rivalry, underlaid by historical, tribal, dynastic, and personality factors, began to take shape. In this meeting, the positions of Qatar and Bahrain showed signs of incompatibility. One example of this bilateral rivalry took shape when the question of drafting a constitution came up. Bahrain nominated Dr. Abdul-Rahman Bazzaz, an Iraqi ex-premier, for the job. Qatar hastened to object, nominating instead its government's advisor, Hasan Kamil, an Egyptian legal expert of considerable stature. Abu Dhabi, however, opted to play a mediating role in this case by nominating yet a third party who easily got the assignment. Furthermore, when the question of a temporary federal council arose, Qatar saw fit to nominate its then deputy ruler, Shaikh Khalifa bin Hamad al-Thani, for the presidency of the proposed council. But Bahrain objected on the ground that the council's presidency is a full-time assignment and a deputy ruler was not likely to devote all his time to the job. However, thanks to Abu Dhabi's mediation, Bahrain was later to shelve its opposition. Other than some procedural decrees, i.e., the appointment of a legal expert, the agreement to rotate chairmanship of the council's meetings, and to designate the place of each future meeting during the session preceding it, no really significant accomplishments could be counted as the meeting ended on July 7.[31]

The second meeting of the Supreme Council was held in al-Doha, Qatar, in October of the same year. At the outset, Bahrain, peculiar as its position was (see below), suggested that the following round of negotiations be held in al-Manama, Bahrain's capital city. Other members objected. Other issues, such as the capital of the federation and the chairmanship of the Supreme Council, were also discussed with little success, due mainly to the seemingly uncompromising demands of some members. The only really significant accomplishment of this round was the council's decision to establish a common defense force, with its land, sea, and air sections, in order to provide for the security of the federating states. Two high-ranking military experts were to be appointed to prepare a study for the realization of this objective. However, as this decree stipulated, the individual emirates would retain the right of maintaining, or establishing, their own individual armed forces.[32]

The third session of the council was also held in Qatar in May, 1969. By that time, the Provisional Federal Council, assisted by several committees, was ready to submit to the conferees recommendations for the setting up of the administrative machinery necessary to run a full-fledged, modern government.[33] But the rulers got themselves entangled in more, seemingly insurmountable problems. Among these were again the site of the federal capital and representation in the Federal Council. On both issues, Bahrain took a stand that contrasted sharply with those of the others. Bahrain argued that building a new federal capital, a highly expensive venture, was wasteful and proposed instead the selection of one of the emirates' capital cities to be the seat of the federal government. But more important was the issue of representation. Having a population almost equal in size to that of all the others put together, Bahrain, not unexpectedly, advocated proportional representation in the Federal Council in place of the fixed formula adopted by the others, notably the smaller emirates. This meeting, like the ones that preceded it, did not fare with much success.

But when the rulers met in Abu Dhabi the following autumn, Bahrain was, for reasons to be cited shortly, in a compromising mood, so much so, in fact, that its position bordered on passivity. Hence, the council, after lengthy deliberations, found itself in agreement on several matters: (1) the election of Shaikh Zayed as the first chairman of the council for two years and Shaikh Rashid as his deputy for the same period; (2) the appointment of Shaikh Khalifa of Qatar as prime minister of the union's government; (3) the selection of Abu Dhabi Town as a temporary capital of the federation pending the construction of a new capital in Wadi al-Mawt ("Death Valley") on the Dubayan-Abu Dhabian border; and (4) the adoption of equal representation in the proposed Federal Council (four delegates from each emirate). However, despite these seemingly tangible results, the meeting ended abruptly when the British political resident had a note delivered to the session in which he urged the shaikhs to get the proposed union off the ground. The resident's seemingly friendly gesture was considered by some members as an unwarranted interference in the council's own affairs. The first to leave the conference table was Sagr bin Muhammed al-Gasimi, ruler of Ras al-Khaimah, followed by the ruler of Qatar.

In two meetings the deputy rulers, aided by several committees, then tried to surmount what the rulers could not. During the latter of the two meetings, held in October 1970, the conferees concerned themselves mainly with an elaborate discussion of the Provisional Constitution prepared earlier. The most salient points of contention in that document also centered on the site of the capital (Qatar wanted it to be specified in the document while Bahrain was in favor of postponing the matter until a permanent constitution was drafted); representation in the Federal Council (Qatar supported equal representation while Bahrain believed it should be proportionate to population); voting in the Supreme Council (larger states, notably Bahrain and Abu Dhabi, supported majority vote while smaller members stuck to the principle of unanimity); and the contribution of each emirate to the federal budget (Bahrain felt that income and size of population should be considered in assigning shares, while Qatar and some other states supported fixed shares).[34]

Indeed, by the end of October, negotiations for getting a gulf union beyond the starting stage had reached a cul-de-sac. One delegate to that last meeting best summarized the situation thus:

> We have now reached the point where some rulers have more or less convinced themselves that a federation is unworkable. Others have

rounded on the British and complained that they should never have set a deadline for them in the first place. . . . And the remainder with minimal bargaining power, appear to be delaying any cooperation until as near the deadline as possible in the hope of stampeding more powerful partners into making maximum last-minute concessions.[35]

During the same year, two developments, one regional, the other international, were of direct bearing on the gulf union negotiations. On the one hand, the long-standing Iranian territorial claim to Bahrain was finally settled through the good offices of the United Nations.[36] This change of situation perhaps goes a long way in explaining the change in the Bahraini position vis-à-vis the union from flexibility and compromise in the October (1969) Supreme Council meeting to a show of clamor and apparent intransigence exactly a year later. From the very beginning of those negotiations, Bahrain had the size and skill of its population as a powerful bargaining card to play. To be sure, it tried to utilize this advantage as a bargaining tool at the beginning of the negotiations, but because its very survival, due to the Iranian claim, was at stake, it logically did not wish to press too much for a status in the union equal to its weight. Instead, it viewed its assimilation by a larger Arab entity, at that time at least, as the best guarantee for the peaceful settlement of this problem. Once a solution was found, however, Bahrain saw fit to adopt a negotiating course that was perceived to be reasonably indicative of its political weight relative to the others.[37]

The other major development that affected the union negotiations in 1970 was the coming to power of the Conservatives to Britain. In earlier utterances, the Tories had promised to reverse the Labour policy of withdrawal from the gulf should they be elected. When Labour lost to the Conservatives, the new government in London, in an atmosphere of uncertainty, chose to send a special envoy, Sir William Luce, to the area in order to consult with all those concerned on what course of action it should take in regard to the previously announced policy of withdrawal. The reaction on the part of most regional powers, namely Iran, Iraq, Saudi Arabia, and Kuwait, was that Britain should honor its promise to disengage at the end of the following year.[38] Once it became obvious that the British were in fact leaving, each emirate began to search more seriously, in the midst of confusion, for some identifiable threads with which to weave its own future. Negotiations to set up a union were the most promising among those threads.

The impasse reached by negotiators by early 1971 invited outside powers—mainly those that visualized in a gulf union the best guarantee for stability in this highly strategic but volatile part of the Middle East—to intervene. In addition to the British envoy, a high-ranking Saudi-

Kuwaiti mission visited the emirates in an attempt to eliminate, or at least narrow, the differences seen as standing in the way of a federation. After some strenuous efforts, the joint delegation was able to reduce the points of dispute to two: the site of the permanent federal capital and representation in the Federal Council. In regard to the latter, Bahrain was even willing to go along with the others in accepting a fixed, but unequal, formula for the number of seats each state should have on two conditions, namely, that such a formula would be specified in the Provisional Constitution as temporary; and that in four to five years, when a permanent constitution would be written, not only would representation in this body be proportionate to the size of population, but also more delegates would be popularly elected rather than appointed by the rulers. The latter seems to have been too radical and premature a step for the others to embrace.

A great part of the blame for the collapse of the Union of Nine in 1971 should go to Qatar and Bahrain. The historical rift between these two states owing to territorial disputes,[39] with tribal-dynastic overtones, naturally spilled over into their attitudes and behavior toward each other at the negotiating table. The rejection of a proposal by one was in some cases less because of its demerits than the mere fact that the other might have sponsored or supported it. Indeed, theirs was a cleavage, not just a gap, and, hence, the incompatibility of their positions had driven negotiations, with increasingly less time left, into a vicious circle.[40]

As the date to abrogate the British protective treaties with the gulf emirates drew near, an atmosphere of urgency prevailed. The ruler of Abu Dhabi, Shaikh Zayed, expressed publicly his emirate's willingness to participate with any number of shaikhdoms in establishing a federation, and matters rapidly came to a head. The response to this invitation came in the form of a meeting of the seven rulers of Trucial Oman in July 1971. Topics discussed at this meeting included the establishment of a common police force, immigration and the means of regulating it, the British withdrawal, and the Iranian claim to the islands of Abu Musa and the two Tunbs.[41] But the most significant achievement of all was the rulers' agreement to establish the United Arab Emirates (UAE). Taking the proposed provisional constitution of the then defunct federation of the nine as a point of departure, six of the seven rulers agreed to modify that document in order to best suit the particular situation of their states.[42] Obviously, the most important modification was the abandonment of the principle of unanimity in the Supreme Council voting procedure in favor of a majority of five, provided that both Dubai and Abu Dhabi were in that majority. This represented a radical departure from the doctrine of primus inter pares under the British-controlled trucial system. In addition, the rulers agreed to contribute a fixed percentage (10 percent) of their individual states' incomes in order to finance the federation. They further elected Shaikh Zayed as the first president of the UAE and Shaikh Rashid as its vice-president, both for a period of five years.

In conclusion, for nearly the entire duration of their involvement in the area, the British had exercised only a minimum of interference in the sociopolitical structure of the gulf emirates. This state of affairs had undoubtedly helped these entities to realize autonomous rule in domestic matters, but it also had the dysfunctional effect of bolstering a spirit of parochialism along tribal and territorial lines. The British-initiated and controlled Trucial Oman Scouts and the Trucial States Council were two Johnny-come-lately attempts on the part of the British to introduce some sense of modern organization and development into an area that for long had been under their protection. Among other things, these two bodies can be said to have somewhat helped in the weakening of the age-old parochial spirit, hence opening the way for later amalgamative efforts.

The British disengagement announcement of 1968 was the major impetus behind the search for a more viable political structure. Upon the rulers' own initiative, a Federation Agreement was signed in the same month by the heads of the nine gulf shaikhdoms. The fact that this nine-member union was nipped in the bud has been attributed in part to the sharp rivalry between Qatar and Bahrain. But other factors from the background of the area, if only indirectly, were also involved. Apart from the varying levels of sociopolitical and economic development, the TSC and TOS, which in my view were both instrumental in preparing the climate for federation, were both limited in their spheres of action with regard to Trucial Oman. Moreover, it is perhaps of some relevance here to recall that the Dubai–Abu Dhabi union agreement of February 1968 had specifically invited the other Trucial rulers to join the proposed union while only inviting the rulers of Qatar and Bahrain to discuss the future of the area. It is conceivable that the two shaikhs, Zayed and Rashid, both of the Bani Yas tribe, lacked the necessary enthusiasm to widen the circle of union beyond Trucial Oman.

The UAE was declared a sovereign entity on December 2, 1971, one day after the official British involvement was terminated.[43] The new federation was later to fulfill all formal requirements for membership in the community of nations.[44] Federation may be looked at as a legal step represented by a common constitution accepted by all the federating states, while integration is a process that can be lengthy and frustrating. Before we get to this process, however, a presentation of the institutional setting of this incipient entity is in order.

The Union: Institutional Setting

Long before the principles and mechanisms of Western democracy were known to the peoples of Eastern Arabia, some tenets of a similar vein had already taken shape in practice as the bases of political rule in the area. Derived essentially from Islamic law and tribal customs, principles such as *shura*, consultation with tribal notables and elders; *majlis*, a tribal ruler's daily audience through which his accessibility to his subjects is assured; and *baiah*, an approval of, and hence a promise of allegiance to, an ascending ruler or an heir apparent by those whom he rules, are obviously the most salient traits on which tribal political culture has often been hinged.[1]

One way of adapting these traditional political principles to a modern mode of rule is to establish a popularly elected representative government in a manner not unlike that followed in Western democracies. Although the Provisional Constitution of the UAE, upon which the union was established in 1971, falls short of realizing this end at present, its preamble nonetheless envisions "a complete representative democratic rule" as the system's long-range objective.

The Provisional Constitution (hereinafter the constitution) incorporates many of the principles of Western constitutionalism relating to the individual's basic rights and obligations into the local Islamic culture, with the latter's emphasis on individual acquiescence and respect for established authority.[2] It further adopts the classical Western model of the trinity of government with legislative, executive, and judicial functions, even though, in this particular case, the balance among governmental organs performing such functions is less emphasized.

In contrast to the many cases of often frustrated ventures at constitution building among new nations (and perhaps old ones as well), the UAE's is apparently a live document. There are at least five basic grounds for this assertion. First, it is the first constitution ever to be promulgated in what was formerly called Trucial Oman. Its novelty has more or less created a sense of enthusiasm bolstered by the notion of securing a more enlightened self-rule. Second, and more significant, this document is based on the voluntary acceptance by local authorities of the seven member units after some lengthy efforts at cajoling and compromising. In a sense, it can be viewed as both an expression of the status quo and a perpetuator of it insofar as traditional authority tries to adapt, cautiously and gradually, to changing times and circumstances.

The third reason the UAE constitution is an important document is that it provides the main basis for political action by both national and local governments. Hence, its subjects are not only individuals, i.e., nationals, as in the case of a unitary system, but, in addition, seven semiautonomous political and administrative entities that ought to look toward the constitution as the sole regulator of their interrelationships, and the only source of their respective powers and individual autonomies.[3] Fourth, whatever promises of material rewards this document purports to deliver to its constituents, individuals and political units, seem to have been faithfully kept by the increasing wealth of Abu-Dhabi, the federation's core-unit and its most influential member. Fifth, and finally, the constitution achieved on December 2, 1976 a new lease on life for another half decade. As years pass, through trial and error, amending and rescinding, this document may well one day achieve a permanent status.[4] It is mainly because of these reasons that a closer look into the constitution, as the basic and most significant document of the union, is warranted.

Concentrating on basically the structural-functional aspects of the union, this chapter deals with a number of questions. For example, what are the prerogatives of the authorities on the two levels of the federation, national and emirate, and how do these two interrelate? In what ways is authority divided on the federal level, and how do the domains of these branches intermesh? How is the legislative process supposed to function as laws and decrees are enacted? Dealing with such questions is essential before we move on to the dynamics of the union's governmental organization—a topic that will be spared for the next chapter.

Two Levels of Government:
Domains and Interrelationships

In its very opening provisions, the constitution sets forth the decision of the six emirates of Abu Dhabi, Dubai, Sharigah, Ajman, Umm al-Guiwain, and Fujairah[5] to establish an Arab federal state that, upon the unanimous approval of the Supreme Council of the Union, will welcome any other independent Arab country to join and "exercise sovereignty on all territories and territorial waters within the international boundaries of the member-Emirates." But it also stipulates that the member emirates shall "exercise sovereignty on their respective territories and territorial waters in all matters that do not fall within the domain of the union in accordance with this Constitution." Moreover, the constitution views the people of the union as "one people" of one nationality, one official language (Arabic), and one official religion (Islam). A permanent capital for the union is [*sic*] to be built on the Abu Dhabi–Dubai joint border within seven years from the date this document becomes operative. Until then, however, Abu Dhabi Town is to be the temporary seat of the union.[6] On the economic plane, the constitution specifically states that member emirates "shall form one single economic and customs unit" within which "the free movement of capital and goods . . . shall be guaranteed and can only be restricted by a Federal law." In addition, "all taxes, fees, excise and royalties levied on the movement of goods from one Emirate to another within the Union shall be abolished."[7]

Before we delve into the allocation of domains between the union and its member emirates, it might be fitting to point out what sorts of aims and purposes the constitution spells out for this amalgamative undertaking. Specifically there are three sets of aims and purposes toward which the union is supposed to strive. On a general and abstract level, the union has the avowed purpose of realizing "a better life, a more solid stability and a higher international status for the emirates and their people."[8] Then, as a preliminary step in the interpretation of these general goals in the national arena, the union is to aim at the preservation of its independence, sovereignty, security, and stability; the repulsion of an aggression against its entity or the entities of the member emirates; the safeguarding of the rights and liberties of the people of the union; the realization of a cohesive cooperation among the emirates on the basis of mutual respect for independence and sovereignty in matters relating to their internal affairs; and the realization of a better life for all the citizens of the federation.[9] The third set of aims revolves around the constitution's prescription of ends toward which the foreign policy of the union is supposed to be geared. In this respect, the support of Islamic and Arab issues and interests and the consolidation of "ties of friendship and cooperation with all states and nations on the basis of the United Nations Charter and the International Code of Ethics" are clearly stipulated.[10]

In a manner not unlike that adopted much earlier by the United States

Constitution, the UAE delegates specific powers to the union government leaving the rest, i.e., any areas that are not designated, to the member emirates. It might be deduced that the delegation of authority to the upper layer of the union by the states would enhance, as is probably the case in the United States, the overall position of the former. However, as we will soon discover in the case of the emirates and their union, a reserved authority can be a lot of authority.

In the area of foreign policy, the constitution charges the union authority with almost all matters ordinarily performed by government in a unitary system. The UAE federal government is alone responsible for planning and directing the foreign policy of the union along with all legislative and executive steps that may be required for the realization of a "sound, efficient, and cohesive foreign policy."[11] With some exceptions to be identified later, the union has monopoly over the conclusion of treaties and international agreements to which the UAE is a party.[12] In addition, it is solely responsible for appointing diplomatic and consular representatives of the union abroad and receiving the credentials of their counterparts accredited to the UAE.[13] The declaration of a defensive war and the protection of union nationals abroad are also the sole responsibility of federal authorities.[14] Finally, the constitution also accords the union the task of defining its own territorial waters along with the regulation of navigation on the high seas.[15]

If the federal government has near-total control over the conduct of foreign affairs, as is the case in many federal systems, the asymmetry is certainly not as pronounced in matters of domestic concern. The emirates' competition with the union government in this arena is, in theory at least, what makes the union of the UAE justifiably a federal entity. In the domestic context, the constitution delegates to the union exclusively all legislative and executive functions pertaining to (1) the federal armed forces and the related matters of defense and security of the federation against all threats, external or internal; (2) matters pertaining to security and order in the permanent capital of the union; (3) affairs of federal employees and the judiciary; (4) union finances, taxes, fees, royalties and general loans; (5) postal, telegraph, telephone, wireless and electrical services; (6) education, public health and medical services; (7) money and currency; (8) measures and weights; (9) construction of roads that the Supreme Council of the Union (SCU) determines are main highways along with the maintenance and improvement of, and the regulation of traffic on, such roads; (10) air traffic control and the licensing of aircrafts and pilots; (11) federal nationality, passports, residence, and immigration; (12) federal property; (13) census and

statistics connected to federal purposes; and (14) federal information.[16]
  On another level, Article 121 of the constitution stipulates that

> The Union shall be responsible for legislation with regard to the
> following matters: Labor relations and social security—estates owner-
> ship and expropriation for public interests—extradition of criminals—
> banks—insurance—protection of animal and agricultural resources—
> major legislation connected with penal laws, commercial and civic affairs,
> companies, procedures before penal and civic courts—protection of
> writers, composers, industrial, artistic and literary copyrights—publica-
> tions—importation of weapons and ammunition unless it is imported for
> the use of the armed and security forces of any Emirate—other aviation
> matters which are not within the domain of the Union's executive
> prerogatives—defining the territorial waters and regulating navigation
> on the high seas.

In regard to the lower layer of the federal structure, the emirates, the
constitution states clearly that all matters not specifically stipulated as
falling within federal jurisdiction are to be considered within the
domain of the member emirates.[17] But the constitution also hastens to
ascertain its supremacy and the supremacy of any federal law, decree, or
decision that may be based on its overall local legislation in case of
contravention.[18]
  With this hierarchical arrangement in mind, the member emirates
have, according to the constitution, sovereignty over their territories and
territorial waters, including control of natural wealth and resources
within their borders. They may maintain their own flags for local
display. They also have the right, upon the approval of the Supreme
Council, to form administrative or political units with one another. And
they are even empowered to raise and maintain their own armed forces.[19]
In the realm of foreign affairs, the member emirates may "conclude
limited agreements of purely local administrative nature with the
neighboring states—provided the Supreme Council of the Union is
notified in advance." In addition, any one of them may retain its
membership in the Organization of Petroleum Exporting Countries
(OPEC) and/or the Organization of Arab Petroleum Exporting
Countries (OAPEC), or they may even join either of these two
organizations any time they so desire.[20] The constitution also prescribes
that federal authorities should consult with any member emirate prior to
the conclusion of any international agreement or treaty that might affect
the status of such emirate. In case of dispute over this matter, referral to
the Federal Supreme Court for a decision should follow.[21]
  We touched above on matters that the constitution reserves

specifically and exclusively for the union government for both legislation and execution. Then, we moved on to areas in which the federal government is empowered only to legislate, leaving the implementation to others. These "others" are actually the emirates. Not only do these entities, through their own administrative machineries, execute federal legislation, but they are also entitled to make laws on such matters as long as they keep in mind the supremacy of federal laws, decrees, decisions, regulations, and, above all, the constitution.[22]

There are several ways to interpret a constitution. One way to read the document that brought seven gulf emirates together in 1971-1972 is to conclude that despite the wide spectrum of powers allotted the member states, the constitution in actuality considers them no more than mere administrative units charged with the execution of federal policy in their respective territories. However, as hopefully will become clear in the next section, the Supreme Council of the Union stands at the apex of both legislative and executive authorities in the union. The council is composed of the seven rulers of the member emirates.[23] Hence, each emirate has tremendous leverage in the conduct of union affairs through its chief executive. Indeed, whether the union is bolstered or retarded, whether it is pushed ahead along the path of integration or left to stagnate, will greatly depend, for some time to come, on the attitudes of the heads of the emirates—the rulers.

The Federal Structure—Unbalanced Tripartition

The principle of the separation of powers adopted in many federal systems cannot be easily identified in the organization of the UAE. The constitution lists the five major structures on the federal level (Fig. 3.1): the Supreme Council of the Union (SCU), the president of the union and his deputy, the Union's Council of Ministers, the Federal National Council (FNC), and the federal judiciary.[24] Beyond the mere fact of these organs' formal existence is the question of which is supposed to perform which legislative, executive, and judicial functions. This is obviously the crux of the matter in this survey.[25]

The Supreme Council of the Union

The Supreme Council of the Union (SCU) represents the highest authority in the land. It consists of all the rulers of the member emirates, or their deputies in case any of the former should be unable to attend for any reason. The council holds its ordinary closed sessions in the federal capital, or in any place of its own choosing, once every two months for an annual term of no less than eight months starting the first week of October. This body can also be convened extraordinarily based on an invitation by its chairman or any of its members. For its meetings to be legal, at least five of its seven members, including Abu Dhabi and Dubai, have to be present. Although each emirate has one vote in the council, not all of these votes are of equal weight. For a decision to be passed on substantive matters concerning the union's general policies, the ratification of international treaties, agreements, and draft laws, the appointment of a prime minister, a declaration of war, the imposition of martial law, and the like, a majority of five, including the two votes of Abu Dhabi and Dubai, is required. However, in the case of procedural issues, i.e., the date and place of the council's meetings, the inclusion of a subject not already on the agenda, the method of voting on a certain issue, whether or not to enter a certain item in the record of the council's session or to invite a certain individual to testify, etc., the rule of a simple majority applies.[26]

The SCU can be viewed in effect as a body of collective leadership that has the final say in almost all matters of significance in the union's authoritative structure. The constitution delegates a wide range of responsibilities to this federal organ whose composition, among other things, reflects a sense of autocracy in a collective form. Whether by itself or in conjunction with other federal authorities, the SCU has several constitutional powers, only the most salient of which are identified here.

First of all, the SCU plans the general policy of the union in pursuance of the aims and purposes set forth by the constitution. In the process of this planning, the common interests and welfare of the member emirates are also to be considered.[27] Second, the council elects among its members both the president and vice-president of the union for a five-year term. This is accomplished by secret ballot and is considered a substantive issue on which five out of seven, including the two veto emirates, have to cast their positive votes.[28] Third, it has the exclusive prerogative of admitting new members into the union. Conditions that apply in this particular case are that a prospective member should be an independent Arab country and that admission should be by a unanimous vote.[29] Fourth, the Supreme Council also has the power to ratify the appointment, resignation, or dismissal of the federal prime minister and the president and member judges of the Federal Supreme Court.[30] Fifth, among the prerogatives of the SCU is also the ratification of international treaties and agreements, in addition to all decrees relating to the imposition or lifting of martial law and the declaration of a defensive war.[31] Sixth, it ratifies, furthermore, all federal laws including those of the general annual budget and the closing account, i.e., a balance sheet indicating actual expenditures.[32] Seventh, because it is at the top of the federal structure, this body is also assigned the task of supervising all union affairs, internal and external. This particular function is stressed by the fact that the prime minister and any member of his cabinet are, collectively as well as individually, accountable politically and in regard to the discharge of their duties not only to the president of the union but the Supreme Council as well.[33] Finally, the SCU's approval must also be secured before any of the member emirates is able to utilize union troops in case of need, before two or more of these states can politically or administratively amalgamate, and before any one of them is able to engage in agreement making with any of the neighboring countries.[34]

In view of the dual roles played by members of the SCU, i.e., the highest authorities in the federal government and also de jure chief executives in their own emirates, and the fact that it ordinarily meets only four times annually, the council according to the constitution delegates some of its powers while not in session to the president of the union and the Council of Ministers together to "issue whatever decrees are necessary." However, ratification of international treaties and agreements, enforcement and lifting of martial law, declaration of war, and the appointment of the president and member judges of the Supreme Court under no circumstances can be delegated.[35]

The President of the Union and His Deputy

The presidency and vice-presidency of the union (the constitution seems to lend the latter no less emphasis) are two legislative-executive posts of great significance. They both are elected by the SCU for a period of five years subject to renewal. They both have to be sworn in before the SCU prior to assuming their responsibilities. The vice-president takes over all responsibilities of the president in case of the latter's absence. If, because of death, resignation, or termination of emirate rule, either of the two posts becomes vacant, then the SCU is to be convened within a month in order to elect a successor for the remaining duration of the term. If, however, both become vacant for any reason, the council is to be immediately convened for the election of a new president and vice-president.[36]

The president of the union has a wide range of constitutional powers. Three categories in this respect can be identified. These are (1) those duties that the president discharges on his own and by virtue of his office; (2) those responsibilities that he exercises either in conjunction with the SCU alone or with this body and the Council of Ministers together; and (3) those powers that he exercises through the Council of Ministers.

In his capacity as the chief executive, and in the first of the three categories outlined above, the president represents the union both domestically and internationally. He also convenes the SCU, presides over its meetings, directs its discussions, and declares an end to its sessions. Furthermore, the president may convoke both the SCU and the Council of Ministers for a conference whenever needed. He also presides over the meetings of the Supreme Council for Defense (SCD) in his capacity as the commander-in-chief of the armed forces.[37] He further signs the credentials of the union's diplomatic representatives abroad and likewise accepts those presented by foreign diplomatic representatives accredited to the union, including their pertinent letters of credence. The president, in addition, is empowered to pardon and/or commute sentences, and no death sentence can be carried out without his approval in accordance with federal laws. Finally, as the chief executive, he confers civilian and military medals and decorations in accordance with laws regulating such matters.[38]

Presidential powers in the second category comprise those that he exercises jointly with, or upon the approval of, either the SCU alone or this body and the Council of Ministers. Here, the president signs and issues all federal laws, decrees, and decisions, including those decrees pertaining to the conclusion of treaties and international agreements, the declaration of war, and the imposition of martial law. In addition, he appoints the prime minister of the union, accepts his resignation, and terminates his appointment. Further, he appoints the president and member judges of the Supreme Court. As noted earlier, SCU's approval is mandatory in the exercise of the last two functions.[39]

The president of the union also exercises some of his prerogatives through the Council of Ministers of the union. In this category, he is responsible for supervising the execution of all federal laws, decrees, and decisions through this council as a group or individually. Besides, the president, upon the approval of the council, appoints all senior federal officials, civilian and military, with the single exception of the president and member judges of the high court. With the advice of the prime minister, the president also appoints a deputy prime minister and the other members of the cabinet as well.[40]

The Council of Ministers

The third federal authority specified by the constitution is the Council of Ministers (or cabinet). This body consists of a prime minister, a deputy prime minister, and a number of ministers, all of whom are to be chosen from among citizens with experience and the reputation for efficiency.[41] The constitution specifies twelve ministerial portfolios to form the first Council of Ministers. In addition to the prime minister and his deputy, these portfolios are foreign affairs, interior, defense, education, public health, public works and agriculture, communications and PTT, labor and social welfare, information, and planning.[42]

The prime minister, according to the constitution, calls for and presides over the meetings of the cabinet. He is also responsible for supervising the activities of his ministers along with the coordination of work between the various ministries and all other federal executive departments. Deliberations of the cabinet are closed to the public and decisions are taken by majority vote. In the event the post of the prime minister becomes vacant, due to resignation, death, or dismissal, then the entire cabinet resigns. However, "the President of the Union may ask the Ministers to stay temporarily in their posts to conduct urgent matters pending the formation of a new Cabinet."[43]

The constitution stipulates that "the Council of Ministers shall be responsible for carrying out the internal and foreign affairs which are within the domain of the union." More specifically, this federal body is charged with several important functions. First and foremost, it initiates federal draft laws. Such laws are then presented to the Federal National Council (FNC) prior to their submission to the president and the SCU for approval and ratification. In addition to proposing draft laws, the council also prepares the various draft decisions and decrees. Furthermore, it has the important function of drawing up all necessary regulations for the implementation of federal laws, including disciplinary regulations and regulations pertaining to the organization of departments and public agencies. It also prepares the federal general budget and the closing account. Another prerogative of the cabinet is the appointment and termination of services for all federal civil servants whose appointment or dismissal does not require a decree.

The Council of Ministers is also charged with supervising the execution of all federal laws, decrees, decisions, regulations, Supreme Court decisions, and international treaties and agreements to which the union is a party. Its supervisory power also extends to gauging the performance of the various federal ministries, agencies, and departments and to disciplining federal employees. Finally, at the beginning of each fiscal year, this federal organ is required to "submit to the President of the Union . . . a detailed report of internal achievements, the union's relations with other states and international organizations, accompanied by the Cabinet's recommendations on the best methods to consolidate the union."[44] In order to best perform its duties, the council is authorized to establish an adequately staffed secretariat and to draw up its own bylaws.[45]

The Federal National Council (FNC)

Another component of the UAE's government is the Federal National Council (FNC). The total membership of this body amounts to forty seats distributed among the seven member emirates, proportional not only to the size of their population but also to the affluence and influence each commands. Accordingly, Abu Dhabi and Dubai each have eight seats; Sharigah and Ras al-Khaimah, six each; and Ajman, Umm al-Guiwain, and Fujairah, four each.[46] Although each emirate is free to determine the method of choosing its own delegates to the FNC, i.e., by appointment, election, or both, a member of this council must be, first, "a citizen of one of the emirates of the union and a permanent resident in the emirate which he represents"; second, twenty-five years of age or older; third, with full civil rights, good reputation, and sound character, and with no criminal record involving honor unless fully rehabilitated in accordance with the law; and, fourth, literate.[47]

According to the constitution, a delegate is to be sent to the FNC for a two-year term that can be renewed for an unlimited number of times upon each expiry. Once selected, however, members are expected to represent not only their respective emirates but the "whole people of the union" as well. While in this council, no member is permitted to hold any other federal post, including those on the ministerial level.[48] In addition to a reasonable remuneration, members of the FNC enjoy commonly granted parliamentary immunities against censorship of ideas and opinions expressed in the line of work, and also against penal procedures during the council's sessions unless the latter's approval is secured. However, this does not include high criminal acts that are committed during such sessions.[49]

The FNC has an ordinary annual session (term) of no less than six months starting the first week in November. But it can also be convened extraordinarily any time the situation so demands. Usually, the federal capital city provides the seat for the council's meetings. However, the council can hold such meetings elsewhere upon the approval of a majority of its total membership and the Federal Council of Ministers. The council's sessions are ordinarily open unless the contrary is deemed necessary by at least one-third of its members, the president of the council, or a government's representative. Deliberations of this body are considered void unless at least a majority of its members are present. Its decisions are passed by a majority vote of the members present except in cases where a special majority is required. With the approval of the Federal Council of Ministers, the president of the union may, by decree,

postpone the meetings of the council for a period not exceeding one
month. No further postponements are permitted, however, except with
the consent of the council itself and for one time only. The federal
president, this time with the approval of the SCU, has the authority to
dissolve the FNC by decree. However, such a decree must include an
invitation for the new council to convene within sixty days from the date
of dissolution. The FNC may not be dissolved more than once for the
same reason, and it may not be dissolved at all during periods of martial
law.[50]

The Federal National Council opens and ends its annual "legislative"
session by presidential decrees issued with the approval of the Council of
Ministers. The constitution emphasizes the invalidity of meetings held
by the council without an official invitation, or held in places other than
those appointed by law. Procedurally, the president of the union is to
declare the official opening of the council's session in a speech delivered
before this body in which he explicates "the conditions in the country,
the most important events and affairs which took place during that year,
and what the Union Government intends to introduce in the area of
projects and reforms during the new session." A reply to the president's
speech is to be prepared by a committee elected by the council from
among its members. This reply should summarize the FNC's
"observations and aspirations" in regard to the way the union is
progressing. After the council approves such reply, it is then forwarded
to the president who, in turn, presents it to the SCU.[51]

Despite its resemblance, in both form and procedures, to legislative
bodies in democracies elsewhere, the FNC has in effect little substance. It
is not a legislative forum and, consequently, it performs no legislative
functions. Instead, this federal organ is essentially a consultative body. It
is intended to produce only recommendations and observations on those
draft laws that are sent to it by the Council of Ministers. Although such
recommendations and/or observations, if incorporated, may in some
cases modify the outcome of law-making processes, they have in reality
no legal obligatory power of their own. Hence, the Council of Ministers
in effect has tremendous leverage over the FNC, inasmuch as it
determines the issues this latter body is allowed to debate.

Among the procedural functions the FNC performs is the election of a
president, two deputies, and two controllers from among its members.
This group of five also forms the so-called Committee of the Council's
Office. In addition, the council is expected to organize its own general
secretariat, prepare its bylaws, and determine the validity of membership
of its members in case any is contested.[52] Beyond these procedural
matters, the FNC is empowered by the constitution to debate all federal

draft laws, including those of financial nature, and either approve, amend, or reject such draft laws before they are presented to the president of the union and the SCU.[53] In addition, the FNC is allowed the opportunity to debate matters relating to the public purse since, according to the constitution, no federal taxes are to be imposed or public loans granted except by a federal law. In regard to the federal annual budget and the Closing Account, however, the council's role is restricted to debate and the attachment of observations.[54] The FNC may also debate any general matter of relevance to the affairs of the federation, provided the Council of Ministers raises no objection on the basis of national security and interests. The communication of such objections if any is facilitated by the constitutional requirement that "the federal government shall be represented at the meetings of the Federal National Council by, at least, the Prime Minister, his Deputy, or one member of the Cabinet," who may respond to questions directed by the council's members on matters of direct concern and in accordance with the FNC's procedures.[55]

In the course of this survey of the institutional setting for the UAE, we have so far identified the structures that are theoretically accorded the constitutional powers to perform the legislative and executive functions—namely, the SCU, the president of the union, and the Federal Council of Ministers. We have also identified the Federal National Council (FNC) not as a legislative body but rather as a consultative one. The fifth and last federal authority to be dealt with in this chapter is the judiciary.

The Judiciary

Among the important provisions relating to freedoms, rights, and public duties, the constitution seems to set the stage for a judicial system with a sense of substance and independence. First, it asserts that "all individuals are equal before the law and there shall be no discrimination between the citizens of the union because of origin, place of residence, religious affiliation or social status." Second, it affirms that "the penalty is personal and the accused shall be innocent until proven guilty in a just and legal trial" and that the right of the accused to appoint a lawyer for his defense during the trial is guaranteed by law. Third, the constitution further guarantees for any citizen the right to "file a complaint to the appropriate authority, including the judicial authority" if and when the rights and freedoms stipulated in the constitution have been violated.[56]

The federal judiciary consists of a Supreme Court and a number of Federal Courts of First Instance. The Supreme Court is naturally the highest judicial authority in the union. The constitution specifies that its justices include a president and no more than four member judges, all of whom are to be appointed, as mentioned earlier, by a presidential decree upon the approval of the SCU.[57] Judges at all levels are considered independent and "shall be under no authority in the performance of their duties except that of the law and their consciences."[58] They are further immune from arbitrary dismissals and, prior to the assumption of their duties, are required to swear an oath before the president of the union and in the presence of the minister of justice to be loyal to the constitution and federal laws and to exercise their judicial authority on the basis of the principles of justice without fear or bias.[59]

Like other federal authorities, the Supreme Court is assigned several functions within the general nature of its domain.[60] First, it adjudicates disputes between any member emirate and the federal government, or between the emirates themselves, provided that a formal request to this effect is presented to the court by either party to the dispute. Second, it determines the constitutionality of federal laws if contested by any of the member emirates and also that of legislation issued by an emirate if contested by any federal authority. Included here are also laws, legislation, and bylaws referred to the high court by any lower court in the union. Third, the Supreme Court has the appropriate function of interpreting the provisions of the constitution upon request by any federal or emirate authority. In such cases, the court's decision is to be binding on all concerned. Fourth, the high court, if so asked by the SCU, may question ministers and other federal officials in matters relating to their performance and official behavior as government employees. Fifth, the Supreme Court also has within its jurisdiction the investigation of crimes committed against the nation and its security, such as currency counterfeiting and the forging of official seals and documents. Finally, the court also rules in jurisdictional disputes between federal and local jurisdictions or between judicial bodies in the member emirates.

In addition to the high court, the union is to establish Courts of First Instance. Jurisdiction of such courts is limited to administrative, commercial, and civil disputes between the union and individuals; crimes committed within the limits of the federal capital; and matters pertaining to personal status and civil and commercial issues between individuals residing in this city.[61] The constitution further stipulates that an attorney general for the union shall be appointed by a presidential decree with the approval of the Council of Ministers. The prerogatives of this official and those of his assistants are to be regulated by a law.[62]

What seems to be reassuring about the union's judiciary is the constitutional stipulation that Supreme Court decisions are final and, hence, binding on all concerned. Accordingly:

> if the Court decides ... that a federal legislation is contrary to the Federal
> Constitution or that any local legislation or by-laws contain a violation of
> the Federal Constitution or of any federal law, then it shall be the duty of
> the Authority concerned in the union or the emirates to take whatever
> steps are necessary to correct or remove the Constitutional violation.[63]

Although judicial bodies in the emirates are to attend to all judicial matters not delegated to federal courts, the constitution provides for the transfer of local judicial prerogatives, or any part thereof, to Federal Courts of First Instance, if so desired by the member emirates themselves.[64]

The Legislative Process—How Laws Are Enacted

In any political system, the identification of who does what in the process of rule making represents the first, and certainly the most important, step in determining whether political power is concentrated or diffused and the extent of such concentration or diffusion. The UAE constitution specifies three types of federal legislation along with the federal authorities empowered to generate them. These types are federal laws, decrees having the power of laws, and ordinary decrees.

The first stage in the process of making federal laws is proposing or initiating such laws in draft form. This important step, as pointed out earlier, is taken by the Federal Council of Ministers. Here, a draft bill is prepared in coordination with the federal ministries or agencies concerned. Or, as the case may be, the various ministries or agencies may choose to draft such bills and then submit them in a suitable legal form to the Council of Ministers for consideration. After a draft law is ready, then the council presents it to the FNC for debate. In the latter, the draft law may either be adopted as it is, amended, or rejected. In any case, it goes back to the Council of Ministers, which, in turn, submits it to the president of the union. If the FNC has adopted such a draft law as is, then the president may approve it and submit it to the SCU for ratification. If, however, the FNC has amended or rejected such a bill, and the president and/or the SCU do not approve of such FNC action, then the draft law, modified or in original form, may be returned by either of the two authorities to the FNC for reconsideration. No matter what action the latter may decide to take vis-à-vis a returned draft law, the president of the union may go ahead and sign and issue the law after ratification by the SCU. Laws have to be published in the *Official Gazette* of the union within two weeks from the date they were signed and issued. Unless otherwise specified, they become operative after one month from their publication.[65]

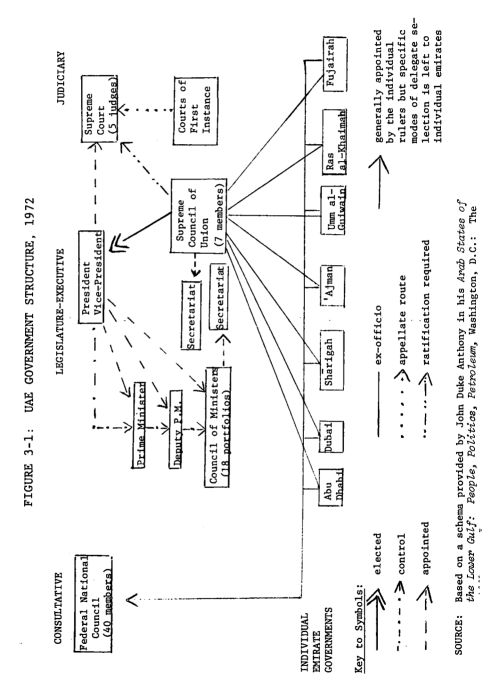

FIGURE 3-1: UAE GOVERNMENT STRUCTURE, 1972

SOURCE: Based on a schema provided by John Duke Anthony in his *Arab States of the Lower Gulf: People, Politics, Petroleum*, Washington, D.C.: The

Another type of federal legislation is the so-called decrees with the power of laws. These in effect are federal laws. Perhaps the only reason they carry different labeling is because they, in the process of being enacted, do not follow the same course as draft laws. According to the constitution, while the SCU is in recess, the president and the Council of Ministers may together issue federal decrees of weight and effect equal to that of federal laws provided there is an urgent need. Of course, such legislation should not come out in violation of the constitution. But the nature of these decrees seems to be somewhat precarious for they

> shall be submitted to the Supreme Council within a week at the most to decide whether to approve or reject them. If the Council approves them, then they shall have the force of law and the Federal National Council shall be notified of such decrees in its first following session.
>
> If the Supreme Council does not approve them, then they shall not have the force of law unless it is decided to consider them valid for the period since their issuance or settle any consequences thereof in another way.[66]

Ordinary federal decrees are proposed by the Council of Ministers and then submitted to the president of the union. Decrees that are constitutionally required to have the approval of the SCU are submitted to this body for such action. Decrees that require no SCU ratification are signed by the president and then issued. What is significant in regard to this type of legislation is the constitutional stipulation that "no decree shall be issued unless approved by the Council of Ministers."[67] This makes the role played by this federal authority in the legislative process extremely pivotal.

Two other forms of law are worthy of brief mention. These are international treaties and agreements and constitutional amendments. In the UAE, treaties and agreements with other states are negotiated, signed, ratified, and issued by a decree by the same authorities that handle federal laws and decrees. The role of the FNC is limited to the mere expression of observations.[68] Constitutional draft amendments, on the other hand, are initiated not by the Council of Ministers but by the SCU. The proposed amendment is then presented to the FNC for debate. A special majority of two-thirds of the votes of members present is required for the FNC's approval of such amendments. There is no specific reference in the constitution as to the weight of the FNC's role in this matter. However, it is stipulated that the procedure for ratifying constitutional amendments is similar to that followed in the ratification of laws. Consequently, similar to the case of lawmaking, the FNC is no more than a powerless participant. Constitutional amendments are

FIGURE 3-2: LEGISLATIVE ROLES OF UAE FEDERAL AUTHORITIES

FEDERAL AUTHORITY

TYPE OF LEGISLATION	Federal Council of Ministers	President of the Union	SCU	FNC
Federal Laws	initiation proposal	approval signing issuance	approval ratification	debating: (1) approval amendment rejection
Decrees With the Force of Law	initiation proposal	approval signing issuance	ratification or rejection within a week	to be notified only if SCU ratifies
Ordinary Decrees	proposal initiation	approval signing issuance	approval (2) ratification	- - -
Treaties & Agreements with Other States	negotiation	approval signing	ratification	to be notified after conclusion
Constitutional Amendments	- - -	signing issuance (in the name of SCU)	initiation proposal	debating (1)

(1) effect of outcome depends on other authorities.

(2) approval and ratification are required only in selected areas of legislation.

signed and issued by the president in the name and on the behalf of the SCU (see Figure 3-2).[69]

To sum up, the UAE emerged as a federal entity of seven Arab gulf emirates based on the voluntary acceptance by the rulers of these ministries of a temporary contractual document called the Provisional Constitution. This document, among other things, regulates the exercise of political authority in the union. It reserves for the federal government alone the undisputed right of performing legislative and executive functions in a specified but extensive array of important fields. Then, it identifies several gray areas where both the union government and political authorities of the individual emirates can share legislative as well as executive powers. What is not specified as belonging to either of these two categories is, according to the constitution, for the member emirates to regulate, each within its own territory. However, in all areas where the latter are accorded the right to exercise authority, the supremacy of the federal constitution, laws, decrees, decisions, and regulations must always be assured.

Among the five federal authorities recognized by the constitution, the Supreme Council of the Union (SCU), the president, and the Federal Council of Ministers are three institutions that have been accorded an almost exclusive control over the legislative and executive domains of the union. These three, each within its own prerogatives, plan and formulate union policy, enact all necessary legislation on the federal level, and execute such policies on all levels. Their interrelation is only partially hierarchical. The Council of Ministers is both formed by and responsible to the president and the SCU. However, without the Council of Ministers' approval, no presidential decrees are possible. In the same token, the presidency and vice-presidency are an extension of the Supreme Council. Between them, they share the powers of approval and ratification in the legislative process in the sense that the chief executive and his deputy are at the same time the two most influential members of the SCU, mainly for the two vetoes they command.

If, as we have seen, the federal judiciary has generally been accorded powers comparable to those usually assigned judicial systems in democratic societies, the Federal National Council (FNC) is a legislative body only on a standby basis. Although its bylaws and above all the constitution render it a parliamentary appearance, i.e., elaborate procedures, immunities, sealing its members from other federal employment, etc., the power of this body in the process of lawmaking is insignificant. Not only are draft bills proposed elsewhere in the federal structure but, in addition, other federal authorities may enact laws in the FNC's absence or issue decrees without its participation. They are even empowered to postpone the meetings of this body or dissolve it altogether. In fact, according to Article 24 of the FNC's bylaws, council members are prohibited from intefering in any of the prerogatives of either the executive or legislative authorities. The "executive" in this context refers mainly to SCU, the presidency, and the Council of Ministers. In short, although theoretically a federal authority, the FNC is in practice only what the Federal Council of Ministers makes out of it.

To begin with, the FNC is not a popularly elected body. Members of this council are all political appointees. Their selection is not necessarily based on their personal qualifications as much as it is on their political loyalties to the rulers of their emirates and also on their social status. Although the official argument is that the rulers themselves thought the time inauspicious for a popularly elected institution due to both the low level of political awareness and education and the critical shortage of legally trained citizens, it is what is at stake politically that makes the rulers insist on appointing these deputies. A popularly elected council member would likely be accountable to those who elected him and not the ruler of his emirate. Consequently, his behavior as a representative of the people might not always coincide with the wishes and expectations of the chief executive in his emirate. This would undoubtedly be different from the present arrangement by which the deputy owes his post to the ruler of his state— something that would influence his official conduct as he remembers the date for the next appointment.[70]

In this chapter, we have dealt with the UAE's federal structure as cast by the Provisional Constitution. The following chapter deals with the union in an institutional developmental sense over the first five years since its establishment.

4
The Union:
Institutional Development
and Integration

The main concern of the previous chapter was to present a detailed account of the constitutional makeup of federal authority in the UAE at the time of its inception in December 1971. It was designed to shed some light on the theoretical institutional foundations of the union. From these foundations, it is only fitting that the institutional development be dealt with next insofar as the spheres of jurisdiction of the emerging federal institutions penetrate the existing frontiers of the member emirates to claim the same force generally accorded local departments. In essence, as we may recall from Chapter 1, this orientation is pivotal in the definitions of integration framed by Deutsch and his associates, as well as those proffered by Haas and Nye, among others.

In contrast to integrative experiences in Western Europe, Latin America, and even East Africa, where fairly well-developed governmental institutions were in existence before integrative efforts were launched, in the UAE new governmental organs had to be created either at the inception of the union or afterward in order to cope with increasingly complex developmental problems. Indeed, it is more a case of integration by emergence than one by merger. At the time the union was consummated, only Abu Dhabi, Sharigah, and, to a lesser degree, Dubai had what might be characterized as modern administrative systems.

Abu Dhabi's oil wealth, though dating back to the early 1960s, was not significantly utilized as an instrument of change until Shaikh Zayed acceded to the emirate's rulership in 1966, hence putting an end to the notoriously sterile rule of his brother, Shakhbut. This date signaled a rapid expansion of the emirate's administration until, by mid-1970, the number of departments reached twenty-eight. In July of the following year, a new administrative reform was introduced, partly in anticipation of the emirate's assuming a leading role in the then-imminent union, and partly in response to the unusually large number of governmental bodies that often reflected a degree of duplication and confusion. Accordingly, the old system gave way to a new setup of thirteen ministries presided over by the emirate's first council of ministers. The new cabinet continued to run the emirate government in uneasy coexistence with the union government until it was finally disbanded in December 1973 in favor of an enlarged union cabinet.

Sharigah seems to have embraced a pattern of administrative organization similar to that of Abu Dhabi before the 1971 reform. Obviously, whether in Abu Dhabi, Sharigah, or any other emirate, the temperament of the incumbent ruler has the most significant effect on the way an emirate is ruled. Sheer material wealth is not sufficient by itself to spark socioeconomic development, and the case of Abu Dhabi before 1966 goes a long way in attesting to this assertion. However, Sharigah, in addition to its relatively more advanced system of education and its status as the former seat of both the British air base and the Trucial Oman Scouts (later the Union Defense Force), has another factor that contributes to its relatively elaborate administrative structure. As will be discussed in more detail in the next chapter, of all the union member emirates, Sharigah has the least contiguous territory, sharing borders with each of the other six sister states as well as the Sultanate of Oman (see map in Chapter 5, p. 101). If nothing else, this territorial fragmentation, or incontiguity, has accentuated the administrative problems of this emirate. By the time the federation was concluded in December 1971, Sharigah had, aside from the Emiri *Diwan* ("office") and Sharigah Municipality, departments for air- and seaports, electricity and water, labor and social affairs, petroleum and mineral affairs, police, post, education, finance, customs, justice, and lands and survey.

Of the three largest member emirates, Dubai is the most administratively parsimonious. The attitude of its enterprising ruler, Shaikh Rashid, in regard to the way a government is structured and run, seems to have been colored by the emirate's long tradition as the unchallenged center of entrepôt trade in the gulf. By mid-1970, only those organizations necessary to run a commercial center were in existence, and even these were only modestly staffed. In addition to the ruler's *diwan* and the Dubai Municipality, there were departments for land and property, customs, oil affairs, accounts, police, and passports and immigration.

But our concept of integration by emergence is even more striking in the case of governmental organization in the four northern emirates of Ajman, Umm al-Guiwain, Ras al-Khaimah, and Fujairah. The paucity of resources, the low level of education, and the intensity of tribal culture in these shaikhdoms had all contributed, in one degree or another, to the virtual absence of modern administrative structures except in a most rudimentary form. In each of these emirates in the early 1970s, the Emiri *Diwan,* which was often considered part and parcel of the ruler's household, and the municipality of the coastal town that had the same name as that of the emirate, dispensed under the direct control of the ruler whatever social services their meager resources could afford. Had these emirates attained the same degree and extent of administrative organization as the other three, the emergence of a cohesive and effective federal structure would have been more difficult.

From this glimpse of the governmental organization of the seven emirates at the time the union was forged, this chapter will trace the process of operationalizing the Provisional Constitution only insofar as integrative or disintegrative trends on the institutional decision-making level can be discerned. This will be accomplished through a discussion of the generally broad areas of cabinet structure and civil service growth, union finances and economic development, social services and social development, and the critical sector of internal security and defense. At the end of the chapter, a brief look into legislation generated by the union government over the first half decade of its existence will help identify areas of emphasis and general trends.

Cabinet Structure and Civil Service Growth

As we have seen in the last chapter, the central role accorded the Council of Ministers in the governmental structure of the union makes recruitment to this body part and parcel of the federal balancing process reflecting the actual distribution of power not only among the member emirates, but between competing power elites within the emirates themselves. Hence, political considerations rather than professional ability often provide the most salient criterion for the distribution of ministerial posts. Although this is not an uncommon practice in other political systems, it has tended in the case of the UAE to inflate the structure of the government by either fragmenting certain ministries or by creating new ones.

The first federal cabinet was announced on December 9, 1971, one week after the union was forged. Aside from the two posts of prime minister and his deputy, it consisted of the following portfolios: foreign affairs, interior, finance, economy and industry, defense, planning, education, public health, justice, labor and social affairs, communications, public works and agriculture, and information. The distribution of these posts among contending interests represented an extension of the whole bargaining process that led to the union in the first place. Thus, aside from the presidency of the federation, won by Shaikh Zayed for a five-year term, Abu Dhabi was assigned six cabinet posts, including the important seats of foreign affairs, interior, and information. Dubai, in addition to the vice-presidency of the union filled by Shaikh Rashid, won the premiership and three additional posts, those of defense, finance, and economy and industry. The rest of the cabinet posts went to the other emirates as follows: Sharigah received three; Umm al-Guiwain and Ajman each received two; and Fujairah, one. Notably, most of the cabinet ministers appointed were either members of the ruling families of the member emirates or citizens aligned with such families in the configuration of tribal politics in the area. Such an occurrence is not unusual, but rather a standard feature of political reality in this part of the world. The clearest case here is that of Dubai, where the ruler's sons, Maktum, Hamdan, and Muhammad, have occupied the vital posts of prime minister; finance, economy and industry; and national defense, respectively. The admission of Ras al-Khaimah into the union, along with the widening scope of federal authority, led to the enlargement of the cabinet early in 1972. In addition to stipulating the jurisdiction of the various ministries, federal law gave birth to four more ministries—agriculture and fisheries, youth and sports, housing, and electricity.[1]

For the opening two years in the existence of this fledgling federation, union ministries, with the notable exception of foreign affairs, education, health, and communications, were in the most part hollow structures lacking in staff and a clear sense of direction. The most useful function these federal organizations were able to perform at this stage was to serve as instruments of coordination among the emirates in their respective sectors. In short, the mere existence of a federal structure did not automatically lead to the spread of federal jurisdiction over the whole territory of the union. Institutional duplication existed in the form of two or more organizations serving the same function and constituency. The best illustration for this duplication was provided by Abu Dhabi. Until 1973, this emirate had its parallel Council of Ministers atop a local government of several ministries.

A major step in the institutional integration and development of the UAE, however, came in December 1973. After an extended study of the whole question of administrative reorganization, Abu Dhabi chose to disband its cabinet and accordingly change its ministries into departments. This in effect meant that Abu Dhabi, a champion of the federal idea from its inception, had decided at this juncture to throw in its lot with the union. Consequently, a twenty-eight-member federal cabinet was formed. Of this relatively large number of ministerial posts, eleven went to Abu Dhabi. The fact that all the eleven Abu Dhabian ministers were members of the disbanded council and that six of the new cabinet posts were without portfolios illustrates the extent to which considerations of political accommodation are important in the formation of this important federal authority.[2]

Concomitant with the new administrative situation was the creation, in January 1974, of three additional ministries. The Ministry of Finance, Economy, and Industry surrendered its economic function to a new ministry of economy and commerce. In addition, a ministry of petroleum and mineral resources and another for Islamic affairs were established, bringing the total to nineteen federal ministries. Later, the Ministry of Labor and Social Affairs gave way to two separate ministries representing the two sectors. And from that time until the end of 1976, not only the size of the federal cabinet and the distribution of its posts remained relatively stable, but, in addition, ministerial turnover was remarkably low.[3]

The UAE civil service, organized by Federal Law 8 (1973), has witnessed a phenomenal growth from less than 4,000 civil servants and employees at independence to over 24,000 by the end of 1976. Although the gradual federalization of otherwise local administrative organs has contributed to this large increase, direct union recruitment has nevertheless been of great significance. In fact, it is this latter factor that reflects the institutional integrative process at its best. As young, skilled individuals desert their poorly paid local employment in pursuit of clearly better opportunities at the federal level, mainly in the capital of the federation, gradual shifts in loyalties are more likely to follow. Even though exact figures are not available, it is estimated that 40 percent of the nationals in the union civil service come from Dubai as opposed to 20 percent from Abu Dhabi—with the remainder recruited from the northern emirates. The relatively small number of federal employment seekers from Abu Dhabi is attributed in part to the extremely generous welfare and social security benefits in this particular emirate, which leave little incentive for the pursuit of public employment.[4]

Another facet of the union civil service structure is the salience of its expatriate elements. Expatriates, Arab and non-Arab, play a major role in the day-to-day operation of the federal machinery, either in an advisory capacity or in the conduct of research, accounting, education, information, health, justice, and other services. In December 1975, for instance, expatriates represented a clear majority of federal employees in at least six ministries. These were petroleum and mineral resources (34 to 22), planning (112 to 33), economy and commerce (55 to 31), information and culture (798 to 348), youth and sports (79 to 47), and justice (244 to 101).[5] The contribution of foreign expertise to the institutional integrative process has been its impact upon the efficiency of the federal government and the training of more citizens in order to cope, at least in the long run, with problems of development.

Federal Finances and Economic Development

The creation of the UAE Currency Board in May 1973 represented a significant integrative step in the financial and economic sector of the union. Prior to this date, and from the time the Trucial States abandoned the Indian Gulf rupee in 1966, various regional currencies such as the Bahraini dinar and the Saudi and the Qatari/Dubai riyals had served as local currencies for one emirate or another. The board was given the authority not only to issue a common currency for the union, but also to exercise central banking functions over the commercial and banking sector in an already overbanked country.[6] The dirham, as the new currency came to be called, was valued at U.S. $0.2533 and an initial money supply of Dh 260 million was put in circulation. One indication of the widening scope of union authority is the growth of its financial capabilities over the first five years of its existence. As Table 4-1 shows, a fledgling federation could raise only Dh 201 million in total revenues in 1972. But this relatively modest figure more than doubled each year until in 1976 it reached fourteen times its original size. As revenues grew so did expenditures. As the same table indicates, federal government spending rose from Dh 164 million in 1972 to an estimated Dh 4 billion four years later. Over the same period, as more institutions were added to the federal fold, a concomitant increase in the union budget was the result. The fact that the development budget jumped from Dh 303 million in 1975 to an all-time high of over Dh 2 billion for the following year reflects an impressive growth not only of the financial clout of the union but of its institutional authority as well.[7]

Income from custom duties, stamps, and investment dividends represented only a small segment of federal revenues. To be sure, the greatest portion of federal income (96 to 98 percent) was contributed by member emirates. And lest this designation be misleading, we hasten to point out that the union's core unit, Abu Dhabi, bore between 90 and 99 percent of this contribution. As Table 4-2 shows, this emirate's support of the federal budget rose from Dh 201 million in 1972 to Dh 4 billion in 1976.

An important question now arises: Why has Abu Dhabi contributed

TABLE 4-1

DEVELOPMENT OF UAE EXPENDITURES AND REVENUES, 1972-1975

(in millions of UAE dirhams)

1 U.S. $ = 3.92 dirhams, approx.

	1972	1973	1974	1975	1976*
A - EXPENDITURES:					
Current and Capital	149	330	568	955	2,141
Development:	15	73	175	303	2,011
Total Expenditures	164	403	743	1,258	4,152
B - REVENUES:					
Ministerial Revenues	5	17	21	50	72
Emirates' Contributions:	196	402	779	1,720	4,128
Total Revenues:	201	419	800	1,770	4,200
C - SURPLUS (B-A):	37	16	57	512	48

*Estimates

Sources: Ministry of Planning, UAE, Annual Statistical Group, 1972-1975 (1976), pp. 214, 215; and Ministry of Information and Culture, UAE, UAE Yearbook, 1976 (in Arabic), pp. 24, 26. The fact that the figures for Abu Dhabi's contribution to the UAE budget (Table 4-2) exceed emirate's contributions for some years, as indicated in this table, might be attributed to the differing bases of calculation utilized by both governments in the sense that Abu Dhabi had extended financial support to some departments and agencies that were not as yet considered fully federal. Or, it might be that figures of Abu Dhabi's support could have been exaggerated.

TABLE 4-2:

BUDGETARY GROWTH IN ABU DHABI, 1972-1976

(millions of UAE dirhams)

	1972	1973	1974	1975	1976
EXPENDITURES:					
Current Budget:	746	966	2,056	2,631	4,300
Capital Budget					
Contribution to UAE Budget	201	403	794	1,600	4,000
Foreign Aid, Grants, Loans, etc.:	328	1,222	2,187	4,234	4,500
Capital Expenditure:	-	243	1,186	655	400
Total Capital Budget:	529	1,868	4,167	6,489	8,900
Development Budget:	461	558	1,541	2,297	5,000
Total Expenditures:	1,736	3,392	7,764	11,417	18,200
REVENUES:					
Oil Royalties:	2,075	3,043	13,703	14,390	18,124
Other Revenue:	106	1,169	473	625	276
Total Revenues:	2,181	4,212	14,176	15,015	18,400

Sources: Emirate of Abu Dhabi, Statistical Yearbook, 1975, pp. 82, 83 and
Ministry of Information and Culture, UAE, UAE Yearbook, 1976 (in
Arabic) p. 26.

so much, to the extent of nearly subsidizing the whole federal venture? Beyond the assertion that the geographical distinctiveness of the Coast of Oman, the shared historical experiences of its people, and their common tribal roots must somehow strengthen a moral obligation to share the area's God-given wealth, something Abu Dhabi's generosity had reflected even before the union,[8] there is a political aspect. Being the federation's core unit and driving force, Abu Dhabi derives from the union's continuity and growth an enhanced sense of hegemonial spirit and fulfillment not unlike that enjoyed by Prussia in the process of German unification in the last century.

From a purely financial perspective, however, the question of financing the union has only recently been settled. At the time the union was forged, the seven rulers agreed each would contribute 10 percent of the total revenues of his emirate to the union budget. As events later proved, virtually only Abu Dhabi kept meeting its obligation. At one point, the latter even went so far as to express its readiness to set aside half of its income for federal support should other member-emirates agree to follow suit.[9] A glance at Table 4-2 leads one to conclude that Abu Dhabi can indeed subsidize the union altogether. In fact, the federal budget is only one item in the list of this emirate's total expenditures, and in no single year from 1972 to 1976 did this item exceed either the emirate's current budget, foreign aid, or development funds. Thus, of a total expenditure of Dh 18.2 billion in 1976, less than 22 percent was contributed to the federal treasury, while over 51 percent was allocated to Abu Dhabi's development and recurrent expenditures and close to 25 percent to foreign aid, grants, and loans.

To discuss the UAE's economy without mentioning oil is perhaps tantamount to writing an essay on the economy of the United States without mentioning tax revenues. Since its production in commercial quantities in Abu Dhabi in 1962, and later in Dubai and Sharigah, oil has undoubtedly been the most significant pacesetter of socioeconomic change in the area. Production of crude oil (see Table 4-3) has increased from an average of over 16,000 barrels per day in 1962 for Abu Dhabi to nearly 2 million barrels per day in 1976 for the three UAE oil-producing emirates. Among the thirteen members of the Organization of Petroleum Exporting Countries (OPEC), the UAE, as Table 4-4 shows, ranked seventh in 1976 with a 6.4 percent share of the organization's oil production and a world share of 3.4 percent. Among Arab oil-producing countries in the same year, the UAE, with an impressive share of 10 percent, ranked fourth, being outproduced only by Saudi Arabia, Kuwait, and Iraq.[10]

As is generally the case with major oil producers in the developing

TABLE 4-3:

PRODUCTION OF CRUDE OIL IN THE UAE

(barrels daily)

Emirate Year	ABU DHABI	DUBAI	SHARIGAH	TOTAL
1962	16,433.9			16,433.9
1963	49,512.1			49,512.1
1964	189,676.7			189,676.7
1965	281,906.1			281,906.1
1966	359,667.4			359,667.4
1967	381,956.7			381,956.7
1968	499,619.0			499,619.0
1969	599,445.7	10,003.0		609,448.7
1970	693,784.2	34,236.0		728,020.7
1971	934,184.6	85,812.0		1,019,996.6
1972	1,052,708.3	125,071.0		1,177,780.3
1973	1,305,968.0	152,848.0		1,462,333.6
1974	1,411,340.3	219,746.0	53,865.6	1,703,503.2
1975	1,403,658.1	254,247.0	38,197.6	1,696,102.7
1976	1,596,243.7	313,794.9	36,995.3	1,947,033.9

Source: Ministry of Petroleum and Mineral Resources, UAE, Oil Statistical Review
(1977), pp. 22, 57. Slight variations of production figures do exist.

TABLE 4-4:

OPEC OIL PRODUCTION, 1976 and 1975

(,000 barrels daily)

Country	1976	1975	1976 Share of World Total (%)	1976 OPEC Share (%)	% Change 1976 over 1975
Saudi Arabia	8,579.5	7,075.4	15.0	28.2	+ 21.3
Iran	5,882.9	5,350.1	10.3	19.3	+ 10.0
Venezuela	2,294.3	2,346.2	4.0	7.5	- 2.2
Iraq	2,184.0	2,261.7	3.8	7.2	- 3.4
Kuwait	2,150.1	2,084.2	3.8	7.1	+ 3.2
Nigeria	2,067.7	1,783.2	3.6	6.8	+ 16.0
UAE	1,942.0	1,663.3	3.4	6.4	+ 16.8
Libya	1,913.8	1,479.8	3.4	6.3	+ 15.1
Indonesia	1,504.2	1,306.5	2.6	4.9	+ 29.3
Algeria	1,050.0	1,020.3	1.8	3.4	+ 2.9
Qatar	487.1	437.6	0.9	1.6	+ 11.3
Gabon	220.0	223.0	0.4	0.7	- 1.4
Ecuador	186.4	160.9	0.3	0.6	+ 15.9
TOTAL	30,462.0	27,192.2	53.3	100.0	+ 12.0

Source: Ministry of Petroleum and Mineral Resources, UAE, Oil Statistical Review (1977), p. 11.

world, the gap between the UAE's oil production and export is extremely narrow. As Table 4-5 shows, while total UAE oil exports in 1972 were less than 440 million barrels, the figure for 1976 reached over 710 million barrels, or over 99 percent of crude oil production. The eight leading consumers in the same year were Japan (28.3 percent), the United States (13.5 percent), France (13.2 percent), the United Kingdom (8 percent), Holland (6.2 percent), Spain (4.8 percent), West Germany (4.6 percent), and Italy (3.3 percent).[11] Income derived from oil has been influenced not only by the gradual increase in oil exports over the years but by changes in the price of this precious commodity as well. Thus for Abu Dhabi alone (see Table 4-2, p. 64), oil revenues have risen from slightly more than Dh 2 billion in 1972 to Dh 18.1 billion in 1976. Understandably, the quadrupling of oil prices in 1974 accounts for the astronomical rise in oil royalties for the same year. Furthermore, the structure of this emirate's revenues, with oil-derived income averaging 92 percent of the total over the five-year period, makes it one of the least economically diversified states in the world.

Institutional integration in the oil sector among the three oil-producing emirates has lagged behind other areas. This might be attributed to the reluctance of some rulers to surrender authority in a matter as vital as oil. Although the Ministry of Petroleum and Mineral Resources was established in 1974 on the federal level with a mandate to "coordinate oil policy" and to "formulate the necessary plans for the best exploitation of oil," little had been achieved by the end of 1976. In fact, when the UAE, along with Saudi Arabia, limited increases in oil prices to not more than 5 percent at the Doha (Qatar) Conference of OPEC oil ministers in December 1976, only Abu Dhabi abided by this limit, while Dubai and Sharigah followed the OPEC majority in adopting higher prices.[12] Nevertheless, the Ministry of Petroleum and Mineral Resources, with a staff force of sixty-two at the end of 1976, and in close cooperation with the better staffed Abu Dhabi Department of Petroleum, continued to serve the union through its symbolic representation in oil matters in the international arena, and, more importantly, by the gathering of oil data and the conduct of research.

The unprecedented wealth brought about by the fairly recent discovery and exploitation of oil has thrust all facets of life in the area into a rapid current of socioeconomic change. UAE national economic policy, which began to take shape roughly in 1973, has endeavored to introduce some sense of balance between the oil-producing emirates and the less fortunate ones. A high-level national planning board was created in the same year in order to "work out a long-term general plan for socioeconomic development in the UAE with major goals toward

69

TABLE 4-5:

TOTAL ANNUAL EXPORT OF CRUDE OIL IN THE UAE

(barrels)

Emirate / Year	ABU DHABI	DUBAI	SHĀRIGAH	TOTAL
1962	5,412,256			5,412,256
1963	18,060,696			18,060,696
1964	67,803,766			67,803,766
1965	102,096,258			102,096,258
1966	132,494,374			132,494,374
1967	137,559,949			137,559,949
1968	181,446,190			181,446,190
1969	218,823,922	3,651,094		222,385,016
1970	253,533,581	30,949,134		284,482,715
1971	339,061,675	45,323,357		384,385,032
1972	384,212,140	55,595,650		439,807,790
1973	472,112,631	81,151,245		553,263,876
1974	511,702,061	88,317,655	8,259,080	608,278,796
1975	514,070,340	91,635,272	13,954,750	619,660,362
1976	580,827,473	115,828,116	13,395,182	710,050,771

Source: Ministry of Petroleum and Mineral Resources, UAE, Oil Statistical Review (1977), pp. 42, 47, 57. Figures for the year 1962 were taken from the 1976 issue of ibid., p. 49.

which all resources, public and private, can be geared."[13]

The emphasis on a more geographically balanced economic development is reflected in the distribution of federal infrastructural projects as they stood in 1976. As Table 4-6 depicts, of a total development price tag of over Dh 6.3 billion, the five oil-poor emirates north of Dubai were marked to receive more than Dh 5 billion, or 80 percent of the total. Allocations for 1976 alone followed a similar pattern. Various federal ministries were empowered to spend 82 percent of a total allocation of more than Dh 1.7 billion on projects that eventually will benefit the five northern emirates alone. Of this sum, nearly 72 percent was earmarked for construction, 14 for machinery and equipment, 1.3 for means of transportation, and 12.5 for studies, designs, and supervision.[14]

Development projects designated as generally serving more than one emirate, and whose share amounted to 7.8 percent of total allocations for 1976 (Table 4-6), pertained either to the consolidation and expansion of the federal establishment through its various agencies, or to programs designed to benefit more than one member state, such as interemirate highways, environmental studies, geological surveys, and so forth.[15]

As the banker of the federation, Abu Dhabi earmarked for development in 1976 more than just the symbolic 2.6 percent shown in Table 4-6. As pointed out earlier, this emirate's development budget for that year alone (Dh 5 billion) did in fact exceed the federal budget in its entirety. In the area of industrial development, for which Dh 1.7 billion were allocated, Abu Dhabi has appropriately concentrated on petrochemicals in addition to electrical power plants and the development of water resources. Agricultural development and the greening of the desert wasteland, especially in the eastern part of the emirate, road construction, improvement of air- and seaports, health facilities and services, public housing and social development were all priority items in 1976.

Like Abu Dhabi, Dubai has the financial capacity to carry out its own ambitious development plan, though to a lesser extent and by different means. Aside from being the center of the gulf reexport trade for roughly the last seventy years, this emirate has the additional blessing of being an oil producer since 1969.[16] Income derived from oil, however, has not been sizable enough to finance the emirate's characteristically ambitious development schemes.[17] So Dubai secures the necessary funds by borrowing from international and domestic sources, and also by encouraging the participation of international financial houses in its projects. Two such projects, well under way in 1976, are the expansion of Port Rashid from fifteen to thirty-seven berths and the

TABLE 4-6:

INFRASTRUCTURAL PROJECTS IN THE UAE
BY SHARES OF MEMBER EMIRATES, 1976

(millions of UAE dirhams)

1 U.S. $ = 3.92 dirhams; approx.

EMIRATE	TOTAL COST	%	COST OBLIGATION REMAINING (Obtained by subtracting what was spent in previous years from total cost)	ALLOCATION FOR 1976	%
Projects Serving More Than One Emirate	600.9	9.4	582.4	138.2	7.8
Abu Dhabi	131.2	2.1	116.0	45.6	2.6
Dubai	527.5	8.3	517.6	128.0	7.3
Shārigah	1,451.8	22.7	1,380.8	357.6	20.3
'Ajman	721.1	11.3	659.7	222.7	12.7
Umm al-Guiwain	545.9	8.5	502.5	196.7	11.2
Ras al-Khaimah	1,133.2	17.8	1,072.5	326.8	18.6
Fujairah	1,270.4	19.9	1,151.0	342.3	19.5
TOTAL	6,382.0	100.0	5,982.5	1,759.9	100.0

Source: Ministry of Planning, UAE, Federal Investment Plan for Socioeconomic Development, 1976 (in Arabic) pp. 47, 48.

construction of a dry dock that will be able, when completed in 1979 at a cost of more than Dh 1.3 billion, to accommodate a million-ton tanker and two others half this size simultaneously.

But by far the most ambitious project in this emirate is the industrial city at Jabal Ali, seventeen miles to the south of the center of Dubai Town. Work began here in 1976. This five-year diversified project includes (1) a seventy-four-berth port with a ten-mile approach channel; (2) an aluminum smelter with a water desalination plant at a cost of Dh 2.4 billion; (3) a steel mill at a cost of Dh 1.4 billion; and (4) an international airport with a capacity of up to 2,000 passengers per hour and twenty-two wide-bodied carriers at a time. The price tag for this project is expected to reach Dh 1.5 billion.

Before oil money began to trickle down to the northern part of the Coast of Oman in the 1960s, people depended on agriculture, boat building, and fishing for their livelihood. Resources were too meager to support developmental programs of the magnitude reached by the two sister states of Abu Dhabi and Dubai. Once in the federal fold, however, these emirates could translate what used to be an Abu Dhabian charitable support into a moral and political obligation. Under the federal banner, the principle of wealth sharing is more emphasized. In addition, geographical balance, as far as socioeconomic development is concerned, is viewed by federal planners as a positive factor in the process of integration.

As can be read from Table 4-6 (p. 71), distribution of development funds among the northern emirates is not even. The three shaikhdoms of Sharigah, Fujairah, and Ras al-Khaimah, in this order, have apparently won the lion's share of federal money for socioeconomic development, whether in the case of total cost or the funds allocated for 1976, with totals exceeding Dh 3.8 and Dh 1 billion, respectively.[18] Of course, these three emirates are the largest and the most populous among the five. But one additional factor might be equally as important. Since the establishment of the union, both Sharigah and Fujairah have been publicly the most enthusiastic of the five about the federal idea and, in addition, were the first, in 1975, to transfer their justice, police, information, and telecommunication departments from local jurisdiction to federal control. Though other states were later to follow suit, at least in part, it is quite conceivable that federal generosity to these two emirates is one way of reciprocating their early support of the federation.[19]

The gradual increase in oil production, and in particular the dramatic rise in petroleum prices in 1974, has brought this commodity to the fore as the single most important factor affecting the balance of trade in the UAE. As Table 4-7 illustrates, the value of exports, predominantly oil,

nearly quadrupled from Dh 7.4 billion (1973) to Dh 27.5 billion in the following year, only to reach an all-time high of an estimated Dh 33 billion in 1976. Of the leading countries at the receiving end of the pipeline in the later year, five accounted for over 61 percent of the total value of exports. These are Japan (28 percent), France (13 percent), the United States (10 percent), Britain (6 percent), and Holland (4 percent).[20] Entrepôt trade, a permanent feature of Dubai commercial eminence, also increased in value nearly fivefold between 1973 and 1976. Over 93 percent of reexports in the latter year went to gulf countries, namely, Saudi Arabia, Iran, Kuwait, Bahrain, Qatar, and the Sultanate of Oman.[21] As the value of exports increased so did imports. Again, Japan led the list of exporters to the UAE (17.5 percent) followed by Britain (17 percent), the United States (14.2 percent), West Germany (7. 3 percent), and France (4.8 percent).[22]

   The economy of the UAE is undoubtedly subject to the vagaries of any economic system that is undergoing extremely rapid change because of the abundance of capital derived from a single commodity. Spiraling inflation, demographic imbalance, and the strain on utilities and the local market caused by the influx of foreign labor are only the most salient drawbacks of such economies. But for the UAE, there is one additional factor whose origins are embedded in the now fading tribal rivalries. It is what we may call "ostentatious duplication," or the inclination of some emirates to build infrastructures just because a neighboring one has done so. The best example of this infrastructural spiral can be found in international airport construction in the country. Dubai has one airport and is in the process of building another seventeen miles away. Sharigah, which is only ten miles from Dubai, has its own international airport. Abu Dhabi and Ras al-Khaimah each have one airport and the former is in the planning stage for another. Seaport proliferation follows a similar pattern. This duplication also occurs in the development of industries that do not benefit from economies of scale due to a limited domestic market. Cement factories, for instance, have been built in Ras al-Khaimah and Abu Dhabi and are under construction in Dubai. The authority of the National Planning Board, as it appeared in 1976, did not transcend the task of dutifully allocating federal development funds. The "duplication" projects we have referred to are obviously the work of local authorities represented by the individual rulers. In most cases, decisions to build or not to build are political, not economic. And until the power of the federal planning board is unleashed in favor of a more genuine coordination incorporating a central plan, the preoccupation with the wastefully spectacular over the economically sound may well continue.

Social Services and Social Development

When a state is endowed with wealth in the magnitude that the UAE is at this stage of its economic development, the distributive aspect of such wealth becomes an overriding governmental function. Government investment in the areas of social services and development, i.e., health, housing, welfare, utilities, and education, is so great that the UAE is becoming a welfare state in emulation of Kuwait in the upper gulf. Figures from the federal budget of 1976, for example, are revealing. The eight ministries most directly connected to social services, welfare, and development, i.e., housing, social affairs, health, communications, information, electricity and water, education, and youth and sports, were allocated 73.2 percent of a total development budget of over Dh 2 billion.

From the perspective of integration, as material rewards in one form or another cross emirates' boundaries and reach down to the lowest level of the social strata in an unprecedented manner, it is likely that a popular stake in the new order, emanating from the promise of a better future, will develop. Elaboration on this point will be reserved for Chapter 6. In order to prepare the ground for such discussion, however, our main concern here will be to explore the extent to which federal institutions are dispensing such rewards in the form of services rendered.

Housing is one area of social services where the union government is visibly active. Aside from long-term, low-interest loans provided by the UAE Development Bank for housing construction, the federal government, through the two ministries of housing and public works, builds houses and then presents them free of charge to citizens. The importance of this sector is underscored by the allocation of 14.8 percent (Dh 297.9 million) of the 1976 development budget for housing alone.[23] Table 4-8 summarizes federal efforts in this socially vital field in the five northern emirates. As can be clearly noticed, the relatively poor states of Fujairah and Ras al-Khaimah were granted the larger share, both for houses already completed and those under construction.

The federal distributive function is also undertaken in the form of health services and welfare. These two areas were allocated 10 percent of the overall 1976 budget. As in other oil-rich states in the area, medical care is provided without cost, and the expansion and improvement of such vital services are tangible benefits brought about by the union. For example, in 1976, seven hospitals (two in Abu Dhabi, two in Sharigah, and one each in Ajman, Umm al-Guiwain, and Ras al-Khaimah), a nursing school (Ras al-Khaimah), four medical centers, and eight general clinics were completed. In addition, work commenced on fifteen

76

TABLE 4-8

FEDERAL PUBLIC HOUSING IN THE
NORTHERN EMIRATES, 1973-1976

Description / Emirate	Public Houses Completed 1973-1975	Under Construction 1976	Number of Applicants for Public Housing 1975	Number of Applicants Granted Public Housing 1975	%
Sharigah	266	730	1358	164	12.0
'Ajman	230	395	412	180	43.7
Umm al-Guiwain	240	375	472	90	19.0
Ras al-Khaimah	536	1493	2743	496	18.0
Fujairah	422	1757	2251	351	15.6
TOTAL	1694	4750	7236	1281	17.7

Sources: Ministry of Planning, UAE, Annual Statistical Group, 1972-1975, (1976) pp. 110, 130, 134, Ministry of Information and Culture, UAE, UAE Yearbook, 1976 (in Arabic), p. 59, and Ministry of Planning, UAE, Federal Investment Plan for Socioeconomic Development, 1976 (in Arabic), pp. 122-205.

new hospitals and twenty-two medical centers and clinics to cover most populated areas in the federation.

But by far the largest single federal investment (19.2 percent) in the 1976 development budget was earmarked for communications.[24] Roads and telecommunications serve a highly significant function not only in the area of economic development, but in the process of national integration as well. A road network connecting all major towns and villages in the union was in the process of completion in 1976. In fact, in the same year, Fujairah, which is the only union member located entirely on the Gulf of Oman, was linked for the first time with the rest of the country when a paved road through the Hajjar Mountains was finally completed. As Table 4-9 shows, by the end of 1976 the federal government was supposed to have built over 700 kilometers of highways. In a relatively small country such as the UAE, with over 80 percent of the population concentrated along a coastline of about 300 kilometers, this is a major accomplishment. Expansion has also taken place in mail and telecommunication facilities throughout the emirates. The latter in particular was consolidated by the transfer of ownership and control in 1976 from six foreign companies to the newly created UAE Agency for Telecommunications.

The distributive efforts of the federal government through the activities of its agencies, in the form of free housing, low-cost utilities, direct welfare benefits, or free medical services, have undoubtedly the implicit purpose of widening the popular base of the new order, the union. Of no less significance, however, is the deliberate and systematic inculcation of the principles of national unity in the minds of the youth through the system of education. Federal planners assign special attention to this vital sector. This attention, for instance, is reflected by the size of federal allocations for education from Dh 62 million in 1972 to Dh 530 million in 1976, making this the largest single item in the overall federal budget for the latter year.

The growth of the educational sector in the UAE is enhanced not only by the fact that education has been compulsory for the primary stage since 1972, but also by the magnitude of incentives provided. Not only is education free at all levels, but most students receive free books, meals, uniforms, transportation, and, in addition, cash allowances. As Table 4-10 clearly depicts, public school attendance over the first half decade of the federation grew from nearly 33,000 students in 1972 to over 71,000 in 1976. Over the same period, the number of classrooms more than doubled and the size of the teaching corps nearly quadrupled. In addition, schools for both sexes increased from 74 in 1972 to 204 in 1976. This does not include centers for adult education and the eradication of

TABLE 4-9:
ROAD AND BRIDGE CONSTRUCTION BY THE
MINISTRY OF PUBLIC WORKS, UAE , 1973-1976

(thousands of UAE dirhams)

Year and Description / Type of Project	1973 - 1975		1976	
	Length (km)	Total Cost	Length (km)	Total Cost (est.)
Highways	347.8	350,800	358	504,500
Internal Roads	47.9	45,347	88	91,000
Studies and Maintenance	--	6,000	145	6,000
TOTAL	395.7	402,147	591	601,500

Source: Ministry of Planning, UAE, Annual Statistical Group, 1972-1975 (1976), p. 109.

TABLE 4-10

THE GROWTH OF PUBLIC EDUCATION IN THE UAE, 1971-1976

Description / School Year	STUDENTS			CLASSROOMS				TEACHERS			SCHOOLS				
	male	female	Total	male	female	Coed	Total	male	female	Total	male	female	Kindergarten	Coed	Total
1971/72	21770	11092	32862	669	333	22	1024	955	630	1585	42	31	-	1	74
1972/73	24508	15685	40193	754	443	93	1290	1381	1005	2386	66	39	11	13	129
1973/74	26154	18118	44272	866	575	63	1504	1678	1279	2957	77	49	7	15	148
1974/75	30264	22057	52321	1015	671	78	1764	2084	1744	3828	73	57	10	27	167
1975/76	34782	27021	61803	1074	809	199	2082	2542	2314	4856	82	67	11	25	185
1976/77	39300	32014	71314	1248	978	226	2452	3058	2908	5966	91	76	14	23	204

Source: based on tables provided by the Ministry of Education (UAE) during this writer's survey.

illiteracy, which, as shown in Table 4-11, have also attracted a sizable attendance over the same period.[25]

Before the federal Ministry of Education took over in 1972, efforts of other countries in the region were largely responsible for formal schooling in the area. Kuwait financed and administered most schools in Dubai, Sharigah, and Ras al-Khaimah, and hence the curricula in such schools were largely based on the Kuwaiti system, which, in turn, was patterned after the Egyptian system. Abu Dhabi, which was not lacking in financial capabilities, administered its own schools, and its curriculum was influenced by the Jordanian model. After the union was formed, the overriding concern of federal educational planners was to integrate these two curricula as the first step in the domestication of the educational system. This task was accomplished in 1974. But since then, a new educational policy emanating largely from the local culture and reflecting the new political arrangement in the area was formulated. In the spring of 1977, a high-level committee of educators was in the process of rewriting the educational material for all levels in a manner that best incorporated the principles of the federal educational policy.[26]

It is perhaps at this stage of sociopolitical development that the role of a centrally controlled media can best be realized. Although a federal ministry for information was established shortly after the union was formed, integration in this sector was not completed until 1976 in the aftermath of an SCU decision by which full control over all audiovisual broadcasting facilities in the country was to be transferred to the federal Ministry of Information and Culture.[27] Thus, through an integrated system of information, comprised of one official daily newspaper, *al-Ittihad* ("the union"), three television stations, and four radio broadcasting facilities,[28] the ministry has a well-defined task to clarify

> the concept of federation in the minds of the people along with the identification of the positive aspects of relations among the rulers as they lay the foundation for a sounder union. . . . Also, to emphasize and depict the significance of the union in the realization of security, stability and prosperity for every citizen.[29]

Defense and Internal Security

Of all the sectors we have discussed thus far, defense and internal security forces were the last to integrate. When the seven emirates established their union, the then Trucial Oman Scouts (see Chapter 2) were immediately put under federation control as the Union Defense Force (UDF), with one of Shaikh Rashid's sons as the federal minister of

TABLE 4-11:

LITERACY AND EVENING EDUCATION IN THE UAE, 1972-1977

Level School Year	SEX	Number of Centers	Number of Students					TOTAL
			Illiteracy	Elementary	Intermediate	Secondary		
1972/1973	male	36	2636	570	146	94		3446
	female	18	1292	269	5	--		1566
	total	54	3928	839	151	94		5012
1973/74	male	68	4628	1215	288	77		6208
	female	23	1839	450	76	--		2355
	total	91	6467	1665	364	77		8573
1974/75	male	71	5390	1665	586	110		7751
	female	27	2165	890	204	7		3266
	total	98	7555	2555	790	117		11017
1975/76	male	74	5209	2188	835	259		8421
	female	29	1583	793	332	38		2746
	total	103	6792	2981	1167	297		11167
1976/77	male	67	3842	2037	1181	332		7310
	female	28	950	574	393	125		2042
	total	95	4792	2611	1574	457		9352

Source: Ministry of Education and Youth, UAE, Education in the UAE (unpublished report presented to the conference of Arab educational statisticians held in Baghdad in the period 5-10 March, 1977), p. 12.

defense. Outside the formal jurisdiction of the Ministry of Defense, however, there were four separate military or paramilitary formations under the direct control of local authorities. The largest and best equipped was the Abu Dhabi Defense Force (ADDF) of over 10,000 men with land, sea, and air branches. Dubai, too, had its own defense force, with a manpower strength of nearly 1,000 men. The two Gasimi states of Sharigah and Ras al-Khaimah formed their own versions of a defense force (the National Guard of Sharigah and the Mobile Force of Ras al-Khaimah), with approximately 250 men each.

The sensitivity of defense and security matters in general may well have contributed to the delay of integration in this sector. However, two specific factors are usually held responsible for this delay. On the one hand, each ruler generally perceived of his defense force, often led by sons or close relatives, as a useful instrument of control and a means for maintaining a stable status quo. To transfer control over such a force to a higher authority might also mean the transfer or, at least, the division of loyalty and allegiance of the men involved, something the rulers were reluctant to accept. The second factor, somewhat linked to the first, involves the great variation in both size and quality of such forces. The ADDF had virtually the characteristics of a modern army with a high command and three integrated branches of service. Other rulers were wary that unifying defense forces would in effect mean a greater ADDF, within which their relatively small detachments would be submerged.

These somewhat subtle, but logical, arguments could not stand the tide of federation for long. Besides the rulers came to realize that, whether in this or other sectors, transfer of control from local authorities to the federal government meant in actuality the transfer of the very heavy cost burden of raising and maintaining armies. Notwithstanding some official declarations by the rulers in which they urged themselves to merge defense and security forces, the first serious attempt in this regard came in mid-1975 when the rulers agreed to invite an Arab committee composed of high-ranking military officers from Saudi Arabia, Jordan, and Kuwait to advise them on the best possible ways of unifying the hitherto disparate defense forces of the member emirates.

Based on the recommendations of this military committee, which were submitted to the president of the union early in 1976, the UAE Supreme Council for Defense, upon the approval of the rulers concerned, decided in May to merge all the armed forces in the UAE. Accordingly, three military commands were created, each led by a son of the ruler in whose state the command was located. These three were the Western Command (Abu Dhabi), the Central Command (Dubai), and the Northern Command (Ras al-Khaimah). Sharigah's national guard was merged with the federal police force under the jurisdiction of the Ministry of Interior.[30] Table 4-12 summarizes the total strength of the UAE armed forces in the aftermath of their merger.

The unification of the armed forces in the UAE represents a significant development in the life of the union. However, it is only the beginning. The realization of full integration, not just formal merger, is contingent upon both the ability and willingness of the central military authority to blend both personnel and equipment across the three military/geographic divisions outlined above in a manner, and to an extent, compatible with the strategic defense requirements of the union as an integrated geographical unit. Furthermore, the preunification motley of defense forces included in their ranks a number of foreign elements from Britons to Pakistanis and Baluchis. Although the expertise of such personnel might be indispensable to the combat effectiveness of these troops at this stage, the gradual domestication of the armed forces by citizen recruitment will perhaps improve their image and help replace personal loyalties with firmer foundations.[31]

Federal control over the so-called public security forces (police, investigation, border and coast guard, and civil defense) has been established gradually through a succession of federal laws and SCU decisions. First, a Nationality and Passport Law was enacted in 1972 regulating matters of UAE citizenship and the conditions under which it can be obtained. One year later, another federal law introduced some uniformity into matters of immigration and residence throughout the union. In 1974, a third law established a "state security force" under the auspices of the Ministry of Interior to "safeguard the federal system against any form of subversion." This law was later (November 1976) amended to put all aspects of state security under the direct control of the president of the union. This amendment was based on a late-1976 decision of the SCU that gave the president full authority to "supervise through federal agencies all matters relating to immigration, residence, and public security and order throughout the land."[32] Thus, by the end of 1976, of all the member emirates, only Dubai had not as yet relinquished control over its police and customs to federal authorities.

We have thus far identified federal institutional development around the three major fields of finance and economic development, social services and social development, and national defense and security in light of the interplay of local and federal structures in these areas. From this survey, apparently only police, customs, and petroleum affairs had, at the close of 1976, escaped full integration under the union central authority. However, one additional domain remains divided between local and central authorities. It is that of the judiciary. Of course, the

TABLE 4-13:

JUDICIAL SUITS HANDLED BY THE FEDERAL SUPREME COURT, 1973-1976

Year Type of Suit	1973	1974	1975	1976	Total
Penal	3	38	212	303	556
Civil, Commercial and Administrative	1	5	3	2	11
Constitutional Interpretative	1	1	-	3	5
Appeal	-	-	-	1	1
TOTAL	5	44	215	309	573

Supreme Court is a federal authority that, as Table 4-13 shows, did handle by the end of 1976 a reasonable load of juridical suits of penal as well as civil, commercial, and administrative nature. But at the lower levels of the judicial system, only the courts of Abu Dhabi, Sharigah, and Fujairah were administered by the federal Ministry of Justice. Obviously, for the other rulers, memories of the ruler judge (whereby the ruler traditionally served both political as well as judicial functions) still lingered. Besides, to some shaikhs, transfer of control over adjudication meant in effect loss of income as well as prestige, something the rulers of Dubai, Ras al-Khaimah, Ajman, and Umm al-Guiwain were not as yet ready to accept at the time they celebrated the union's fifth anniversary.

At the beginning of this chapter, we suggested that the relative poverty of institutional organization in most member emirates of the UAE has probably helped, though in a passive way, in the process of institutional integration through what might be called "the emergence effect." The erection of a federal edifice usually proceeds in a certain manner. First, a federal law is enacted establishing a certain organization to perform a particular function. Tables of procedures are then drawn. Recruitment of personnel commences. Once this is accomplished, the organization, be it a ministry, a department, or an agency, begins to discharge its duties authoritatively. Where there is no equivalent on the local level, a gradual diffusion of such institution's authority may be accepted on the basis of novelty as well as socioeconomic returns. If, however, a member emirate has a reasonably well-established structure in such a sector, i.e., police, defense, municipalities, etc., integration proceeds at a slower pace, involving perhaps the highest level of the decision-making structures on both federal and local levels.

Federal Legislation: Scope and Emphases

The typology and volume of laws, decrees, and decisions generated by the union government over a specified period of time should provide some insight into the scope of its authority, the degree of its performance, and, possibly, the direction in which it is heading. During the first half decade of the UAE's existence, 65 laws, over 300 decrees, and more than 40 decisions by the Council of Ministers were enacted. Although only 47 of the laws were specifically approved by the Federal National Council (FNC), the Council of Ministers did play the central role in the enactment of almost every piece of legislation the federal legislative system was able to produce.

Federal legislation can be arranged in such a way as to reflect areas of emphasis in the most general terms. In Table 4-14, for instance, each of

TABLE 4-14:
RULE-MAKING IN THE UAE
(Typological/Chronological)

		1971	1972	1973	1974	1975	1976	Totals
DECISIONS OF THE COUNCIL OF MINISTERS	National Security & Defense				2			2
	Social Services, Security, Benefits & Development				2	5	3	10
	Finance, Trade & Economic Development			1	1	3		5
	Organization/Regulation of Federal Agencies & Institutions		3	4	4	4	2	17
DECREES	International Cooperative Agreements		19	10	21	21	20	91
	National Security & Defense						4	4
	Social Services, Security, Benefits & Development				1		1	2
	Finance, Trade and Economic Development		1	1	1		1	4
	Organization/Regulation of Federal Agencies & Institutions		3	2	1	1	6	13
LAWS	International Cooperative Agreements		1	1			1	3
	National Security & Defense	1	1		1		4	7
	Social Services, Security, Benefits and Development		6	3	5	4	3	21
	Finance, Trade, and Economic Development		2	2	2	2	6	14
	Organization/Regulation of Federal Agencies & Institutions	3	6	5	3	3		20
	YEAR	1971	1972	1973	1974	1975	1976	Totals

the three types of legislation was enacted in any one of five general areas of interest.[33] These areas are organization and regulation of federal institutions; finance, trade, and economic development; social services, security, and development; national security and defense; and international cooperation. Federal laws in the first category, for example, range from the organization and reorganization of federal ministries to the regulation of immigration and residence to spelling out the rules by which private medical practice is allowed. The establishment of the Supreme Council for Defense in 1972 is naturally a national security matter, whereas regulating private schools or making primary education compulsory in the same year pertain to social development. The decree by which the UAE joined UNESCO in 1972 is clearly an international cooperative venture, whereas the decree by which it joined the Arab Postal Union (APU) a year later is obviously a regional cooperative undertaking. Likewise, according to this categorization, the decree by which directors were appointed for the UAE Monetary Board in 1973 is a matter of financial concern to the union, whereas those by which this country joined the IMF and the World Bank for Construction and Development clearly belong to the area of international cooperation. Moreover, the decision of the Council of Ministers to establish a ministerial committee for education, culture, and information in 1974 is apparently a social development matter, whereas its 1976 decision to form a permanent committee for projects is one of an economic developmental nature.

In sum, one finds laws, decrees, and decisions along the lines just described in almost all aspects of life typically undertaken by any modern government. Federal legislation in the domestic arena has generally revolved around the establishment, expansion, and consolidation of federal authority vis-à-vis domestic forces that have not always been positive. Similarly, through a spate of decrees either concluding or acceding to all sorts of international agreements, bilateral and multilateral, regional and global, the UAE has sought to establish itself as a full-fledged member of the international community. Before we discuss the UAE from regional and international perspectives, however, a look into domestic integrative and disintegrative variables is in order. This is the subject of the next two chapters.

Part Two
Integration and Disintegration
on the Local Level

5
Disintegrative Factors in the Union's Internal Environment

The year 1976 was supposed to inaugurate a new constitutional era in the union of the seven Arab gulf emirates. After five years of experimentation, a permanent constitution, incorporating a consensus reached through compromise among the contending political elites, was supposed to have been adopted. As it turned out, however, the seven rulers and the coteries of advisers behind them failed to reach an acceptable final form for their partnership. Accordingly, the Provisional Constitution, as its terminus ad quem of December 2 approached, was given a new lease on life for another half decade along with the hesitant acceptance by Shaikh Zayed of the presidency for another five-year term.

In the midst of the circumstances that finally led to the extension of the Provisional Constitution, Shaikh Zayed sent letters to fellow rulers in which he outlined the major obstacles facing the federation. Although these letters were not made public, it is apparent that among these obstacles were the reluctance of the more affluent member emirates, namely Dubai and Sharigah, to share in the financial burden of the union and, more importantly, the lack of integration in the vital areas of defense, public security, and information.[1]

In other words, the president was saying that although the union was still holding, it was nevertheless stagnating. Other member emirates were receiving more than they were willing to give—not so much in material aspects as in political power. The other rulers were not willing to surrender to federal authority in order to give it more meaning and spirit. Shaikh Zayed's bitterness over the obstructive tactics of some of his fellow rulers came out into the open when he said, "[T]he problem is the spirit with which my brother rulers are tackling the problems which face the federation."[2]

In fact, given the financial clout of Abu Dhabi relative to the other union members (see Chapter 4), it is likely that the issue of sharing the financial burden was brought up only as an instrument of pressure. Shaikh Zayed's objective was probably to convey the message that should the other emirates fail to give in on the broadening of federal authority, Abu Dhabi's financial commitment to the federation might be reconsidered. As it turned out, a great deal of bargaining and persuasion, both domestically and regionally, was required before Shaikh Zayed's conditions, i.e., the unification of defense and security forces and the integration of the information media, were met, leading to his acceptance of the presidency for another five-year term under a provisional constitution.

Parallel to the issue of Shaikh Zayed's presidency, there was the matter of promulgating a permanent constitution. The major stumbling blocks that eventually led to abandoning the idea late in 1976 revolved around the rulers' inability to reach a compromise on three issues: (1) the method of recruiting members of the Federal National Council (FNC); (2) the abolition of the individual emirates' prerogative under the Provisional Constitution to raise their own defense forces; and (3) the abolition of the veto in the SCU that was constitutionally accorded the two larger states of Abu Dhabi and Dubai.

Obviously, from the point of view of most rulers, with the probable exception of Abu Dhabi's and Sharigah's, to abandon the prerogative of appointing members to the FNC was tantamount to inviting a serious imbalance in the local distribution of power. To these rulers, appointing members to this federal body not only meant having a loyal leverage at the federal level, but also allowed more room in the process of distribution of political favors—a significant feature of politics in the area. Two compromise solutions between the extreme choices of election by the populace and appointment by the rulers were debated. One specified that a ruler would appoint half the council's membership, with the other half to be popularly elected. The second allowed the rulers to nominate 200 individuals who, in turn, would elect from among themselves the 40 deputies called for in the constitution. Both were rejected, and thus the rulers retained their right of appointment.

With regard to the other two stumbling blocks, the right of the member emirates to raise their own individual armies has since been abolished, but veto power for the two sister states of Abu Dhabi and Dubai in the crucial SCU remains. Thus, if one looks at the entire array of issues involved here, Abu Dhabi and Dubai emerged with relatively more influence in union affairs than they already had. Though smaller emirates saw their ideas prevail in matters of recruitment to the FNC and in the entire issue of a permanent constitution, they nevertheless gave up control of defense and security forces and information facilities in favor of federal authorities, and acceded to the retention of Abu Dhabi and Dubai's veto power in the SCU.

The tug of war between centralism and parochialism reflects a dialectical interaction between two currents of opinion that have been operating in the local environment ever since the idea of a federation was born. On the one hand, there are the *wahdawis*, unitarians, who idealistically view the union concept in totalistic terms. They argue that step-by-step integration is a sign of weakness and is tantamount to surrender to narrow parochial interests. Hesitation in this matter, they add, is a betrayal of the ultimate Arab goal of total unity. In their view, the union tends to transcend the physical borders of the member emirates, joining ideologically with Arab nationalism and the seemingly arrested drive for unity. To them, unity must be an end by itself and not a means to certain narrow ends. Being generally outside the political establishment, the *wahdawis* hope that the realization of a unitary system will weaken the traditional brand of rule, which has limited meaningful political participation to the ruling families and their upper-class allies. On the regional level, the *wahdawis* argue, a strong and solid union in this strategic part of the Arab homeland might not only protect the eastern flank of the Arab world, thereby preserving the Arab character of the peninsular side of the gulf, but also serve as an example for other Arab states to emulate. On the whole, the proponents of this approach are generally antiestablishment but not necessarily revolutionaries in the classical sense.

At the other end of the spectrum, one finds the *ittihadis*, or federalists, who primarily believe that a step-by-step federation is the most promising course of action in view of the sociopolitical dynamics of the area. These gradualists argue that any integrative step should be adopted only after the voluntary acceptance of such a step by the federating states. This, they feel, is the best guarantee against reversals along the federal path that might find their origins in coercive politics at one time or another during the crucial early stages of such ventures. To underscore this point, the gradualists point to examples of unsuccessful amalgamations in the Arab world, e.g., the unity between Egypt and Syria (1958-1961). From another perspective, the proponents of gradualism visualize the union as a perpetuator of the status quo; that is, it is a means to continue traditional rule, rather than a means to weaken it. They tend to resist the pressure to widen political participation and favor preserving the traditional power structure, particularly on the local level. In short, then, those who embrace the step-by-step approach look at the union as one of convenience, and hence are likely to judge its success not so much by the magnitude of their sacrifices for its sake as by the easy rewards they get in its wake.

The two different approaches to union politics have been portrayed in abstract terms. In reality, however, proponents and opponents of both positions may not be as vocal nor their positions as clear-cut as just portrayed. This is especially true for the unitarians, who, although they are generally more politically articulate, may find espousal of their cause in public inhibited by the authoritarian nature of political systems on the local level. Although it is difficult to generalize, a few tentative observations are nonetheless worth mentioning. The first is that, except for Abu Dhabi, the political establishments of the member emirates have adopted an incremental attitude toward the union. The special position of Abu Dhabi within the federal structure (see Chapter 6) makes it a direct political beneficiary of any further integrative undertaking. Second, given the low level of political awareness and participation in all the emirates, the select few who make the major political decisions and generally shape an emirate's position vis-à-vis the union are not likely to be influenced by the opposition, however intense. Third, exponents of the totalistic approach tend to be younger, better-educated, and more politically articulate. They include university graduates, intellectuals, and junior civil servants. They represent a fast-growing minority among the indigenous population in the union. Further, their political views on the union are more likely to be colored by the nature and extent of their education than by the attitudes of their home states toward the federation. For instance, despite the renowned phlegmatic attitude of Dubai vis-à-vis the union (see below), a son of a Dubayan merchant who has received a university degree abroad and then returned to work in the federal government is likely to have an orientation more favorable to the enhancement of union power than to the isolationist attitude this emirate tends to project.[3]

The draft of the permanent constitution contains a substantial curtailment of the powers of individual emirates. In view of the fact that, by the end of 1976, it had failed to enlist the support of most rulers, one must conclude that further unification will be gradual and slow-paced. This conclusion, however, must be qualified. As pointed out earlier, some of the issues of contention at the time the draft was debated had in fact been settled in favor of the union central authority even before the first term of the Provisional Constitution expired. Although inter-emirate pressures and counterpressures at the ruling elites' level did contribute to this outcome, it further attests to the observation that gradualism in union matters is a relative term.

Both *wahdawi*s and *ittihadi*s operate within a cultural context that impedes speedy integration within the UAE. Tribalism, local territorial disputes, the paternal and personal nature of political leadership, and immigration are the key contributing factors. The first three are sociopolitical characteristics that are deeply rooted in the cultural milieu of the area. Immigration, on the other hand, is a phenomenon brought about by economic expediencies owing to the discovery and exploitation of oil. These factors interrelate in a manner that evokes a limited sense of cause and effect. For example, tribalism is a product of the historical, ethnic, cultural, and environmental makeup of the region. It promotes a paternalistic view of political power and may, in addition, perpetuate conflict over territorial matters. However, tribalism can be weakened not only by modern education but also, and more so, by immigrants who, in addition to their skills, bring ideas that erode traditional values and outlooks among the indigenous population, at least in the long run. The effect of this erosion, again in the long term, will probably reach to the very essence of parochialism and authoritarianism, the two most salient manifestations of tribalism. Finally, there is one more external factor of relevance here. In the span of nearly one and a half centuries of involvement in the area, Britain either kept aloof as these factors operated or else helped sharpen and aggravate them in a manner and to an extent perceived to be in its best colonial interests.

Tribalism, territorial disputes, political paternalism, and immigration all antecede the union and, hence, each is a carry-over from an earlier era. How did these factors develop? Why are they considered disintegrative? How does each one of them affect the federal venture negatively? These are the types of questions I propose to discuss at this particular juncture.

Tribalism

Tribalism has been a feature of human existence in the Arabian Peninsula since time immemorial. The tribe has traditionally served as a cultural and ethnic frame of reference for the individual tribesman. It has further provided him with a sense of identity and physical security against a characteristically hostile environment. In the past, tribes of varying sizes and statures roamed the desert spaces of Eastern Arabia in search of pasture, depending on the erratic and unpredictable behavior of natural precipitation from year to year. This pursuit was all too vital since rain, when it fell, gave rise to the sort of life upon which nomads sustained their animals, the mainstay of a traditional tribal economy. The encounter of many of these tribes with the sea to the east during the seventeenth and eighteenth centuries led to the gradual rise of a more settled life along the gulf coast, characterized by new modes of economic activity such as seafaring, fishing, pearling, and subsistence agriculture. In addition, a number of city-states emerged along tribal lines. Later on, the discovery and exploitation of oil in the area was to give the greatest impetus for the development of what one observer has referred to as "urban tribalism."[4]

In historical terms, tribalism has traditionally developed certain characteristics that are in harmony with the physical, cultural, and political nature of the environment within whose bounds the tribes have lived. First, tribal organization tends to be hierarchical. This kind of vertical fissility starts with the family, then the section, the clan, the tribe, and, occasionally, the tribal confederation, with considerations of ethnicity and security as the main dictates of the latter. Tribal authority has traditionally been entrusted to a tribal chief who is chosen by the elders on the basis of the venerated qualities of hospitality, bravery, and honesty. As the tribal states along the gulf peninsular coast were emerging, so was the phenomenon of the tribal ruling family. But because no state was ever exclusively composed of the members of a single tribe, tribal pluralism became the norm. The numerically superior tribe or tribal confederation provided the ruling family, from which a semihereditary ruler was chosen as the paternalistic ruler of the state, and the paramount tribal chief, to whom other tribal heads in the state looked for support in exchange for loyalty. As Table 5-1 shows, of the seven member emirates of the UAE, only Ras al-Khaimah fails to meet the criterion of numerical superiority as a precondition for rule.

Through the custom-honored and religion-revered practices of *shura* and *majlis*, a ruler exercised his authority, with the protection of the community and the adjudication of disputes according to Islamic law and tribal customs as the raison d'être of his rule. Furthermore, as one observer puts it,

> reciprocal reinforcement on the side both of ruler and kinsmen which determined relative authority was based on size of family, degree of kinship, size and relationship of the generations, force of character, personal ties, vague or specific threats of deposition and almost institutionalized liquidation.[5]

Loyalty of a tribesman has traditionally resided in the family, then in the tribe, and finally the state. What is important here is that in the case of the latter, loyalty was often granted the ruler as a person, not the position of rulership or the territorial frame called the state.

Another traditional aspect of tribalism in Eastern Arabia is

TABLE 5-1

TRIBAL POPULATION IN TRUCIAL 'OMAN, 1968

EMIRATE / TRIBE OR TRIBAL CONFEDERATION	ABU DHABI	DUBAI	SHĀRIGAH	'AJMAN	UMM AL-GUWAIN	RAS AL-KHAIMAH	FUJAIRAH	TOTALS
Bani Yas	4,597*	3,913*	1,424	213	1	290	27	10,465
al-Sharguiyyīn	80	65	116	69	25	82	8,372*	8,809
Shihuh-Habus	147	74	74	13	-	5,845	244	6,397
Al Ali	60	155	508*	85	2,862*	1,445	3	5,118
al-Gawāsim	101	108	3,592*	8	3	1,055*	14	4,881
al-Manasīr	3,224	275	49	21	-	38	-	3,607
Z'aab	22	27	710	7	4	2,455	-	3,225
al-Dhawāhir	2,844	42	109	41	-	9	57	3,102
Mazāri	1,287	271	293	17	38	1,062	76	3,044
Al bu Shāmis	370	769	689	190	12	408	-	2,438
Bani Kitāb	617	156	1,458	21	6	112	-	2,370
al-Nu'aym	325	171	219	616*	25	968	10	2,334
al-Nagbiyyīn	16	-	1,345	-	- .	541	3	1,905
al-'Awāmir	1,721	69	37	7	19	34	5	1,892
Other (less than 1,000 each)	2,339	1,769	2,146	303	214	3,597	327	10,695
TOTALS	17,750	7,864	12,769	1,611	3,209	17,941	9,138	70,282

Source: 1968 Trucial States Census (unpublished).

*The tribe or tribal confederation to which the ruling family in the Emirate belongs.

geographical mobility. The desert is a seemingly endless expanse of desolate and inhospitable land. The only promise of survival required the nomads to chase pasture whenever and wherever the unstable weather patterns in the area allowed rain to fall. Out of this mobility evolved the problem of control over tribal grazing land, or *dirah*s, and water sources, which later came to be an irritating factor in the determination of territorial boundaries between the emirates.

Violence is yet another characteristic of tribal life in the area. It was generally part of the quest for survival in view of the scarcity of resources. Disputes among tribal states, or between the tribes within them, arose over issues such as access to and control over grazing lands and water holes, trade, fishing and pearling rights, and, more recently, with the coming of the oil era, over territorial jurisdictions. In fact, the history of these shaikhdoms over the past two centuries is replete with incidents of rapacious plunders, raids, and reprisals characterized by tribal alliances that were as shifting as the sand beneath them. One example of violent interemirate clashes that had tribal overtones occurred as recently as 1940, when Dubai and Sharigah fought each other for several months with significant loss of life before they came to accept the mediation of Ras al-Khaimah for a truce. Six years later, Abu Dhabi and Dubai engaged in a fierce war that lasted over a year with Shaikhs Zayed and Rashid leading the two opposing camps. Although both wars were sparked by territorial disputes, historical tribal enmities and dynastic rivalries were at their base. The British policy of minimum interference in matters of domestic concern to the emirates had not only allowed such patterns of violence to continue, but in effect had helped aggravate them simply by insulating and protecting the sociopolitical structure of the shaikhdoms against outside currents in the region. It was only after Britain had acquired a major material stake in the area in the form of an oil investment and had established the air base at Sharigah after World War II that it initiated an interemirate peacekeeping force, the Trucial Oman Levies, in the early 1950s (see Chapter 2).

Another aspect of tribal existence in the lower gulf is the incidence of tribal flight. This type of contested mobility occurs when a tribe attempts to escape an unfavorable situation by moving en masse away from the jurisdiction of one ruler and on to another's. In view of the scarcity of population in the area, this phenomenon has often had the result of exacerbating interemirate relations. One early example of such flight took place in 1835 when the al-Gubaisat tribe, a branch of Bani Yas, migrated in force to al-Odaid at the base of the Qatari Peninsula. This new settlement was for two years both a source of and a target in the hostilities between Abu Dhabi and Qatar until the tribe was brought forcibly back to the Abu Dhabian fold in 1837.[6] More recently, in the late 1960s, the al-Zaab tribe (see Table 5-1 above) virtually vacated Jazirat al-Hamra (the Red Island) just off the Ras al-Khaimah coast in a mass migration to Abu Dhabi after their differences with the ruler, Sagr bin Muhammed al-Gasimi, over the distribution of the emirate's income became irreconcilable. Apparently, the Zaabis struck a better deal with Shaikh Zayed as they settled in Abu Dhabi Town.

Although tribalism is a fact of life in Eastern Arabia, our contention here is that it is obstructive to integration among the emirates in at least four of its aspects. First, tribalism is by its very nature factionalistic and divisive. It encourages a sense of mobile parochialism and ethnic (lineal) exclusiveness. Second, as pointed out earlier, loyalty among tribesmen is primarily and firmly a family and tribal preserve. At the state level, it becomes both personal and elusive. Indeed, it is on this level that incidents of loyalty shifts, whether or not accompanied by tribal flights, are most common. In the past, these loyalty shifts were often accomplished in a manner tantamount to commodity transaction depending on the highest bidder. Nowadays, although the breakdown of the traditional tribal structure may have already been overshadowed by the emergence of the modern state, political loyalty to one's tribe has not as yet given way to loyalty to the state as an abstract political concept. The broadening of this concept to include the union authority as the most encompassing will not only have to await the outcome of a rigorous and lengthy process of education, but will, in addition, largely depend on developments at the top of the federal structure as it shifts between progress and stagnation.

Third, tribalism is by nature aversive to any outside central authority. This traditional rejection of control from above is an outgrowth of the tribal tradition of mobility in pursuit of desert sources of life wherever available. Finally, tribal history in Eastern Arabia is replete with incidents of violence of varying magnitude. In the background of this conflictual situation, rivalries, personal and dynastic, have often been a significant factor. Although this pattern of violence is now virtually a thing of the past, its impact on the interaction among top political elites of these tribal political units still lingers.

Territorial Disputes

The jurisdictional conflict over interemirate frontiers has recently evolved as one of the most disruptive factors in the development of a federal entity. Behind the current territorial disputes in the area is an interplay among a variety of variables, traditional, economic, and political. Traditionally, as one British student of the area has summarized,

> the concept of territorial sovereignty in the Western sense did not exist in
> Eastern Arabia. A ruler exercised jurisdiction over a territory by virtue of
> his jurisdiction over the tribes inhabiting it. They, in turn, owed loyalty to
> him and not to the shaikhdom, amirate or sultenate in which they dwelt.
> Political allegiance to a territorial unit, such as implicit in the European
> state system, is unknown to the Arabian tribesman. His loyalty is personal
> to his tribe, his shaikh, or a leader of greater consequence, and not to any
> abstract image of the state.[7]

Of course, throughout the history of the area, the tribes and tribal states did quarrel over grazing ranges and water holes to the extent that such contests were often regarded as a casus belli for violent skirmishes. But it was the potentiality of oil discoveries and the concomitant Western interest in prospecting for this valuable mineral in the postwar era that aggravated the territorial issue not only on land but offshore as well. Britain, as a de facto protecting power long before that time, had made no serious attempt to reconcile conflicting tribal territorial claims. One is even led to contend that a strange coincidence of foreign control and domestic parochialism may well have contributed a great deal to reinforcing the small-frame mentality characteristic of the local political situation.

It was not until the mid-1950s, with the granting of oil concessions by the shaikhs under way, that the British government sent a diplomat, Julian Walker, to the then Trucial States with the difficult task of drawing a plan for the definition and, if possible, the demarcation of interemirate frontiers. After six years of survey and negotiations, Walker was able to reconcile only some of the conflicting territorial claims and counterclaims definitely; the rest were to be depicted on the map as *frontières de convenance* pending final settlement. The result was a tribal political map (see Figure 5-1) of intertwining jurisdictions and confusingly scattered enclaves. The latter in particular developed out of Walker's approach to determining jurisdictional authorities among the shaikhs, which does not seem wholly unsensible. According to one observer at the scene, the British official would drive to isolated villages and tribal encampments and then ask the elders there to which one of the seven rulers, in addition to the sultan of Oman, they owed allegiance. A consensus on this matter would prompt Walker to simply encircle such a village or encampment, utilizing whatever landmarks were available. He would then submit to British authorities his recommendations as to which of the states this piece of land should belong.[8]

FIGURE 5-1:   *101*

INTERNAL FRONTIERS IN THE UAE

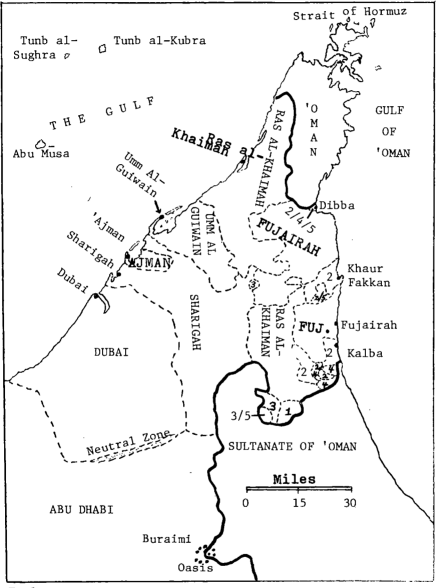

Enclaves:

Dubai:	1	Fujairah:	4
Sharigah:	2	'Oman:	5
'Ajman:	3		

Today, local jurisdictions in the UAE are so fragmented that only Abu Dhabi and Umm al-Guiwain have all their territories contiguous. But territorial fragmentation, had it been settled on a de jure basis, is not problematic in view of the relatively small size of the country as a whole. The source of friction within the union is actually the dozen or so territorial disputes, both land and sea, that characterize almost every internal frontier. These disputes have arisen, for example, between Dubai and Sharigah over the land boundary line; Sharigah, Ajman, and Umm al-Guiwain over offshore jurisdictions and rights of granting oil concessions; Umm al-Guiwain and Ras al-Khaimah over land and sea borders; Sharigah and Fujairah over the boundary line between them.[9]

The sensitivity of such matters, and their ever-existing potential for invoking violent skirmishes, was demonstrated early in 1972 in an incident that posited a major threat to the fledgling union at the time. This incident started when the late Shaikh Muhammad al-Shargui, ruler of Fujairah, apparently motivated by political and economic factors, announced that he had decided to present Shaikh Zayed, the president of the union and ruler of Abu Dhabi, with an orchard in his territory as a gift. The significance of this gift giving lies in the fact that the well that waters this garden was used for years by both Sharigan and Fujairan tribesmen. So the former felt that the shaikh had no right to give away the garden and its well without prior consultation with them. Consequently, fighting broke out between the two emirates until order was restored, after numerous fatalities, by the stationing of federal and Abu Dhabian troops in the "unfulfilled gift" area between the combatants. Eventually, the federal government coped with the issue by purchasing title to the orchard and allowing equal utilization of its well by both sides.[10] More recently, in the summer of 1975, a dispute over the Dubai-Sharigah border came close to triggering a violent confrontation between the two emirates because of Sharigah's expressed intention of building a major shopping complex. The site of the planned structure happens to be claimed by Dubai astride the *frontière de convenance* between the two. The reported resort of the two sides to arbitration by a European power, probably France, is indicative not only of how seriously the individual shaikhs view such disputes, but also the precarious position of the federal government in its inability to act as a credible arbitrator.

In sum, territorial and jurisdictional disputes among member states of the UAE have substantially contributed to the existence of an atmosphere that is nonconducive, in fact inimical, to sociopolitical and economic development, stability, and, above all, integration. The frustration of union officials over this issue was expressed recently by Zayed in the following terms:

> I spent nearly a week in the northern emirates in an attempt to settle some border disputes of minor consequence, yet they are a source of conflict among the member-states. . . . I can say, with both bitterness and sorrow, that their disputes often involve a few tens of meters, and do you believe that we have not been able to build a hospital on a piece of real estate because two emirates claim sovereignty over it? Abu Dhabi, for one, had territorial disputes with neighboring countries such as Saudi Arabia, Qatar and Oman, but they were resolved through understanding, flexibility and brotherly discussions.[11]

Of course, the best resolution of internal frontier problems in the UAE is to have no frontiers at all. This is at least what more recent official maps of the federation reflect. However, it takes more than just the printing of frontierless maps to settle this seemingly perennial issue. It will probably take a feat of large-scale territorial exchange that may involve federal financial compensation and that should involve a spirit of compromise and flexibility. Until this occurs, the map of UAE internal frontiers will remain fragmented and will continue to be a disruptive factor.

Paternalism

The ruling family is the cornerstone of the political power structure in the gulf's small littoral states. Its evolution around prominent tribal chiefs took place gradually as the mode of life changed from nomadic to sedentary. As the economic status of such families improved, thanks to oil royalties, their character began more and more to change to that of ruling aristocracies. In each of the seven member emirates of the UAE, the ruling family belongs to the most prominent clan of the most powerful tribe in the shaikhdom. Its overriding function is to elect a ruler who, once elected, becomes not only the ruler of the emirate but the head of the ruling family and the paramount tribal chief. This triple role has traditionally made these individuals the center of political influence and the source of all authority in the emirate. In addition, sovereignty has to these rulers nearly the same meaning it had to the "absolute" monarchs of post-Renaissance Europe insofar as it resided in the person of the ruler himself, not in the state in an abstract sense. However, in view of the highly regarded rule by religious law and tribal customs, along with the time-honored practice of consultation, this system can hardly be described as dictatorial in the classical sense. Instead, it

represents a brand of authoritarianism, paternalism, and conservatism
that characteristically "allows the exaltation of a privileged few [with
no] significant procedure of control by the governed."[12]

Rulers go about choosing this "privileged few" according to a delicate
formula that takes into consideration the whole question of intertribal
and interclan politics within the emirate and beyond. With personal
relationship to the ruler as the principal factor, important positions in
the government are usually assigned to leading members of the ruling
family. In addition, influential members of the nonruling families in
the same tribe, prominent members of other leading tribes in the
emirate, influential merchants, *ulama* ("religious scholars"), and a
select group of expatriates are likely to be on the top of the list for
possible recruitment to less influential posts in a typical shaikhly
administration. Except in a handful of cases, birth into a ruling family is
generally a precondition for the attainment of high positions of power.[13]
This type of ascriptive elitism has substantially narrowed the base of the
power structure and restricted meaningful political participation to the
few at the top of the social scale. As one keen observer summed up the
situation in the mid-1970s,

> political power in the Shaykhdoms continues to be wielded mainly at the
> top by an assorted coterie of cousins, sons, brothers and uncles of
> semihereditary tribal rulers. In the meantime, those interest groups that do
> exist—the ruling families, other families of the ruling tribes, important
> nonruling tribes, influential merchants, venerated religious leaders and
> selected representatives among the community of expatriate advisors—
> appear content with, and have positive interests in the survival of,
> shaykhly rule.[14]

One aspect of this shaikhly rule is the problem of succession. While
still in power, most shaikhs ordinarily prepare the way for a smooth
succession by designating a son, usually the eldest, as the heir apparent.
This is normally accomplished by a behind-the-scenes process of give
and take not unlike that which accompanied the accession of the ruler
himself. In cases where a ruler has no male offspring, or if a son has not
as yet reached maturity, a relative, close or distant, is usually appointed
as a deputy ruler. Despite this system of seemingly institutionalized
succession, transfer of rulership by palace coups has always been a fact of
political life in the emirates. Four of the seven rulers at present have
acceded to their respective positions by takeovers or in the aftermath of
assassination. Shaikh Ahmad of Umm al-Guiwain came to power
following the murder of his father in 1929; Shaikh Sagr of Ras al-
Khaimah, by deposing his uncle in 1948; Shaikh Zayed of Abu Dhabi, by

takeover in 1966; and Shaikh Sultan of Sharigah, upon the murder of his brother by a previously deposed ruler in 1972. Indeed, in the political history of the shaikhdoms, many rulers died with their heads up and sandals on. In a tribal society such incidents of violence tend to generate chain reactions of their own. Their imprints do not easily fade away with the passage of time.

The political history of the emirates is also replete with cases that support the assertion that the most likely source of threat to a ruling shaikh springs from among his close relations. The most illustrative example in this regard can be drawn from the fairly modern history of Abu Dhabi. After a fruitful long rule of over fifty years, Zayed bin Khalifa died in 1909, leaving behind seven sons but no heir apparent. The Al Nuhayyan family elected Khalifa, Zayed's eldest son, for the rulership, partly for his age and partly for his close relation, via his mother, to al-Manasir, a prominent tribe in al-Buraimi Oasis. Khalifa declined, however, leaving the position to Tahnun, a younger brother. The death of this ruler of natural causes in 1912 brought to power yet another brother, Hamdan. After a decade of relative tranquillity in the princely household, this ruler died violently at the hand of a brother, Sultan, who shot him in the back as he was leaving the latter's home after attending a dinner banquet. Sultan's act triggered a period of quick rulership succession by means of fratricide, which in only a half decade (1922-1927) brought the end of three rulers.

Sultan succeeded his murdered brother, but failed to win the support of the ruling family and leading tribal chiefs. In 1925, he was in turn assassinated by his brother, Sagr, who shot him in the back as he was on his way to the sunset prayers. Sagr's usurpation of rule not only complicated tribal politics in the emirate, but, in addition, heightened his own sense of personal insecurity, causing him to plot against the life of Khalifa. Although Khalifa was leading a private life, he was the choice of many Abu Dhabian tribal chiefs, especially those of the al-Manasir tribe, for ruler. These tribal chiefs, learning of the impending assassination, counteracted by arranging and bringing about Sagr's violent end in the fall of 1927. At this particular time, the Al Nuhayyan ruling family, conscious of the adverse effect of this chain of violence on its status, brought to the center of power a low-key young shaikh, Shakhbut bin Sultan, the eldest son of the second slain ruler. A relatively long period of political calm ensued in Abu Dhabi until, in 1966, Shakhbut's younger brother, Shaikh Zayed, came to power in a nonviolent palace coup.[15]

Of far greater bearing on the union, however, is a more recent incident of dynastic squabbling involving the ruling family of Sharigah. Back in

1951, Shaikh Sagr bin Sultan acceded to the rulership in Sharigah in the aftermath of a dynastic dispute. He was later deposed by the British in 1965, partly for his persistent criticism of their policies in the area and partly for his apparently strong pro-Egyptian orientation. Sagr was succeeded by Khalid, a nephew who belonged to another line of the Gasimi dynasty. In late January 1972, less than two months after the union came into being, Sagr returned to Sharigah from exile in Egypt and Iraq, accompanied by eighteen of his followers. What ensued then was an attempted palace coup against the incumbent ruler that, although it resulted in his death, was nevertheless doomed due to the quick response of federal authorities, who dispatched a contingent of the Union Defense Force (UDF). The uprising was swiftly crushed and Sagr was arrested. A university-educated younger brother of the slain ruler, Sultan, was chosen by the federal government to succeed to the rulership.[16]

   This incident represents more than just an assertion of the pattern of dynastic violence; it has had a far-reaching effect on the essence of the union as a whole. First, the coup attempt represented the first real challenge to union authority since it was forged. The cooperation of the two most powerful members of the Supreme Council, Shaikhs Zayed and Rashid, in first dispatching the UDF to put an end to the coup and, second, in appointing a successor to the slain ruler is indicative of how determined the inner core of the union power structure has been to keep things under control. Second, and of no less importance than foiling Sagr's attempt, was the nagging question of what type of action the federal government should take in regard to the arrested shaikh who, by attempting to regain his former position of power, committed a capital offense against a duly established ruler. A complicating factor in this whole affair is that less than two months earlier Khalid had acquiesced to the landing of Iranian troops on the Sharigan island of Abu Musa (see Chapter 7). This made Sagr appear to many Sharigans a patriotic prince rather than a power-hungry usurper. Had Sagr been tried and convicted, federal punishment, however light, might well have been interpreted in tribalistic and not in civic terms, thereby inflaming the faintly simmering historical tribal enmities between al-Gawasim and Bani Yas, a risk both Zayed and Rashid were not willing to take.[17] Finally, the fact that Khalid's successor was chosen by the SCU and not by the elders of the ruling family, as customary, goes a long way toward setting a precedent that may eventually lead to the erosion of tribal influence in the affairs of the federation.

   The concentration of power at the top in each of the political systems in the UAE underscores the dependency of these emirates' interrelations on the personal factors conditioning the rulers' attitudes toward each other. In the words of one student of politics in the area,

> a ruling shaykh, for example, perceives his counterparts in the other amirates in terms of such considerations as geographical location, regional trade, kinship links, historical fears and animosities, irredentist sentiments and recent instances of conflict or cooperation at the ruling family or tribal level.[18]

Although personal rivalries and jealousies are important ingredients of shaikhly politics in the UAE, it is probably the territorial factor, a subject of contest along most frontiers, that most adversely affects the interrelations of emirates with common borders. To a ruling shaikh, more territory means more population, better prospects for oil discoveries, and, hence, more prestige.

These factors, coupled with each ruler's own temperament and perception of his emirate's role and interest in the union, are to a great extent responsible for the variation in these emirates' orientation toward the federal experiment. Abu Dhabi, Sharigah, and Fujairah are generally more positively oriented toward the union than the other member emirates. Being the core and the backbone of the federation, Abu Dhabi's consistent support is understandable. The two rulers of Sharigah and Fujairah, in addition to being by far the youngest and best educated among the incumbents, seem to have developed an early interest and personal involvement in union affairs. They both depend on Abu Dhabi's largesse for developing their own states, and Shaikh Sultan even owes his accession to the rulership primarily to the union top authority.

Given the current distribution of power within the all-powerful Supreme Council of the Union (SCU), one is tempted to look at it in microcosmic terms as an epitome of the power structure in the individual political systems of the emirates themselves. In this council, the two rulers of Abu Dhabi and Dubai make up the inner core of the federal power structure not only by virtue of being the president and vice-president respectively, but also, as noted earlier, because of their veto power and control over the important posts in the federal cabinet. Despite numerous instances of cooperation between them, notably in the two crises of the Sharigan succession of 1972 and this emirate's territorial dispute with Fujairah in the same year, the two rulers are historical and dynastic rivals and, in addition, temperamentally different.[19] Rashid seems resentful of any federal intervention in free commercial enterprise upon which Dubai thrived long before the advent of the oil industry. Besides, this ruler expressed his dissatisfaction, at least in one instance, with the manner by which federal ministerial posts are filled. The present method of distributing ministerial portfolios in order to achieve a sense of dynastic balance is bound, in Rashid's view, to bring to top federal positions individuals with dubious qualifications and professional competence. Even though his eldest son is the prime minister, Shaikh Rashid has expressed his disappointment over the fact that he (the premier) has had little role in selecting members of his cabinet.[20]

Notwithstanding its influential position within the federal power structure, Dubai has consistently embraced a more conservative stand vis-à-vis the broadening of federal authority. Officials in this emirate, with Shaikh Rashid as the foremost, hold the view that further integration in the fields of utilities and public services at this stage, for instance, will inevitably lead to the inefficiency of the federal administrative machine. However, the Dubai ruling family's involvement in the ownership and management of most utilities goes a long way to explain this emirate's reluctance to merge this vital field. Rulers who sympathize with Rashid's phlegmatic stand within the SCU, namely, Rashid of Ajman, Ahmad of Umm al-Guiwain, and Sagr of Ras al-Khaimah, do so mainly because of their grievances and resentment over their inferior position in union affairs relative to the more affluent and populous states of Abu Dhabi and Dubai. However, as will be discussed in the next chapter, the economic poverty of their emirates, and, hence, their need for Abu Dhabi's financial support, makes them grudgingly accept this hierarchy of power.

The highly personalized patterns of rule in the Coast of Oman make these systems less conducive to the achievement of a smooth and genuine integration. Political power is chiefly concentrated at the top of the social strata in a carefully selected coterie of sons, brothers, cousins, and aligned kinsmen and merchants. The union was in effect the doing of such elites, isolated from any significant popular participation. Hence, under the present circumstances, these very elites seem to have the same capacity to undo their experiment should it become detrimental to their interests. The absence of a diffusion of power, brought about mainly by these elites' preference for ascriptive over achievement values, may well encourage the growth of political radicalism. In turn, either such radicalism by itself, or the reaction against it, may lead to viewing the current federal experiment in a totally different light.

From another perspective, since the extension of its Provisional Constitution late in 1976, the union has become in a sense open-ended. As more integrative steps are taken, the point will no doubt be reached when either the union will be condemned to stagnation or else the power of individual rulers will be curtailed. These rulers have understandably inherited and been conditioned by traditional structures and hence are reluctant to watch their authority gradually melt into a larger entity that, despite their influence, would be beyond their exclusive individual control. It is precisely the thought that "the union's gain is my loss" that adds to the precariousness of the federal experiment as it passes its early stages.[21]

The phenomenon of rulership succession is a persistent variable that can affect integration in one way or the other. Patterns of accession in the dynastic history of most of the emirates, whether violent or peaceful, may well bring to power rulers with quite new ideas about the union. At this stage of federal development, parochial loyalties are still strong and the appeal to tribal sentiments may well hit responsive ears. In addition, the distribution of power, institutionalized or not, within the SCU under the present arrangement brings to the fore questions that may touch upon the very survival of the union. For example, were Shaikh Zayed to leave the political scene on a permanent basis, his son and heir apparent, Shaikh Khalifa, would probably succeed to Abu Dhabi's rulership and Shaikh Rashid to the union presidency. Under these circumstances, would Abu Dhabi continue to support the union at the same level, given her relatively inferior position in its power structure? Or, should Khalifa succeed his father to the union's top post, given his age and relative political inexperience, would the other rulers, especially those of Dubai and Ras al-Khaimah, acquiesce in such an outcome? Besides, three of the seven incumbent rulers are in their seventies. This makes a power changeover in these emirates a distinct possibility in the near future. What types of personalities will ascend to these rulerships, and how will they react to the union? Personality factors are indeed crucial, as they have always been, in the determination and distribution of power in the area. At this stage in the existence of the union, they are even more so.

Immigration

The scarcity of indigenous populations in an area of remarkable oil-based affluence may have the statistical advantage of boosting the per capita GNP in the small entities astride the Arab gulf littoral, but it has certainly invoked an immigrant imperative of a magnitude seldom paralleled elsewhere. Scores of expatriates from widely divergent cultural backgrounds pour into the Coast of Oman each day with one purpose in mind: to exchange their skills and physical powers for material benefits in a substantially capital-surplus land. Although figures of work permits issued to citizens of foreign lands and those depicting actual arrivals are seldom one and the same, the former nevertheless reflect both the magnitude and relative distribution of the immigrant population among the member states of the UAE over a specified period of time. As Table 5-2 shows, of nearly 240,000 work permits issued in 1976, over 91 percent were to fill the needs of the three oil-producing states of Dubai, Sharigah, and Abu Dhabi, in that order, with the Indian subcontinent (India and Pakistan) accounting for 65.8 percent of these permits. Perhaps more significantly, total figures of work permits for 1976 reflect an increase of 87.2 percent over the preceding year.[22]

Partly due to the nature of work opportunities provided and partly because of Britain's policy of insulating the area under its de facto protection from Arab nationalist currents by its deliberate encouragement of immigration from the east of the gulf, the Arab expatriate community in the emirates has always been a minority among foreigners in general. There are mainly two categories of expatriate Arabs in the UAE. On the one hand, there are those who occupy a wide range of professional and skilled jobs in both private and public sectors. These jobs are reasonably well paid. Examples in this category are administrators, doctors, nurses, teachers, legal and political advisers, judges, technicians, construction engineers and superintendents, personnel supervisors, accountants, national defense and security officers, and the like. Here, one finds Egyptians, Lebanese, Syrians, Jordanians, Palestinians, Iraqis, and Sudanese.[23] On the other hand, there are Yemenites and Omanis who generally engage in semiskilled and unskilled jobs such as taxi drivers, porters, domestic servants, street cleaners, watchmen, gardeners, and security and defense personnel. Arabs in this category, as well as those from Jordan and Sudan, are generally more trusted by local regimes as they occupy numerous positions of varying levels in defense and public security forces.

Non-Arab immigrants make up the largest segment of the total population in the emirates. Occupying a wide spectrum of economic activity, they too can be divided into categories. First, there are numerous Westerners, mainly British, and a handful of Indians who hold highly skilled jobs in the oil industry and advisory positions at the highest level of government. In the second category, one finds a sizable number of expatriates from Iran, Pakistan, and India who engage in trade, craft, accounting, storekeeping, banking, and engineering. In yet another category fits the lowest, but largest, stratum of the labor force. This category is comprised of the bulk of Asian immigrants, who

TABLE 5-2:

WORK PERMITS ISSUED BY UAE MEMBER EMIRATES
TO EXPATRIATES BY COUNTRY, REGION OR CONTINENT, 1976

COUNTRY / EMIRATE	ARAB COUNTRIES	INDIA	PAKISTAN	REST OF ASIA	EUROPEAN COUNTRIES	NORTH & SOUTH AMERICA	AFRICAN COUNTRIES	AUSTRALIA AND NEW ZEALAND	TOTAL	%
Dubai	13,296	55,338	30,898	6,362	7,160	1,593	399	133	115,179	48.0
Sharigah	9,516	24,669	11,512	1,831	5,969	635	42	170	54,344	22.7
Abu Dhabi	21,519	10,205	11,106	3,737	2,320	396	48	51	49,381	20.6
Ras al-Khaimah	2,200	6,051	2,717	428	862	313	12	9	12,592	5.3
'Ajman	1,189	2,248	1,181	540	220	39	6	5	5,428	2.3
Umm al-Guiwain	606	521	213	32	68	9	2	1	1,452	0.6
Fujairah	182	610	253	59	61	11	2	1	1,179	0.5
TOTAL	48,508	99,642	57,880	12,988	16,660	2,996	511	370	239,555	100.0
%	20.2	41.6	24.2	5.4	7.0	1.3	0.2	0.1	100.0	

Source: Ministry of Labor and Social Affairs, UAE, Annual Statistical Report, 1976. (in Arabic), p. 16.

generally engage in manual labor at the lowest point on the wage scale. At this level, job security is lacking, social conditions are substandard, and discrimination is more salient than at other levels.[24]

Before any consideration of the negative effect that immigration may have on integration, a few general observations on this phenomenon are in order. First, the expatriate community in the emirates is extremely heterogeneous, generally unorganized, and largely mobile. In the same vein that expatriate Arabs range, for instance, from Lebanese to Yemenites, who in turn may be Christians, Sunni Muslims, Zaidis, or Shafiites; so the Pakistanis could be either Pathans, Urdu, or Baluch, speaking different languages or dialects; and the Iranians Farsi-speaking northerners, Baluchis from the east, or Muhawwalah ("of Arab origin") from the south, and so on. These immigrants, especially in the lower strata, are highly mobile, comprising a gulf littoral labor force from Kuwait in the north to Oman in the south. Second, these immigrants, as noted earlier, are solely motivated by economic concerns. Being predominantly male and young, they aim at earning a means of livelihood to keep them and their families back home afloat.

Another observation in regard to the expatriate community is that its members play crucial roles in each and every facet of economic life in the UAE. Indeed, one may venture to assert that without their expertise and physical power, socioeconomic development in the emirates would probably come to a halt. Fourth, although many carefully selected members of the expatriate community play important political roles as advisers at the highest level of the power structure, immigrants are officially outside the political system as far as de jure political rights are concerned. Moreover, the ever-existing fear of deportation makes the great majority of immigrants politically acquiescent and passive. The Iranians, for instance, maintained a passive attitude toward the Iranian occupation of the three small gulf islands of Abu Musa and the two Tunbs (see Chapter 7) on December 2, 1971, the eve of the emirates' independence. Finally, and most importantly, expatriates on the whole are far superior numerically to the indigenous population. In fact, the number of work permits issued in the year 1976 alone (see Table 5-2 above) may have already exceeded the number of UAE nationals. The problem is most acute in the case of the three oil-producing member emirates. Although official figures are not available, the most reliable estimates put foreigners as comprising between 70 and 80 percent of the populations in each of the three emirates of Abu Dhabi, Dubai, and Sharigah.[25]

The phenomenon of immigration in the lower gulf is relatively recent and certainly of a transient nature. More importantly, however, unlike tribalism, territorial disputes, and paternalism, it thrusts upon the whole system from the outside. Its negative effect on integration lies not so much in the internal polaristic tendencies the other factors tend to enhance as in its potential of creating unfavorable linkages with the external environment. More specifically, a foreign minority, whether inclined or disinclined, may well be used by the external power to which this minority belongs as a pretext for unwarranted interference, either to promote its own interests at home or else to give credence to ambitions of grandeur that might be detrimental to the survival of local sociopolitical arrangements. Furthermore, the magnitude of this phenomenon is alarming if only for the fact that UAE nationals happen to be a minority in their own land. Although massive foreign presence has been brought about by the deliberate action of local political elites, the sense of insecurity among the local populace is generally heightening. In the long run, due to political deprivation and unfavorable living conditions, these laboring masses may become clandestinely organized and may provide a receptive soil for internal subversion that might be instigated from beyond the border. This situation, if and when reached, would be to say the least a factor for instability.

To conclude, tribalism, frontier disputes, paternalism, and immigration have all been approached here from the perspective of their negative impact upon the integration of member emirates in the UAE insofar as they impede the emergence and realization of a solidly founded federal political culture and a sense of political community. The negative impact of such variables varies. Tribalism's most salient unfavorable aspect is its parochial and factionalistic orientation; frontier disputes, their magnitude and conflictual linkage to personal and dynastic rivalries; paternalism's, its precarious nature and effect on the scope of political power; and immigration's, its seemingly uncontrollable size and potentially unfavorable linkage with the external environment. As time elapses, some of these factors may get weaker, and others may intensify or remain stable. Alongside all of this is a process of interaction with factors of different origin and nature. The latter operate in the local environment in varying ways and to extents that are generally favorable to integration. The following chapter concentrates on what these factors are and why they are considered integrative.

6
Integrative Factors in the Union's Internal Environment

The preceding chapter was an attempt to identify factors that have been operating in the internal environment of the union with an impact that is characteristically disintegrative. There are certain aspects of tribalism, territorial disputes, paternalism, and immigration that operate negatively, and in varying degrees of intensity, upon the integrative process. These factors can hardly be viewed as entirely unique to the area of the Arab gulf littoral even though they may reflect some characteristics of a special nature owing to the local culture. Tribalism, territorial disputes, and paternalism cannot be ruled out as crucial factors in the postwar African integrative ventures, for example. However, they do not appear to have created problems in similar ventures in Western Europe or Latin and Central America, where national, rather than tribal, sentiment has been more influential as a disintegrative factor.

As two well-known students of regional integration assert, aspects of integration and disintegration can both operate simultaneously in a dialectical or nondialectical fashion.[1] Thus, to the extent that the process of European integration is a drive for the realization of a federated Western Europe, the expansion of the EEC membership from six to nine (by the admission of the United Kingdom, Norway, and the Republic of Ireland earlier in this decade) can by itself be interpreted as a disintegrative step that occurred simultaneously as members of the community were trying to unify their currencies or widen the scope of authority for the European Parliament. By the same token, the attempts by some countries in Central and Latin America and East Africa to reduce or eliminate trade barriers among themselves are integrative factors, whereas simultaneous power seizures by military generals may be disintegrative if they bring to power individuals with ultranationalistic orientations. Recent military takeovers in Uganda, Peru, and

Argentina may be cases in point.

Within the United Arab Emirates, integrative as well as disintegrative factors operate on each other in a generally dialectical fashion also. At least seven main factors in the federation's internal arena are treated here from the point of view of their positive effect on the emergence and development of the union. These are (1) the quest for political survival, (2) a sense of a grand national mission, (3) material improvement in the general standards of living, (4) the gradual and cautious approach to integration adopted by political elites, (5) the existence of an overwhelming and seemingly determined core, (6) geographical contiguity of the federating states, and (7) commonality of culture in the area. These seven factors do not necessarily operate at the same level, nor do they influence the process of integration to the same degree. In addition, the nature of these variables differs. Survival and the sense of mission, for instance, may be aptly classified as causative in the sense that they lie at the very foundations of the union. Improved life standards and gradualism, on the other hand, may be viewed as reinforcement variables. Although not significant in the forging of the union, the first, as a tangible benefit, and the second, as a widely acceptable political style, nevertheless support the integrative trend. The existence of a powerful core within the union can be looked at as both a catalytic and volitional variable. The latter sense depicts the core power as determined to preserve and strengthen the federal experiment. Finally, geographical contiguity and cultural commonality are both contextual factors that, albeit anterior to the emergence of the union, have nevertheless affected its emergence, and will probably continue to influence its development in a positive manner.

The main argument of this chapter is that these seven factors have, in one way or the other, contributed to the formation of the UAE and, furthermore, continue to be positive aspects in their growth. How and to what extent each operates integratively is what we will attempt to clarify next.

Survival

Underlying the triple purpose of "providing a better life, a more solid stability, and a higher international status," which the preamble of the federal Provisional Constitution sets forward as the main justifications behind forging the union, is the more fundamental question of survival—survival in a certain form. Before we attempt to specify this form, however, a glimpse at the history of these states' relations with Great Britain might be useful.

The evolution of British influence in the gulf region (see Chapter 2) may be said to have passed through three general stages before it officially ended in 1971. First, there was an infiltration stage on a purely trading basis along with other European powers through the sixteenth, seventeenth, and eighteenth centuries. This was followed by a period of defensive penetration during which Britain sought to protect the sea lanes to its newly acquired empire in India through a system of maritime control. This era took up the last few decades of the eighteenth and most of the nineteenth centuries. It was also during the latter century that the third stage of British presence began with the continued consolidation of position, which finally led (in the 1890s) to a virtual British monopoly of foreign control in the area that continued until independence. Through the so-called Exclusive Agreements with the tribal states along the Coast of Oman, which best epitomized this monopoly, Britain obtained exclusive jurisdiction over the foreign and defense affairs of these states. By concluding these agreements, and other ones as well, with each ruling shaikh separately, Britain, in effect, reinforced the atomistic nature of a tribal society. Furthermore, British exclusive control over the foreign relations of these states, along with Britain's consistent policy of noninterference in the sociopolitical organization in the area, contributed to the evolution of a spirit of dependence and internal political insecurity that were to complicate the political situation once the controlling power departed.

Thus, the British Labour government's decision in 1968 to terminate Britain's treaty obligations east of Suez three years later caught the seven rulers of Trucial Oman by surprise. None of them welcomed the decision. Behind this reluctance to throw off the shackles of foreign control was the fact that, at this particular juncture, the alternative was frightening. The idea of independence in a complex world found the shaikhs unprepared and, hence, invoked fear on two levels. On the one hand, there was the level of capabilities. The responsibilities of statehood are tremendous. None of these seven emirates, with the possible exception of Abu Dhabi, had in 1968 the financial and human resources sufficient to carry out the multifaceted functions of a modern, independent entity. As Table 6-1 shows, public revenues of the six northern shaikhdoms were simply minuscule. What kind of independent state would Ajman, for instance, establish with 5,000 inhabitants and less than a quarter of a million dollars in revenues? The same question could be raised in regard to any of the six. Would such resources be adequate to raise armies or establish diplomatic missions in foreign countries on an individual basis? In view of the fact that such meager resources could only cover limited recurrent expenditures dispensed by the different rulers, a negative answer would be required to such a question. Most of these states still are in reality coastal towns and villages that have traditionally subsisted on fishing, limited agriculture,[2] and pearling. Their evolution into this lilliputian condition may be attributed to cultural characteristics, imperial control, and sociopolitical organization.

Still another indication of these emirates' capabilities was the low level of socioeconomic and political development most of them had managed to reach by 1968. As previously noted (see Chapter 4), only a semblance of institutional organization was visible in the smaller emirates at that crucial time. This administrative underdevelopment and ineptness could hardly be counted on to run a full-fledged, modern state. Whatever Britain had done in the way of development was too little, too late. In fact, it was as early as 1951 that Britain established a law-and-order force to protect foreign oil concessionaires and force headquarters at Sharigah, but not until 1965 (three years before the British withdrawal announcement) that a Development Fund was established for the purpose of financing limited infrastructural projects here and there. The benevolent intent of establishing this fund was belied, however, by the circumstances. It was in fact a reaction to the attempt by the Arab League to break the insular nature of the area by making inroads under the pretext of development.[3]

The economic conditions of most states in the Coast of Oman in 1968 were sufficient reason to support the logic of pooling resources in order to afford the luxury of an independent status. But even with the seven amalgamated, the new entity could not possibly pose, on sheer material capabilities, as a significant match under any criterion for any of the major regional powers. What a union could attain, then, was psychological security, not necessarily material.

Behind their decision to unite, then, was the psychological element, inherent in the new era after a long period of dependence, which went beyond the material facade down to the sociopolitical dynamics of the area as a whole. For example, the ruler of Abu Dhabi offered to reimburse Britain's costs if it would keep its troops in the area beyond the deadline date. Since Abu Dhabi did not suffer from a lack of material resources, it is likely that the psychological element was the motivation behind this offer. Local rulers' perceptions of regional ambitions in light of unresolved territorial disputes at that time are likely to have played a major role in the fateful decisions formulated between 1968 and 1971.

In addtion, and perhaps more significantly, the shaikhs were in search of a tool that could protect their systems against domestic threats. The fear of local disarray instigated by internal tensions such as historical and tribal enmities as well as dynastic and personal rivalries may have haunted these traditional elites as their partnership was in the making. To them, the union could perhaps provide a higher sense of purpose under which the status quo might be preserved in the midst of socioeconomic change. This is where a specific mode of survival ties in: the survival of the traditional form of rule, which the British had for long not only maintained but encouraged.

Thus, with the British declaration to terminate their official presence behind, but with the existing low level of socioeconomic development, the rulers of the seven states along the Coast of Oman saw in a loose union of their tiny emirates the most logical and promising step for the very survival of their regimes. To federate is to get relatively bigger, to be bigger is to be more visible, and to be more visible is to be psychologically less vulnerable to internal as well as external odds and, hence, is to be more viable.

Sense of Mission

The preservation of traditional rule was a fundamental factor underlying all efforts that finally led to the emergence of the union. The view that such an amalgamation could somehow fill the void of British protection was not unheard as traditional elites struggled over the technicalities of their impending partnership. More deeply felt, however, was an abstract sense of mission. Traditional elites, too, are generally imbued with a sense of Arab nationalism. "There was a consensus among ruling elites," in the words of one participant, "that the union ought to underscore the message of averting a catastrophe for the Arab nation in its eastern flank as the one in its heart."[4] This sense of mission has been expressed time and again by members of the ruling elite, and it served recurrently as a catalyst in the drive for integration. The tempting idea that traditional regimes could succeed where the "progressive" ones have so far failed, even though on the edge of the cauldron, was understandably worth pursuing.

The conception of this federal experiment in wider Arab terms seems logical insofar as the union is perceived as a factor for stability in this part of the Arab world. But the implication that such an amalgamative step should only be the beginning—that other Arab states, whether gulf littoral, peninsular, or Levantine and North African, might consider joining—is a remote possibility.[5] The length of time it took to conclude the present union and the fact that two states (Qatar and Bahrain) of the original nine have opted for independence support the assertion that as long as the preservation of the status quo remains the underlying task, only regimes with similar systems might consider joining, and even these may not be as enthusiastic.

Improved Standards of Life

If the conception of the union as a fulfillment of some abstract Arab purpose was looming in the horizon as traditional political elites were forging their partnership, the improvement of life standards of every citizen after its emergence may well be the most concrete and reinforcing factor in the existence of the federation. To belong to a large entity may be psychologically gratifying, but it is the flow of material rewards across emirate frontiers after a long deprivation that tends to magnify the relevance of the union on every level. Wherever one travels in the emirates, the union's imprints are clearly in evidence in schools, hospitals and medical clinics, housing projects, roads, utilities, and so on. How can these be identified as federal projects? Simple. The four-color flag of the union provides the background of the sign on which details of the project are depicted.

Federal endeavors in the field of socioeconomic development have been dealt with in detail in Chapter 4 and, hence, need not be repeated here. However, a few observations on their magnitude and effects on integration are appropriate. First, the transfer of rewards under the union banner has taken many forms on all levels. This flow has taken a drastic turn upward of unprecedented proportion, particularly since 1974 when the global energy picture was drastically altered, thereby resulting in more wealth for the oil-producing states. In addition, transfer of material benefits, thanks to the great wealth and generosity of Abu Dhabi, has proceeded in one direction. Second, this extensive but unidirectional flow of benefits from the federal center to member states has the potential of influencing interemirate relations by the role it plays in encouraging a state of dependence rather than interdependence in these relations.[6] In this area of great but accidentally unequal material wealth, the more expectations of the peoples of the less fortunate shaikhdoms rise, the more likely they will look toward the center within the framework of the federation for the satisfaction of such demands.[7] Additionally, one aspect of this dependency syndrome as an integrative factor is institutional diffusion resulting from the proliferation of central institutions (see Chapter 4), which, as time goes by, may undermine local control if only by virtue of monopoly over administrative skills.

A third consequence of the unprecedented material penetration by the central authority is the attempt by local rulers to compete with such authority in order to woo the individual citizen. Rulers are fearful that developmental programs of a socioeconomic nature that are directly planned, financed, and managed by federal authorities have the risk of eroding their own traditional control within their respective territories. Indeed, in the history of this area, tribal allegiance has often been granted to the source of rewards, giving reciprocity its basic, true meaning. The direct linkage between those who benefit from such projects and those who initiate and implement them is by itself an integrative trend since it tends to undermine parochial authority.[8] Finally, this federally initiated revolution in infrastructural development may have also given rise to a popular stake in the federal system through numerous federally sponsored entrepreneurial ventures that are designed to attract local capital on the popular level.

In sum, the widening scope of socioeconomic development and welfare benefits since the establishment of the union brings to the fore the question of integration by dependence—or, if you will, by material abundance. As federal authorities compete with local leaderships in the presentation of material rewards, the gap between "theirs" and "ours" will narrow. Traditional loyalties on the parochial level will probably be weakened, leading in the long run to the diffusion or the broadening of the concept of integration by dependence and perhaps even to the gradual change in its nature from personal to institutional. Although it is too early and perhaps even too difficult to ascertain the validity of this assertion, the mere transfer of purely material rewards from the federal center to its constituent units on such a large scale makes embracing the union perhaps overwhelmingly advantageous and strictly a cost-benefit operation.

Gradualism

Tribal antagonisms, personal and dynastic rivalries, the low level of socioeconomic development, and the great variation in human and material resources have been traditionally the most salient ingredients of internal tension along the Coast of Oman. For this reason, they also account for the suitability of a gradual, step-by-step approach to the federal venture, rather than a comprehensive one. This approach, in essence, entails a process of interaction among the parties to the union through which they become gradually convinced that whatever integrative steps are to be taken are in their best interest. To be sure, a consensus does exist among traditional elites that gradualism constitutes the best guard against setbacks. However, disagreements arise over what really constitutes a gradual approach between those who want the union to steadily develop and those whose conception of the idea borders on stagnation or stalemate.[9]

The process of merging the armed forces in the UAE provides the best illustration of how cautiously the ruling elites approach the whole question of their federal experiment. Separate defense and security forces around each ruler safeguard his political life. Given the less institutionalized pattern of rule, then, soldiers can best serve as instruments of control.

The first step along the path of merging the different military elements in the UAE was the creation of a Union Defense Force (UDF) by a federal law three weeks after the union was consummated. Composed essentially of the Trucial Oman Scouts, the new force was put under the direct supervision of the federal defense minister with the paramount task of safeguarding the federation against threats, external or internal. This law further enjoined the newly established force not to interfere in matters of concern to the member states except as stipulated in the constitution. When the jurisdictions of federal ministries and the authorities of ministers were spelled out by law in February 1972, the Ministry of Defense was empowered only to supervise the UDF and to "coordinate cooperation between the Union Defense Force and the defense forces of member-emirates for the purpose of providing for effective defense against any foreign aggression."

The second major step in the integration of defense forces in the UAE came late in 1972 with the establishment of the federal Supreme Council for Defense (SCD). Empowered to advise in matters of concern to the UDF's organization, armament, preparedness, and deployment, the SCD was composed of the president of the union (chairman); the vice-president; the prime minister; ministers of foreign affairs, defense, finance, interior; the commander-in-chief of the armed forces; and the chief of staff. According to the federal law that established this council, the president of the union acts at the same time as the supreme commander of the armed forces (land, naval, and air) and, accordingly, has the prerogative of making the necessary decisions for the defense of the union and the maintenance of its stability and security. In view of the manner in which federal cabinet posts are distributed, however, only Abu Dhabi and Dubai were represented in the council.

Thus, with the Union Defense Force, a federal ministry, and a supreme council for defense in coexistence with the defense forces and national guards of Dubai, Sharigah, Ras al-Khaimah and Umm al-Guiwain, in addition to the sizable and well-equipped Abu Dhabi Defense Force, further integration in this area was delayed for nearly three years. As the end of the provisional term approached, despite the sensitivity of such matters in a political atmosphere charged with mutual suspicions, more cautious rulers, namely those of Dubai and Ras al-Khaimah, gradually and reluctantly accepted Abu Dhabi's view that unless further integrative steps in the area of defense were taken, the following phase of the federation in general would be adversely affected.

The invitation of an Arab military committee (see Chapter 4), the conditions put forward by Shaikh Zayed for renewing his presidential term, and perhaps his support of the union all foreshadowed the major military developments of 1976. These developments started with the appointment of a Jordanian major general as the chief of staff of the Federal Armed Forces—not the UDF. The major step, however, came in early May when the Supreme Council for Defense, based on the approval of the SCU, decided to unify the armed forces of all member emirates under one central leadership composed of three commands (western, central, and northern), the Yarmuk Brigade (former UDF), and naval and air branches. Military colors, badges, and dress were also uniformed. At the same time, powers of the chief of staff were spelled out, and decrees were issued by which Khalifa bin Zayed, Sultan bin Zayed (both sons of the union-president), Ahmad bin Rashid (a son of the ruler of Dubai), and Sultan bin Saqr (a son of the ruler of Ras al-Khaimah) were appointed as the deputy supreme commander and commandants of the Western Command (Abu Dhabi), Central Command (Dubai) and Northern Command (Ras al-Khaimah), respectively. Further integrative measures followed later in the year when a constitutional amendment was enacted giving the federal government the sole prerogative of forming armed forces of any kind, and, when a federal law was passed, prohibiting the importation of arms, ammunition, and explosives for other than the use of the armed forces, except by a license issued by federal authorities.

Although officially merged, the various military formations in the UAE can hardly be said to have been fully integrated as the second provisional constitutional term commenced in December 1976. The establishment of three commands along geographical political lines, with each dominated by the military forces of one emirate and led by the son of its ruler, not only points to the relative fragility of this merger but also underscores the delicate nature of this sector. The respective rulers' conception of these commands as crucial guardians of the status quo still prevails. For this reason, the surrender of nominal, not real, control over these elements seems to have been the maximum most rulers could tolerate at this critical stage of their union.[10] Moreover, the few steps taken along the integrative path up to that date, limited though they may have been, may not all have been embraced out of a voluntary acceptance by some rulers and, hence, may well defy our criterion for the graduality of integration. In this, as well as in other sectors, behind-the-scene politics of coercive persuasion, i.e., cajoling, bargaining, etc., are likely to have been among the major determinants of outcomes along the federal trail. Hence, consideration of what has been accomplished in the way of integration in this field is more on the basis of the time it took rather than the degree of its voluntary acceptance. After all, in this delicate balance of tribal, dynastic, personal, and environmental factors, it is probably myopic to push hard or to expect too much too soon. Nevertheless, the line between gradualism and stagnation is often fine, and the right definition of each in the life of the union is a crucial federal, as well as local, task.

The Existence of an Overwhelming Core

In addition to being two organizations on opposite sides of the fence, the two military pacts of NATO and Warsaw have one more thing in common: each contains in its membership an overwhelming power that not only plays a central hegemonial role within the pact but also molds the pact's existence to express its own interests and the interests of the bloc as it perceives them. In other contexts, the United States also plays a leading role within the Organization of American States (OAS), and Britain has been for long, and still is, the central power within the British Commonwealth. Prussia, in the course of German unification in the latter part of the nineteenth century, and Aden, with respect to the ill-fated South Arabian federation a century later, are two examples of cores that in the final analysis opted for the absorption of the periphery instead of preserving it. Although it is too early to tell, the emirate of Abu Dhabi as a core unit within the UAE seems to fall somewhere between the British Commonwealth example and that of Prussia. Although analogies of this kind can be misleading, the role Abu Dhabi plays inside the union approaches faintly that which England exercises within the United Kingdom or that which Soviet Russia (Russian SFSR) undertakes within the Soviet Union.

Abu Dhabi's position within the union seems to be directly influenced by the weight of the natural attributes of power it controls. This emirate controls over 86 percent of the union's total area and 40 percent of its population, and has been consistently providing over 90 percent of its finances. Thanks to one natural resource, oil, Abu Dhabi is not only by far the richest member of the federation (see Chapter 4), but has the highest per capita income in the world. Even before the union was established, this emirate provided over 80 percent of the British-sponsored Trucial States Development Fund, which was largely responsible for whatever infrastructural development was accomplished by the end of the 1960s. Furthermore, Abu Dhabi's great financial resources have apparently enabled it to raise the largest and best-equipped military force in the lower gulf. This force now represents nearly 70 percent (men and equipment) of the Federal Armed Forces.

The union came about largely at the initiative of Abu Dhabi's ruler, Shaikh Zayed. Since it was established, this emirate has persistently been the driving force behind its development. Abu Dhabi's financial contribution to the union over the first half decade of its existence has been largely determined by the pace of growth in its own wealth as well as by the degree of receptivity on the part of other member states to allow for increasing federal authority relative to theirs. In addition, Abu Dhabi has made this contribution, and continues to contribute more, not only because it can afford to do so, but also because of the conviction of local political elites that it is somewhat aberrant not to share such wealth with less fortunate kin and neighbors. Indeed, it is Abu Dhabi's overwhelming wealth that has been largely responsible for the physical integration as well as the narrowing of gaps between the "haves" and the "have nots" in the area, and for this reason it is considered here as integrative. If integration means survival to the impoverished states of, say, Umm al-Guiwain and Fujairah, Abu Dhabi may view such a step as an opportunity to assert its hegemonial control in a more stable atmosphere. Abu Dhabi has invested a great deal in the federation, in both skills and treasure, and surely would opt not only for its preservation but for its growth and consolidation as well. In response to a question that generally touched on this theme, Shaikh Zayed came close to echoing Abu Dhabi's determination vis-à-vis the union in the following terms:

> Secession [from the union] is illegal and, hence, is out of the question. It cannot take place because he who wants to secede is a minority compared to those who prefer to stay and cooperate. Decisions [in the union] reside with the majority. I, for one, despise disunity and never, never, never will I believe in it. I believe in cooperation even with little capabilities. Power comes from cooperation. . . . As I see it, whoever wants to secede is like a child who has not as yet reached his majority and, hence, must be guided. . . . After all, does the one who enters paradise want to desert it and go to hell? Or, that who enters the shade would like to abandon it in favor of the summer sun on the burning sand? Is this logical?[11]

The extent of Abu Dhabi's involvement in union affairs, mirrored by the great and vital role it plays in the federal power structure, is largely in harmony with, and an expression of, the magnitude of its financial as well as political support of the amalgamative experiment from the moment of its inception. This vital role is largely manifested through the presidency of the union, a veto power in its supreme council, control over several important ministerial posts, and the fact that Abu Dhabi Town is more and more becoming the permanent capital of the union. Indeed, the significance of the last fact in enhancing the centripetal orientation of the federation in the future cannot be overemphasized.[12] Is it likely, then, that the union, as some observers have suggested,[13] is becoming more and more "a greater Abu Dhabi"? It is probably inaccurate to answer such a question affirmatively without adding some qualifications. Whether this trend will continue is largely contingent on at least two factors. These are, first, the continuation of Abu Dhabi's material abundance vis-à-vis its relative shortage elsewhere in the union and, second, and perhaps more importantly, the vicissitudes of Abu Dhabi's rulership successions. Shaikh Zayed is a remarkably shrewd leader and able statesman. Will his successor maintain such a standard in the face of Dubai's countervailing rivalry? As has been emphasized time and again in this study, personal considerations play an extremely crucial role in the political power structures and dynamics in the area. Given the intricate power relationships within the union in relation to its immediate environment at this early stage, it takes a highly capable leadership to steer this federal experiment along a safer path. That is primarily why the question of succession to the rulership of the federation's principal power is of great importance.

Geographical Contiguity

In the history of international amalgamations, physical territorial contact among relevant political units has never been a necessary condition for unions to emerge. Nor has it been sufficient for unions to hold. Former East Pakistan, for instance, maintained nearly a quarter century of partnership with West Pakistan despite a thousand miles of interposing, generally hostile, territory, with religion as the only cultural denominator. However, geographical distance only aggravated the eventual collapse of this partnership with the emergence of Bangladesh in 1971. On the other hand, the East African and South Arabian federations, both British-sponsored, did not fare well with success despite geographical contiguity. And in the case of the United Arab Republic (1958-1961), geographical distance might have been a contributing factor in the breakup of the union insofar as it helped aggravate the administrative situation in a highly centralized governmental apparatus.[14]

Although the conception of the Coast of Oman as one geographical entity might have reasonably crossed the minds of those who negotiated the formation of the UAE, it is rather paradoxical that geographical contiguity among member emirates has often been a source of aggravation in their interrelations. As noted in the previous chapter, territorial irredentism among immediate neighbors plays a major retarding role in the development of healthier relations and, hence, is considered as disintegrative.[15] The consideration of geographical contiguity here as an integrative factor centers on its impact on the vertical relations between the central authority and member states insofar as such proximity may enhance administrative control and minimize the likelihood of isolation by exposing any of these units to outside influence. Besides, territorial disputes are generally of a transient nature, and their resolution may well take place in the not-too-distant future.

Cultural Commonality

Like geographical contiguity, commonality of the cultural milieu is a contextual factor that can render a more conducive atmosphere for integration. The geographical area known as the Coast of Oman supports inhabitants who share the same cultural orientation, whether in their religious affiliation, linguistic practices, historical experiences, future aspirations, life-style, or even ethnic makeup. Even though all seven member emirates of the UAE trace their political systems back to various tribal or dynastic roots, those tribes or dynasties are nonetheless part of one national heritage. These are not tribal nations but rather varying manifestations of the same nation. Islam and Arab nationalism provide for the individual useful identity references that have been historically inseparable despite the increasingly apparent conflictual nature of their orientations. The first is a system of spiritual beliefs and rituals, as well as a way of life, with a universal outlook, whereas the second is mostly a secular political ideology with ethnic, exclusivist emphasis. The debate on how to harmonize these two concepts still continues, however.[16]

As already noted in earlier chapters, the political systems in the lower gulf are elitist in the sense that the power base in these systems is extremely narrow. Only a few select groups of mostly consanguineously related individuals determine choices and make vital decisions with far-reaching effects. The existence of a common culture seems to have molded the political culture of these elites in a certain way. Their political ideology and outlook are more or less identical. They seem to share similar views on the locally cherished political values of conservatism, preservation of the status quo of traditional rule, security, economic freedom, and the like. Such values, for instance, could not be logically shared in toto with, say, the Iraqi revolutionary regime, in view of the basic ideological differences between the two systems. In sum, then, traditional elites in the lower gulf tend to reflect identical self-images and values from which a common interest in the preservation of a traditional brand of rule emerges. Such ideological compatibility among these elites may well help create the sort of political atmosphere most conducive to the type of integration with which we have been dealing.

To sum up, the survival of the traditional patterns of rule, a sense of a higher national purpose, the remarkably extensive tangible benefits enjoyed on all levels under the federal banner, the incremental approach adopted by traditional elites vis-à-vis the nascent union, the centripetal role played by Abu Dhabi as the federation's most powerful member emirate, in addition to geographical contiguity and cultural common-ality, have all, in varying ways and to certain extents, played upon the emergence and development of the union and continue to affect its existence today. To ensure the survival of the traditional regime, in particular, has been a strong motivation to a degree that has dwarfed deep-seated tribal hostilities and dynastic and personal rivalries, and thus may have been a sufficient cause behind the conception and consummation of this federal experiment in the first place. It must be borne in mind, however, that these factors are neither necessarily exhaustive nor are they considered integrative except in the sense and to the degrees noted here.

In the emergence of this federation of ministates, and in its existence since then, the regional environment has played a crucial role. Indeed, factors of survival and growth and of integration and disintegration in the domestic arena are only matched by other no less crucial ones that interplay on the regional level. The next chapter centers on precisely this interplay.

7
The Regional and Global Contexts:
Support and Disruption

The gulf region's strategic location and spectacular mineral wealth make it one of the most important spots on earth. Along the coast of this vital arm of the Indian Ocean, which extends from the strategic Strait of Hormuz in the south to Shatt al-Arab in the north, lie eight political entities, of which the United Arab Emirates is the newest. Iran, Iraq, and Saudi Arabia form, by almost all accounts, the major gulf powers. In contrast to the other five (Kuwait, Bahrain, Qatar, Oman, and the UAE), they are individually much larger and more populous; they control greater shares of the material wealth in the area; they are militarily superior; and they have longer histories of political independence. Given the shallowness of the gulf waters (which wholly fall within the limits of a continental shelf) and both actual and potential offshore oil discoveries, the length of the coastline a state happens to control can easily add to its strategic and economic importance. Of the five small gulf states, the UAE (Figure 7-1) controls the third longest coastline, exceeded only by Iran and Saudi Arabia, in that order. Two characteristics distinguish the gulf states from the rest of the Middle East. They are all oil-producing countries, although their production capacities vary greatly; and, with the exception of Iraq, they are politically conservative countries where political power has resided in ruling families that have tribal/dynastic roots. Table 7-1 gives some basic updated information about these countries.

The emergence of the United Arab Emirates as a federal entity has been encouraged as much by regional factors as by local initiative and British support. Regional vicissitudes from 1968 to the present have greatly influenced the making and the growth of the union in almost every aspect. When the UAE is viewed as an amalgamative venture within both regional and global contexts, it is evident that the regional context has played, and continues to play, a far greater role in the

FIGURE 7-1

THE UAE: A SMALL STATE IN A VITAL REGION

union's consummation and early development than the global one. If one compares the UAE with the European Economic Community in this particular aspect, the two cases contrast sharply for three main reasons. First, the EEC emerged at the height of the cold war in a tightly bipolar international system where security on a global scale was very much at issue. The United States perceived the community as a means of enhancing Western security, whereas the Soviet Union viewed it as a threat to its interests in Central Europe. Hence, the circumstances under which each emerged were totally different. Second, from its inception, the EEC included the two principal continental powers of France and Germany, thereby dwarfing outside influence within its immediate environment. Again, this contrasts sharply with the UAE, where the

TABLE 7-1

BASIC ECONOMIC DATA FOR THE EIGHT GULF STATES

	IRAN	IRAQ	SAUDI ARABIA	KUWAIT	UAE	BAHRAIN	QATAR	OMAN
Est.Area (sq.miles)	636,300	173,000	830,000	6,880	30,000	256	4,000	105,000
Est. Population	33,810,000 (1976)	11,490,000 (1976)	5-6,000,000 (1976)	1,065,400 (1976)	655,937 (1975)	266,078 (1975)	190,000 (1975)	766,000 (1975)
Oil Production 1976 (000 b/d)	5,882.9	2,184	8,579.5	2,150.1	1,942	56.7	487.1	360.7
Est. Oil Revenues (billions of US $)	22 (1976)	8 (1975)	30 (1976)	6.5 (1976)	6.3 (1976)	less than half a million (1976)	2 (1976)	1.4 (1976)
Est.Crude Oil Proven Reserves, 1976 (billions of barrels)	63	34	113.2	70.6	30.5	0.3	5.7	5.8

Source: Compiled from The Middle East and North Africa 1977-78 (London: Europa Publications Limited, 1977). Figures for oil production and reserves were taken from Ministry of Petroleum and Mineral Resources, UAE, Oil Statistical Review, 1977, pp. 5-6.

federating states are the smallest in a region of "big powers." Third, Western Europe was the center of the cold war and is now presumably the center of détente. The gulf region is geographically too remote to have been enmeshed in the former or covered by the latter.

The overriding importance of the regional context to the federation makes a closer look into its dynamics a matter of direct relevance. The UAE ostensibly plays a small part in its ongoing interaction with other gulf powers, large and small. This interaction is greatly influenced by strictures and opportunities of a regional nature, which will be approached in this chapter from four angles. These are the political hegemonial dimension, the territorial dimension, the collective security dimension, and the radical connection. As we will find out later, these areas often interlock. The territorial aspect of regional relations, for instance, can influence and be influenced by the political hegemonic aspects. Likewise, the radical connection is in part a function of the political makeup of the region and, moreover, has a lot to do with territorial matters. In sum, it is only for the clarity of discussion that these aspects are separated.

The Political Hegemonic Dimension

Under an authoritarian rule, such as exists in the gulf region, domestic constraints upon the formulation and pursuit of foreign policy objectives are either minimal or virtually absent. The role played by personal leadership is heightened. Recognition is extended not so much to an internal consensus of politically effective interest groups as to the limits of a state's material resources, and even the latter may be overextended, as in the case of Egyptian President Nasser's military intervention in North Yemen in the 1960s or perhaps the unprecedented Iranian military buildup in the present decade. A leader acting within such political systems does not have to cater to varying interest groups, share with other governmental institutions responsibilities of state, or worry about periodic public support at the ballot box.

Predictably, the conduct of foreign policy in this manner makes instances of turnabouts in bilateral relations more frequent and therefore adds to the complexity of predicting a nation's behavior as it interacts with neighboring or distant countries. The resolution of the Shatt al-Arab dispute between Iran and Iraq in 1975 after sixteen years of generally poor relations and the Saudi–South Yemeni rapprochement one year later are only two recent examples of such turnabouts in bilateral regional relations. Therefore, to understand the context within which the UAE has evolved, one must appreciate first, the tremendous

influence exerted upon the determination and conduct of foreign policy
by one man or a small group of policymakers; second, the leaders' virtual
insulation from domestic constraints; and, third, the somewhat baffling
sharp foreign policy shifts that sometimes reverse regional interrelationships.

The official demise of Pax Britannica in 1971 after more than a
century of supremacy in the gulf has intensified the quest of major
powers seeking to play a leading role in shaping the area's political
future in a way compatible with their own interests. Iran, Iraq, and
Saudi Arabia have been involved in a tripartite interactional situation
that has reflected instances of both competition and cooperation. The
economic and military resources of each of these regional powers, the
degree of determination on the leadership level, and the strictures and
opportunities in the wider Middle Eastern and global contexts have all
been salient factors in the determination of the outcome of this
interaction. In addition, regional interrelationships in the gulf can best
be understood when viewed as occurring within the context of two rival
nationalisms, Persian and Arab. Both, though very old, have only
recently experienced a sense of upsurge that, especially for Arab
nationalism, involves the wider context of the Arab world.

How does each of the three major gulf powers assert itself in the
immediate region, and what sorts of interests may guide this assertion?
How did each react to the union, first, as an idea and, later, as a reality?
How are the smaller gulf states likely to behave in such a tripartite
situation? These are the types of questions around which the remainder
of this section will revolve.

Iran

Iran's involvement in the gulf has historically fluctuated in intensity
depending upon the character, the fortunes, and the military
capabilities of its rulers.[1] The consolidation of the former Iranian
regime of Muhammad Reza Pahlavi (hereinafter the shah) took
Iran through some turbulent years, which extended roughly from the
Second World War until the mid-1960s and further involved a complex
interplay of global, regional, and domestic factors. Once Iran emerged
from domination by the Great Powers during the war and its immediate
aftermath, as well as the ensuing politico-economic crisis that almost led
to the downfall of the monarchy in the early 1950s, the Iranian sense of
security, political as well as military, was greatly heightened. Until
roughly 1960, however, the threat to Iranian security was generally
perceived to be emanating from Moscow. This explains in part the
shah's enthusiasm for the extension of the concept of containment as a

cold war strategy from its origin in Western Europe to the Middle East. Iran acceded to the Baghdad Pact (now CENTO) in 1955, endorsed the Eisenhower Doctrine two years later, and concluded a bilateral defense agreement with the United States in 1959.

This Iranian policy of direct alignment with the West inescapably led to a clash with Nasser's brand of Arab nationalism since the latter was staunchly opposed to foreign military alliances under any guise and, further, because Nasser sought to realize Arab unity under Egyptian leadership. The overthrow of the monarchy in Iraq in 1958 represented, at least from the Iranian point of view, the most significant development in the gulf region up to that date. In the shah's perception, Iraq would no longer serve as a buffer and ally against the rising power of Nasser, especially after Egypt's unity with Syria was consummated earlier in the year. It was understandably at that juncture that the emphasis in Iranian foreign policy shifted from the traditional preoccupation with a perceived Soviet threat to a greater attention to the gulf.[2]

Iran's determination to play the leading role in the gulf dates back to roughly the late 1950s. In 1959, the shah asserted that "Iran's supremacy over the Persian Gulf is a natural thing," emphasizing further that Iran had already reached that stage and would "enhance it in the future."[3] This enhancement has extended over more than fifteen years since then and has been pursued on various levels. On the diplomatic plane, Iran adopted a pragmatic course that best served its foreign policy interests. The shah's pledge not to allow foreign missiles on Iranian soil in 1962 removed the most important obstacle to a rapprochement with the Soviet Union.[4] The relaxation of Irano-Soviet tensions has fitted nicely within the Iranian strategy of more concentration on the gulf, particularly that aspect that pertained to a perceived Egyptian threat to Iran's interests. To this end, Iran sought to improve its relations with its CENTO partners as well as conservative Arab states, notably Saudi Arabia, Jordan, and Lebanon. Furthermore, the shah opposed Egyptian military intervention in the Yemeni civil war in the early 1960s to the extent of reportedly dispatching military advisers to aid the royalists in the battlefield.[5] The shah in essence saw an Egyptian success in that war as opening the door for the cultivation of Egyptian influence in the gulf, which was in turn perceived as a potential direct threat to the shah's regime.[6]

The Iranian quest for regional supremacy in the gulf has yet another equally significant facet. After introducing extensive socioeconomic reforms in 1963 and successfully cracking down on domestic opposition to his rule during the same year, the shah launched a military buildup campaign (see below) that has continued up to the present day. This buildup initially involved the reorganization of the armed forces by the creation of a third army corps with more emphasis on southern and eastern defenses, the strengthening of the navy by commencing the construction of a naval base at Bandar Abbas near the Strait of Hormuz, and the purchase of more sophisticated military hardware from the United States and Britain. Justifications for such steps revolved primarily around the constantly perceived threat to Iranian interests in the gulf by revolutionary Arab regimes in Baghdad and Cairo, coupled with little faith in the utility of CENTO or of the bilateral agreement with the United States in regional conflicts, as the Indo-Pakistani war of 1965 clearly demonstrated.

By the time Britain's momentous decision was announced by the Labour government in January 1968, Iranian strategic interests in the gulf centered mainly on three aspects. First, freedom of navigation in this waterway at all times was essential, for Iran, unlike Saudi Arabia and Iraq, depended upon the gulf as the only outlet for its oil exports and was at this time emerging as the leading oil producer in the area. Second, Iran needed to exploit its offshore oil resources and to protect not only its extensive oil installations at Kharg Island and elsewhere in the gulf, but also its oil cargo for the entire length of the waterway. Third, the preservation of the political status quo astride the gulf was necessary to prevent takeovers by revolutionary elements that, as the shah perceived, would not only affect the two essential requirements above negatively but might threaten the survival of the present regime in Iran as well. If by no other means, such takeovers could be accomplished through the encouragement of internal subversion in such a heterogeneous society as that of Iran. It is only fitting to mention that the pursuance of a diplomatically active foreign policy and the unprecedented military buildup throughout the decade were both designed to guard and further national interests.

The initial Iranian reaction to the federation of the nine was, to say the least, unenthusiastic. According to one observer,

> the shah was perplexed by attempts to create a federation of oil sheikhdoms in the Persian Gulf in the light of Britain's experience with federations in South Arabia, Nigeria, and Rhodesia. He felt that tribalism and federalism were incompatible, and the Persian Gulf federation would go the way of Aden and South Arabia.[7]

But more significant than the shah's doubts about the viability of a federation of tiny states were Iran's long-standing territorial claims in the gulf involving the Bahrain archipelago and the three strategic islands near the Strait of Hormuz (see below). Iran made it clear that its recognition and support of such a union were contingent upon the resolution of such claims to its full satisfaction. According to a statement issued by the Iranian Foreign Ministry in July 1968, "The creation of a so-called confederation of Persian Gulf Emirates embracing the Bahrain islands [was] absolutely unacceptable to Iran."[8] However, the shah's abandonment of the Iranian claim to the sovereignty of Bahrain in the spring of 1970 and the Iranian occupation of Abu Musa and the two Tunbs in November 1971 (see below) seem to have cleared the air for Tehran's recognition of the smaller entities in the area. Accordingly, diplomatic missions were exchanged at the highest level with Bahrain, Qatar, and the UAE upon independence.

From another perspective, the three-year period between the British declaration and official evacuation from the area witnessed an unprecedented acceleration of Iranian diplomatic activity and military buildup through the addition of American F-4 fighter-bombers and British Rapier missiles and Chieftain tanks to Iran's inventory of military hardware. Relations with nongulf regional states were improved, and the shah paid a visit in the fall of 1968 to King Faisal of Saudi Arabia. At this time the two monarchs coordinated their policies and explored means of closer cooperation in the area as the British were preparing to leave.[9] By the end of the 1960s, it became obvious that Iran was in effect preparing to assume, either by itself or in cooperation with other regional powers, the same role Britain played for over a century: a guardian of stability. The illusion of a power vacuum was tempting, and the shah felt that the disinclination of either of the superpowers to step in left Iran as the most appropriate candidate for the job. This conviction was expressed by the shah himself late in 1971 when he said, "I believe that the Persian Gulf must always be kept open—*under Iranian protection*—for the benefit of not only my country but the other Gulf countries and the world."[10]

Iran's emergence in 1971 as the gulf's most powerful state was greatly assisted by favorable circumstances that involved the wider context of the Middle East as a whole. Perhaps to a degree greater than the U.S.-Soviet cold war (which brought Iran within the perimeter of Western containment strategy), the Arab cold war and divisions of the 1960s allowed more room for Tehran's diplomatic and military action in the gulf than there would have been had the Arab front been solidly united. This cold war first pitted Egypt and Iraq as bitter rivals for most of the two decades following the Egyptian revolution; then, in 1962, Iraq and Kuwait argued over territorial sovereignty, Egypt and Saudi Arabia argued over North Yemen, Iraq and Saudi Arabia split on grounds of ideological incompatibility, and, finally, the Arab-Israeli conflict raged, particularly the war of 1967. Iran's determination to play the role of the principal power in the gulf in this decade has manifested itself primarily in the two important dimensions of regional collective security and radicalism. Both will be discussed later.

Saudi Arabia

Saudi Arabia controls nearly four-fifths of the entire area of the Arabian Peninsula and is the only country in the Middle East with direct access to the two strategic waterways of the gulf and the Red Sea. In 1976, this country produced more than one-third of the gulf region's crude oil and had by far the greatest proven oil reserves in the world.[11] This, if nothing else, makes it the most important political entity on the peninsula and one of the gulf's principal powers.

However, Saudi Arabia, unlike Iran, was slow in developing a cohesive gulf policy. A twofold explanation comes to mind. On the one hand, the gulf has generally been viewed within the context of the Arabian Peninsula as a whole. The peninsula represents a distinctive geographical unit with widely shared ethnic, cultural, and historical characteristics among its people. Indeed, were it not for Britain's atomistic, protective policy astride the periphery of this territorial mass, the whole peninsula might have been brought under one political leadership four or five decades ago. The clash between Britain and Saudi Arabia over the latter's territorial claims in Eastern Arabia in the 1950s and the Yemeni civil war, which drove Saudi Arabia and Egypt closer to a point of collision for most of the 1960s, give some indication as to where on the peninsula the center of attention of Saudi foreign policy was, at least until the British declared their intention to leave the gulf. On the other hand, Saudi Arabia (again in contrast to Iran) was and still is far more involved in the Middle East's seemingly perennial conflict over Palestine, with all the constraints and diversions as well as the demands on diplomatic, financial, and military resources such a strong attachment may entail. Part of this linkage with the Arab East has been the inescapable involvement in the postwar Arab political rivalries and divisions that are becoming more and more a permanent feature of the Middle Eastern political scene.

Saudi foreign policy toward the southern part of the peninsula over the last two decades can be characterized as remarkably pragmatic in view of the deep-seated political conservatism of the Saudi regime. An identifiable pattern can hence be depicted, revolving essentially around, first, the outright rejection of a situation perceived as undesirable, followed by, second, a gradual accommodation. The case of the two

Yemens is an interesting illustration. When a 1962 revolution brought a republican regime to power in North Yemen (the first ever in the peninsula), Saudi Arabia rejected such a development vehemently. The Egyptian military intervention on the side of the republicans in the ensuing civil war was certainly a factor, but it was the great aversion to leftist radicalism in general and the perception of its potential threat to the form of traditional political rule in the peninsula that hastily put Saudi Arabia and Britain on the same side despite differences over Saudi territorial claims in the gulf. However, when the republican regime moderated its policies and the Egyptian forces were withdrawn in 1967, Saudi Arabia's attitude toward North Yemen changed to one of accommodation.

This rejective-accommodative pattern seems to have reappeared in the case of South Yemen. The British withdrawal from Aden in 1967 brought to power (after a dose of violence, to be sure) a rigidly doctrinaire, communist-oriented regime. A communist version of leftist radicalism is something of an anathema in view of the Saudi grave aversion to an atheistic communist ideology under any banner. Relations with the new republic were extremely strained and the two countries even fought a brief war in the fall of 1969. South Yemen's support of revolutionary movements whose avowed purpose inci- dentally was to "liberate" the entire gulf region from traditional rule (see below) was an aggravating factor in Saudi–South Yemeni relations for nearly a decade until diplomatic relations were restored in the spring of 1976. Obviously, a number of factors might have contributed to this accommodative development. The untiring Kuwaiti mediatory efforts, the increasing realization on the part of the South Yemeni regime of the futility of its hitherto continued isolation on the peninsula, the decline of South Yemen's interest in supporting the Dhufari rebels, and the Saudi strategy of countering, and, if possible, rooting out any form of Soviet influence not only on the peninsula but in the Arab world as well are all relevant factors.[12] But it is the contention of this writer that a factor of no less significance in this rapprochement has been the Saudi reluctance to accept any form of foreign intervention in peninsular affairs. The hostile attitude Saudi Arabia adopted toward Nasser's intervention in North Yemen might have reasserted itself less intensely and more cautiously as the Iranian troops landed in Oman a decade later (see below).

Viewed within a peninsular context, Saudi Arabia's reaction to the 1968 Whitehall decision to withdraw from east of Suez by the end of 1971 was positive. Moreover, the Saudis enthusiastically supported the proposed federation of the nine gulf states as a significant move toward stability in the area. King Faisal is reported to have told an interviewer in May 1968 that "there need be no vacuum in that area [the gulf] when the British leave in 1971 as long as the Federation receives the support of the United States and its [the federation's] neighbors." He further expressed Saudi Arabia's unconditional support for the proposed union.[13] In pursuance of this objective, as noted in Chapter 2, Riyadh in collaboration with Kuwait invested a great deal of effort to bring the Union of Nine to fruition. The fact that both Bahrain and Qatar finally opted for independence was something of a disappointment to the Saudi policymakers, who had hoped the Saudi intimate relations with these two emirates would be translated into a stronger Saudi influence inside the union had they in fact joined. When a union of six, later seven, gulf states was forged in 1971 as the UAE, Saudi Arabia chose to maintain a sense of aloofness despite close relations with some UAE members, namely Dubai and Ras al-Khaimah, until its territorial claim to a part of Abu Dhabi was amicably settled in 1974. This development opened the way for closer cooperation between the two gulf littoral states in almost every field. Indeed, in matters relating to its territorial claim, Saudi Arabia, unlike Iran in the case of the three islands (see below), seemed to have ruled out the use of force as a means of settlement and, instead, chose the diplomatic path.

Saudi foreign policy toward the gulf in the 1970s has been a manifestation of its perceived strategic interests in the area. Having the second longest gulf coastline, Saudi Arabia is apparently determined to play a major role in gulf affairs. It shares with all gulf littoral states an aversion to any form of superpower domination or rivalry in the region, embracing instead the doctrine of gulf security by local gulf powers. Riyadh, like all other gulf states, has a profound interest in maintaining free navigation in the waters of the gulf so the region's oil can flow to its distant markets, and international trade, for so long a permanent feature of gulf life, may prosper. It further shares with all governments in the area, with the possible exception of Iraq, a vital interest in and concern for defending the political status quo against subversive activities of any form.

Iraq

A principal gulf power of considerable resolve, Iraq has nevertheless been a frustrated participant in the political arena of the region since a republican regime came to power in 1958. This frustration has not been without reasons. Among them have been political instability and a bloody Kurdish rebellion at home, a bitter dispute with Iran over Shatt al-Arab to the east, isolation from the main current of Arab politics through personal and partisan rivalries to the west, and failure to establish a genuine working relationship with political elites in other gulf regimes to the south, mostly because of ideological incompatibility. The Iraqi Baathist regime pursued, until the mid-1970s at least, a gulf policy that was inconsistent at best and erratic at worst.[14] To be sure, Iraq joined the other two major gulf powers in applauding the British decision to terminate its official presence, and the Iraqis viewed the proposed 1968 federation at the time as "a logical step . . . adequate to confront the covert and overt schemes against the Arab character of the Gulf and its nationalism."[15] But the Iraqis seem to have adopted a double-standard foreign policy for most of the decade prior to 1975. On the one hand, they maintained reasonably proper diplomatic relations with other gulf regimes on the official level. At the same time, Baghdad extended rhetorical, and sometimes material, support to clandestine organizations of the left whose long-range aims were to overthrow such regimes through revolutionary violence. Iraq recognized the sovereignty of Kuwait in 1963, but later reasserted its claim to Kuwaiti territory to the point of using force in 1973.

Iraq undoubtedly shares with other gulf states a genuine interest in maintaining free navigation in the waters of the gulf. Its efforts at cultivating political influence in the area by different means, however, might be attributed to a gravely felt isolation in the face of a profoundly perceived threat of Iranian hegemony in the gulf. The Iraqi-Kuwaiti territorial dispute may well be understood in this light. Controlling only a forty-mile stretch of gulf coastline, the Iraqis need more room at the head of this waterway in order to safeguard what they consider vital national security interests. More profound, however, is the issue of accepting Iraq as a full-fledged gulf power by an often wary and suspicious gulf community. In the words of the Iraqi foreign minister, the real issue, whether with Kuwait or other gulf states, is "whether Iraq was to be a Gulf state or not."[16]

The amicable resolution of the Shatt al-Arab dispute in the spring of 1975 obviously heralded significant changes in Iraqi foreign policy toward the gulf and the Arabian Peninsula. Closer relations were reestablished with Iran, and the Iraqis not only terminated their support of subversive groups in the gulf, but also persuaded South Yemen to do likewise. Iraq also initiated a restoration of diplomatic relations with Oman and sought closer links with Saudi Arabia. Suddam Husein, deputy to the chairman of the Iraqi Revolutionary Command Council, visited Riyadh in the spring of the same year (the first visit by an Iraqi official at this level since 1958) and later expressed his satisfaction with Saudi Arabia's readiness to understand the Iraqi point of view "particularly [in regard to] the preservation of the Arab character of the Gulf."[17] All in all, by the end of 1976 Iraq was apparently becoming more and more a status quo state by ostensibly abandoning its earlier policy of covertly augmenting anti–status quo elements in the area and instead striving for better relations with the established political order.

The Smaller Gulf States

One approach to the study of the regional politics of the smaller gulf states is to conceive of such atomistic entities as operating in a political milieu dominated by a tripartite rivalry. Accordingly, one is tempted to propose that the greater the intensity of such rivalry, the greater the room for diplomatic maneuvering these states will have. Writing in 1973, Enver Koury has observed that

> the inter-Shaikhdom rivalries give rise to a search for allies and protectors in the macrocosm of Arab politics. The dominant powers of the Gulf area are so divided that for the present the rulers of these Shaikhdoms are able to play off these powers against each other and maintain their delicately balanced independence.[18]

However, events since 1975 have somewhat weakened this assertion. Indeed, in today's gulf politics, the only clearly identifiable case of such a playoff is probably that of Kuwait in its relations with both Iraq and Saudi Arabia, and only insofar as Kuwait has taken advantage of the profound ideological antipathy between the two larger powers in securing a Saudi deterrent against the Iraqi threat to Kuwait's sovereignty.

But it is the other side of the coin that seems equally plausible. Larger powers, now that their interrelations have greatly improved, are always capable, individually or collectively, of taking advantage of the many personal, dynastic, and tribal rivalries of the ministates, thereby influencing the smaller states' internal political development or swaying their foreign conduct in a manner and to a degree compatible with their own. Such a regional constraint is exemplified by the inability of the smaller states, with the exception of Kuwait, to establish diplomatic relations with any of the East bloc states despite repeated attempts along these lines.

The UAE is distinguishable from other gulf states in that its federal structure of seven not yet solidly connected entities makes it a more suitable target for external influence than, say, its neighboring unitary political systems. In other words, one may venture at this particular stage in the development of the union to suggest that the looser the partnership among member emirates of the union, the easier it is for regional political influences to penetrate such a system and hence affect its behavior in one way or another. One implication here, of course, is that an understanding of the possibility of penetration might have an impact on the effectiveness and determination of the UAE government as it interacts with other states, particularly those in its immediate surroundings. Despite this vulnerability, however, the UAE has managed to maintain, especially since 1974, seemingly excellent relations with all regional states—a case that is scarcely applicable to them all.

The smaller gulf states share with the major ones a genuine interest in maintaining the stability and freedom of navigation in the gulf as a whole. In addition, they understandably tend to reflect a greater sensitivity in matters pertaining to their territorial integrity and to the protection of their systems of rule against internal subversion. Rather than playing the major powers off against one another in the intricate local gulf politics, the small states, or some of them at least, have adopted other, low-risk means as instruments of foreign policy. In addition to the use of material wealth in the form of aid for the cultivation of good will, the tool of mediation is gradually becoming a recognizable feature of gulf and Middle Eastern politics where patterns of political antagonism are rife. To mediate is to narrow the gap between two or more opposing views on a certain issue. To have the image of a troubleshooter in such a volatile region is to cultivate good will, enhance one's own prestige, and escape the embarrassment of being drawn to either side should a dispute reach an explosive stage.

Kuwait, for one, seems to have mastered the technique of mediation as a convenient instrument of its foreign policy. This state utilized its good offices toward the rapprochement between Iran and Egypt in the late 1960s, mediated between Saudi Arabia and South Yemen in the mid-1970s, and offered to mediate between Iran and South Yemen when an Iranian F-4 fighter-bomber was shot down by South Yemeni ground fire in November 1976.[19] Kuwait also helped improve relations between the two Yemens on more than one occasion, and between Oman and South Yemen as well.

The UAE has recently shown an interest in following the Kuwaiti example. Shaikh Zayed, the president of the union, has helped in the efforts that have finally led to improving South Yemeni relations with neighboring countries. He also played a personal mediating role between Egypt and Libya in an effort to repair the more recent rift between the two countries. In short, although diplomatic mediatory initiatives have always been resorted to at all levels and in all regions as a benevolent instrument of international relations, their salience in gulf politics is a consequence not only of the high frequency of local political antagonism, but also of the favorable, low-risk results they produce for the smaller states.

The Territorial Dimension

More than any other factor, the territorial issue has been the most significant in shaping regional bilateral relations and has thereby exerted the greatest influence on gulf politics in general. At one time or another, territorial disputes, major and minor, have permeated almost every gulf frontier, land and sea, from the Strait of Hormuz in the south to Shatt al-Arab in the north. In addition, the relatively recent discovery and exploitation of oil have further aggravated such disputes by sharpening local awareness of the potential economic advantages an otherwise desolate expanse of desert might yield. By the end of 1976 most territorial issues were amicably settled. But others remain. And although the political aftereffects of some of those resolved still linger, it is those that remain that pose a potential threat to stability in the region. In international politics irredentism has never been, and will never be, a stabilizing factor in any situation.

Four major territorial disputes will be briefly discussed in this section. These have centered on al-Buraimi Oasis in Eastern Arabia, Shatt al-Arab between Iraq and Iran, Abu Musa and the Tunbs islands in the gulf, and the border between Iraq and Kuwait. Each of these problems has involved one or more of the major gulf powers directly, and two, those of al-Buraimi and the three islands, have directly involved members of the United Arab Emirates. The disputes over al-Buraimi and Shatt al-Arab were amicably resolved in 1974 and 1975, respectively. The remaining two, however, are still in want of a resolution that satisfies all interested parties.

Al-Buraimi Oasis Dispute

Al-Buraimi is an oasis of nine small villages in the eastern part of the Arabian Peninsula on the edge of the great sand stretch known as al-Ruba al-Khali or the Empty Quarter. The oasis and its surroundings have historically been adopted as both home and grazing area for several major East Arabian tribes, the most prominent of which are Al bu Falah (a branch of the Abu Dhabian tribal confederation of Bani Yas) and al-Nuaim (a tribe that has traditionally given allegiance to the sultan of Oman).

The Saudi Arabian claim to this territory has its roots in the eighteenth and nineteenth centuries. During various periods in the past, the last of which ended in 1869, the Wahhabis of Central Arabia succeeded in establishing control over the oasis, including obtaining tribal allegiance from at least some of the tribes. Although Saudi Arabia had reasserted its claim on this basis earlier, until mid-1952 a small Saudi military detachment occupied Hamasah, one of the nine villages, as an expression of its determination to restore sovereignty over the whole oasis. The shaikhdom of Abu Dhabi and the Sultanate of Muscat and Oman, the other two parties to the dispute, were under de facto British protection and, accordingly, had surrendered the conduct of their external relations to Great Britain (see Chapter 2).

The Saudi occupation of Hamasah invoked an immediate British reaction, and minor skirmishes between the Saudi force and the British-led Trucial Oman Levies ensued. In October 1952, Saudi Arabia and Britain signed an armistice agreement in Riyadh and the two countries later agreed to resort to international arbitration as the best means of resolving the matter. A tribunal of five members (a Saudi representative, a British representative, and three judges of international stature) was formed. However, during this panel's second meeting in Geneva late in 1955, the British representative, alleging violations of the armistice agreement by Saudi Arabia, tendered his resignation from the tribunal and the arbitration attempt for all practical purposes failed. Late in October 1955, the British-led Trucial Oman Levies evicted the small Saudi force, thereby ushering in a period of considerable strain in Saudi-British relations that continued up to the early 1960s. The issue was then temporarily relegated to a minor order of importance in Saudi foreign policy as the Yemeni civil war drew Riyadh and London closer in an attempt to check Nasser's influence in Southern Arabia.

With the Yemeni civil war behind it, Saudi Arabia renewed its claim to al-Buraimi in 1970, which, though less extensive than the original claim, nevertheless embraced approximately one-third of the Abu Dhabi territory. However important this claim was, with the 1971 deadline for the British withdrawal approaching, Riyadh was determined not to allow its territorial grievances in the area to preclude its efforts to push the proposed Union of the Nine to a successful conclusion. When this broader venture failed and the UAE was established, however, the Saudis withheld formal recognition of the fledgling entity until the summer of 1974, when an agreement on the twenty-two-year-old dispute was reached during a visit to Riyadh by the UAE president and ruler of Abu Dhabi, Shaikh Zayed.

The Faisal-Zayed agreement of August 1974 was not as yet formalized in an international treaty by the end of 1976. Problems of land surveys and demarcation may have contributed to this delay, or the Sultanate of Oman might have raised some questions in regard to the UAE's territorial concessions in accordance with the agreement. Be this as it may, the highlights of the Saudi-UAE agreement include: (1) Saudi Arabia is to renounce its claim to the Buraimi Oasis; (2) the Saudis, in return, will get an outlet to the sea fifteen to twenty miles in width encompassing Kaur al-Odaid at the base of the Qatari Peninsula; and (3) the Saudi-UAE border will undergo minor adjustments in favor of Saudi Arabia. The revised border (see Figure 7-2) starts at a point on the gulf coast to the east of Duwaihin opposite to Ghaghah island and commences in a southeasterly direction to Ras al-Mihradh, then to al-Ribadh and on to Umm al-Zumul, where the borders of Saudi Arabia, the UAE, and Oman converge.[20] According to this agreement, the rich al-Zarrarah oil field will now be within Saudi territory. It is unknown, however, whether its oil is going to be exploited jointly or whether either country will own it.[21]

The Shatt al-Arab Dispute

Perhaps more than any other political dervelopment in recent years, the amicable resolution of the Shatt al-Arab dispute between Iraq and Iran, thanks to the energetic mediation of Algiers, has contributed not only to the improvement of the political atmosphere in the gulf but to the general stability of the Middle East as a whole. The name Shatt al-Arab is given to a fifty-mile-wide waterway that is formed by the confluence of three rivers, the Euphrates, Tigris, and Karun, as they pour into the gulf. Since this waterway extends along the Irano-Iraqi border, the center of the long-standing controversy was exactly where the borderline should be drawn. The treaty of 1937 between the two countries assigned to Iraq a far greater share of the Shatt waters by depicting the border along the Iranian shore for most of the length of the waterway. More than once in the last three decades, Iran protested that the earlier arrangement was unfair, claiming that its earlier acceptance of the arrangement was brought about by British pressure. The Iranians felt that because of changed circumstances, a more equitable division of the Shatt waters on the bases of the *thalweg* ("a river's line of fastest current or greatest depth") principle was urgently needed. Negotiations to this effect were in progress when the Iraqi revolution broke out in 1958.

The assumption of power in Baghdad by an ideologically incompatible regime and the subsequent Iraqi defection from the Baghdad Pact, thus leading to a drastic departure from this country's past foreign orientation, were viewed by Iran as seriously complicating factors

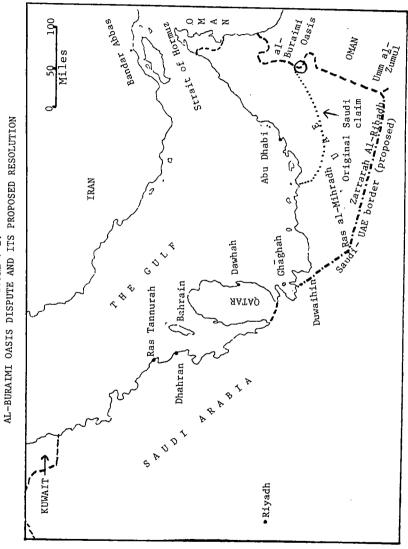

FIGURE 7-2:

AL-BURAIMI OASIS DISPUTE AND ITS PROPOSED RESOLUTION

affecting the border controversy. In 1959-1960 and again in 1969, the issue came very close to the point of violent eruption with wide-ranging local and regional implications. In addition, throughout the period up until 1975, the Shatt al-Arab dispute played a central role in the two countries' external relations not only in regard to the gulf region, but also in the wider context of the Middle East and beyond. Also, throughout this period of more than one and a half decades (1958-1975), Iran from time to time utilized the Kurdish rebellion in northern Iraq as a means of pressuring Baghdad. Iran not only extended material aid and offered sanctuaries, but also acted as a conduit for the flow of arms sent to this national minority from other countries, notably Israel.[22]

The Iranian government went a step further in aggravating its seemingly perennial crisis relations with Iraq by declaring, in the spring of 1969, that the 1937 treaty was null and void. The Iranians justified this act by referring to the alleged Iraqi failure to live up to the treaty provisions regarding joint adminstration of the waterway and the utilization of collected dues. Under these circumstances, the Iranians also succeeded in establishing a precedent by sailing an Iranian cargo vessel, despite Iraqi objections, from the gulf to the port city of Khorramshahr on the upper Shatt. This de facto division of the Shatt waters continued to be an aggravating element in Irano-Iraqi relations until the Algiers Accord of March 5, 1975, brought to an end decades of tension. According to this settlement, the two countries agreed to demarcate land frontiers between them, to divide the Shatt on the basis of the *thalweg*, and to bring to an end all acts of subversion against one another.[23] Among the immediate results of this rapprochement were the termination of the Kurdish rebellion against Baghdad and, as pointed out above, a significant moderation in Iraq's policy toward the gulf.

Abu Musa and the Tunbs Islands

There are generally two aspects of the gulf as an international waterway that tend to set it aside as noticeably different from other closed seas elsewhere. First, the entire body of this waterway is far shallower than the 600-fathom limit established by the United States in 1945 as the depth below which the continental shelf of a contiguous state ends. More specifically, the gulf in its entirety falls within the continental shelf of the littoral states, for it seldom goes below 300 fathoms in depth. Second, the seabed in the gulf is rich in mineral resources and the advent of high-complexity petroleum technology has made exploitation of such resources possible since roughly the late 1950s. It is these two aspects, particularly the second, that have often made the division of gulf waters, and the control of some of its islands, a matter of contention.

   Although offshore boundaries between Iran, on the one side, and
Kuwait, Saudi Arabia, Qatar, and Bahrain, on the other, were drawn in
1965, 1968, 1969, and 1971, respectively,[24] it is the Iranian occupation of
the three strategically located islands of Abu Musa, Tunb al-Kubra and
Tunb al-Sughra (Greater and Lesser Tunbs) on November 30, 1971, that
remains up to this day a potentially destabilizing issue in gulf politics.
Abu Musa and the Tunbs are located near the strategic Strait of Hormuz
(see Figure 7-3), but, as one student of gulf politics puts it, control over
these islands is "neither essential to block sea traffic in the Gulf, nor
sufficient in itself to frustrate a determined naval power from pursuing
that objective."[25] Abu Musa was recognized by the British as under the
sovereignty of the shaikh of Sharigah, while the other two islands were
historically part of Ras al-Khaimah. At various times since 1920, Iran
reasserted its claim to these islands on a historical basis. However, a
more serious Iranian interest in them surfaced only in the aftermath of
the 1968 British decision. Negotiations on the future of these islands
were conducted throughout the three-year period from 1968 to 1971, and
a quid pro quo situation is reported to have prevailed when Iran
renounced its long-standing claim to Bahrain in the spring of 1970.[26]
   The Iranian official argument in regard to these islands is that they
were in fact Persian before Britain transferred their sovereignty from the
Persian emperor to the shaikhs of the Trucial States some eighty years
ago. But it was the political-strategic factor, not the territorial-
historical, as one observer rightly suggests,[27] that weighed heavily in the
Iranian quest for their acquisition. Abu Musa and the Tunbs are, in the
shah's words, "of strategic importance to us as much as to the Persian
Gulf states and to the peace and security of our region."[28]
   The Iranian determination to take over the islands was underscored
when the Iranian government made the settlement of its claim a
precondition for its recognition and support of any federation of gulf
emirates. But it was not until mid-1971 that such determination reached
the point of a threat to use force should peaceful means fail.[29] The shah is
reported to have said in October 1971: "Those islands . . . are ours. We
need them. We shall have them. No power on earth will stop us."[30] Less
than two months later, on the eve of the deadline for the British
withdrawal, Iranian troops landed on the three islands in a manner not
entirely peaceful. Only in the case of Abu Musa did the two parties reach
some form of compromise. Although both Iran and Sharigah insisted on
their respective sovereignty over the island, the two apparently agreed
that (1) Sharigah would maintain jurisdiction over the inhabitants of
the island through its police and other pertinent offices; (2) Iran would
deploy troops on agreed-upon sites on the islands; (3) the two parties

FIGURE 7-3:

THE GULF PROPER--DISPUTES AND DEMARCATIONS

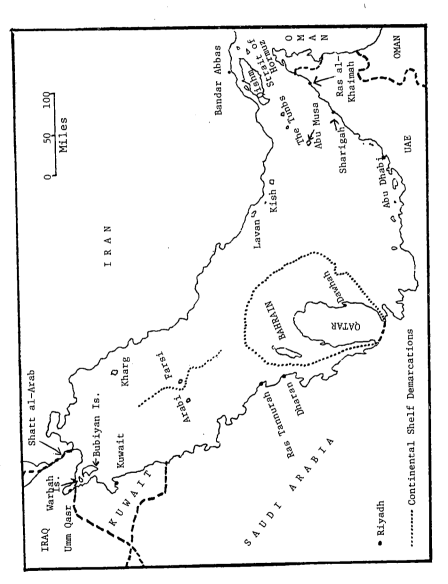

would equally share income derived from oil and other minerals; and (4) Iran would extend financial aid to Sharigah in the amount of 1.5 million pounds sterling per annum for nine years or until Sharigah's annual oil revenues reached 3 million pounds sterling.[31]

Iran's forceful occupation of the two Tunbs, with the few human fatalities involved, invoked varied reactions from Arab capitals depending on the predispositions of each regime toward Iran and its intentions in the gulf region. Ras al-Khaimah, the state most directly affected by the occupation, witnessed an outburst of public anger and indignation that resulted in some losses to property owned by Iranian and British interests. Shaikh Zayed, the head of the then just-formed UAE (of which Ras al-Khaimah was incidentally not as yet a member) is reported to have said, "We protest against Iranian aggression on her neighbors and her occupation of the islands, and are awaiting Arab states to help the . . . Union of Arab Emirates to regain our rights."[32] Except for South Yemen, Iraq, and Libya, the Arab states in general reacted mildly to the incident with regret and disappointment that a neighboring state such as Iran had chosen to use force in pursuance of a weakly founded claim. Libya and Iraq, however, went a step further. The former, accusing Britain of collusion in the affair, went ahead and nationalized a segment of British oil interests on its territory. The latter reacted by severing diplomatic relations with both Iran and Britain as a protest and further called for a concerted Arab action to block what has been described as Iranian expansionism.

The direct linkage between the Iranian occupation of the islands and the shah's perceived guardian role in the gulf after the British had departed was clearly stated by the shah himself in response to a question on the Abu Musa affair after the Iranian troops had landed. In that interview the shah justified the Iranian action thusly: "Our forces were sent to the island to take up positions on strategic heights there so that they could ensure the stability of the region. You have no doubt been told that it is nothing new for us to ensure the control of the Persian Gulf and the Strait of Hormuz."[33]

The three Arab islands of Abu Musa, Tunb al-Sughra, and Tunb al-Kubra continue to this day under Iranian military occupation or presence. Until their permanent status is settled to the full satisfaction of both sides, they will probably continue to be a potential source of regional tension. Even in the case of Abu Musa, where agreement was reached before the Iranians landed, the fact that both sides claim sovereignty over the island makes its future no less uncertain.[34]

The Iraqi-Kuwaiti Border Dispute

Another outstanding territorial controversy with far-reaching implications for gulf politics is the one between Iraq and Kuwait. This dispute goes back to the early 1960s, when the republican regime of General Kasim in Baghdad put forward an Iraqi claim to the whole of Kuwait based on the pre-1919 period when both Iraq and Kuwait were part of the Ottoman Empire. The Iraqi threat to invade Kuwait shortly after the latter's independence in 1961 first invoked the reaction of the British (who hastily dispatched some elements of their forces in the gulf and elsewhere to Kuwait) and later that of the Arab League. An Arab deterrent force of Saudi, Jordanian, and Sudani detachments was stationed on the border between the two countries until 1963, when Kasim's regime in Baghdad was toppled and a more conciliatory military junta came to power. Accordingly, Iraq recognized Kuwait's independence, but this recognition fell short of effecting a border demarcation between the two countries.

The coming to power of a rigidly doctrinaire Baathist regime in Baghdad in 1968, the subsequent conclusion of the Soviet-Iraqi Treaty of Friendship and Cooperation in 1972, which led to the granting of port facilities to Soviet naval ships at Umm Qasr, and Iraq's increasing need for a deep-water terminal to replace the relatively shallow port at Fao have all combined to contribute not only to the resurfacing of the Iraqi-Kuwaiti territorial issue but, in addition, to a change in its locus from land to sea. Following a border clash between the two countries in 1973,[35] the Iraqis offered to abandon their claim to Kuwait if the latter agreed to cede to Iraq sovereignty over the two strategically located islands of Warbah and Bubiyan at the entrance to the Iraqi port of Umm Qasr in the upper gulf (see map above). In addition to their obvious strategic importance to the security of Iraq, the two islands, if acquired by Baghdad, will doubtless give the Iraqis a greater share in seabed oil under a new formula of continental shelf demarcation. At the end of 1976, however, the two countries seemed to be holding widely divergent views on the issue. The Kuwaiti acting prime minister at the time, Jabir al-Ali, denied his country's abandonment of the two islands and stated that their "absolute ownership . . . by Kuwait is defined in accordance with the 1932 agreement between Kuwait and Iraq and confirmed by a document signed in Baghdad on October 4, 1963."[36]

The two territorial problems of the three islands of Abu Musa and the Tunbs in the lower gulf, on the one hand, and Bubiyan and Warbah in the upper gulf, on the other, involve a principal gulf power against a smaller one. It is precisely a situation of this sort that tends to cloud the repeated efforts at concluding a security pact among gulf states. To this question we now turn.

The Collective Security Dimension

When the security umbrella provided by Pax Britannica was officially removed from the gulf region in 1971, the search for an acceptable regional defense system that could fill the British void was well under way. At stake here was the stability of the region against acts of disruption, from within or from without, in view of its strategic significance particularly to Western Europe and Japan—the two areas most heavily dependent on this region's oil. Although both the United States and the Soviet Union later came to accept the principle of regional security by local powers (especially the United States, for which this principle is a direct expression of the Nixon Doctrine enunciated at the time), the oscillation of regional relations between competition and cooperation with nationalistic and ideological overtones has been primarily responsible for the absence of a security arrangement in the gulf up to this day. Major questions of definition and identification have often posed as stumbling blocks along this path. For example, who is really the adversary against whom a regional pact should be concluded? Is it foreign intervention, internal subversion, or both? Is the preservation of the status quo part of this security system? Which state or states should be allowed to play the role of a core power and who should be the junior partners?

Iranian Military Buildup

A corollary of the failure of the gulf principal powers, Iran, Iraq, and Saudi Arabia, to reach a definitive understanding on the question of regional security in the aftermath of the British announcement and, later, withdrawal, has probably been the unprecedented arms race among these powers that still goes on. Taking the three countries individually, as Table 7-2 shows, Iran has ostensibly fared far better in matters of military capabilities than the other two combined.[37] Determined to assume the leading role in the gulf once the British left,[38] the shah has put Iran on an extensive military armament track since roughly 1965. This military buildup started with the modernization of the navy and the creation of a Third Army Corps in 1967, but continued to accelerate with the accumulation of an arsenal of highly sophisticated weapons and weapon systems that, with scheduled deliveries as of late 1977, has placed Iran, according to one observer, comfortably ahead militarily of either France, Britain, or West Germany.[39]

A key to the understanding of the Iranian military buildup is obviously the shah's perception of the role Iran should play in the region and how the security of the present Iranian regime can best be

TABLE 7-2

MILITARY BALANCE AMONG THE THREE MAJOR POWERS OF THE GULF AREA, 1976

	IRAN	IRAQ	SAUDI ARABIA
area (sq miles)	636,300	173,000	830,000 (est.)
est. population	33,810,000	11,490,000	5-6,000,000
est. GNP	$ 56.8 billion (GDP, 1975)	$ 13.4 billion (1975)	$ 24.8 billion (1974)
defense expenditure	$ 9.5 billion (1976/77)	$ 1.191 billion (1975/76)	$ 6.771 billion (1975/76)
total armed forces	300,000	158,000	51,500
ARMY:			
1) personnel:	200,000	140,000	40,000
2) formation:	3 armored divisions; 4 infantry divisions; 4 brigades; 1 SAM battalion with HAWK; and Army Aviation Command	3 armored divisions 2 mechanized divisions; 4 infantry divisions; 1 Republican Guard mechanized brigade; and 1 special forces brigade.	1 armored brigade; 4 infantry brigades; 1 parachute battalion; 1 Royal Guard battalion; 3 artillery battalions; 6 AA battalions; 10 SAM batteries with HAWK.
3) major equipment:	500 Chieftain, 400 M-47/-48, 460 M-60 A1 tanks; 2,000 M-113 and BTR-50/-60 Armored Personnel carriers; 650 guns and howitzers (75 mm, 105 mm, 130 mm, 155 mm, 175 mm SP, 203 mm, 203 mm SP); 64 M-21 RL; 106 mm RCL; ENTAC, SS-11, SSH2, TOW ATGW; 650 23 mm (20 SP), 35 mm, 40 mm, 57 mm, and 85 mm AA guns; HAWK SAM. Army Aircraft include: 45 Cessna 185; 10 0-2A; 6 Cessna 310; 60 AH-1J, 100 Bell 214A, 20 Huskie, 52 AB-205A, 15 CH-47C helicopters.	1,200 T-62, T-54/-55, 90T-34 medium, 100 PT-76 light tanks; about 1,600 AFV; 700 75 mm, 85 mm, 100 mm, 120 mm, 130 mm, 152 mm guns/howitzers; 50 SU-100, 40 JSU-152 SP guns;120 mm, 160 mm mortars; RL; FROG, Scud SSM; 800 23 mm, 37 mm, 57 mm, 85 mm, 100 mm AA guns; and SA-7 SAM. Army Reserves: 250,000	300 AMX-30, 25 M-47 medium, 60 M-41 light tanks; 200 AML-60/-90, Staghound and Greyhound armored cars; Ferret scout cars; 105 mm guns; 75 mm RCL; SS-11, Harpon ATGW; AA guns; HAWK SAM. On Order: 100 AMX-30, 250 M-60 medium, 250 Scorpion light tanks; AMX-10P AFV;

	On order: 1,480 Chieftain and 250 Scorpion tanks; Fox scout cars; Dragon, TOW ATGW, ZSU-23-4 SP AA guns; Rapier SAM; 187 Bell 214A and 142 AH-1J helicopters. Army Reserves: 300,000		250 APC; guns/howitzers; AMX-30SA SP AA guns; Rapier, Chahinn and HAWK SAM.
NAVAL AND NAVAL AIR:			
1) personnel:	18,500	3,000	1,500
2) formation & equipment	3 destroyers (1 w/Seacat, 2 w/1 standard SAM); 4 frigates; 4 corvettes; 25 patrol boats; 5 minesweepers; 2 landing ships; 2 landing craft; 2 logistic spt. ships; 14 hovercraft; 1 maritime reconnaissance squadron with 6 P-3F Orion; 1 ASW helicopter squadron; 1 transport battalion; and 3 marine battalions. On order: 3 Tang-class submarines, 6 Spruance-class destroyers, 12 FPBG with Exocet SSM, 2 landing craft, and 6 S-5A helicopters.	3 SO-1 submarine chasers; 8 Osa-class FBPG with Styx SSM; 12 P-6 torpedo boats; 2 minesweepers; and 3 patrol boats.	3 FPB (2 Jaguar-class, 1 ex-US coastguard cutter). On order: 6FPB, 4 MCM, and 4 landing craft.
AIR FORCE:			
1) personnel:	81,500	15,000	10,000
2) formation & equipment:	317 combat aircraft: 10 fighter-bomber-squadrons with 32 F-4D, 141 F-4E with	299 combat aircraft: 1 bomber squadron with 9 Tu-16	97 combat aircraft: 2 FB squadrons with 30F-5E;

Sidewinder and Sparrow AAM, Maverick ASM; 10 Fighter, ground-attack squadrons with 12 F-5A and 100 F-5E; 1 fighter squadron with 15 F-14A Tomcat; 1 reconnaissance squadron with 4 RF-4E and 13 RF-5A; 4 medium transport squadrons with 57C-130E/H; 1 tanker squadron with 12 Boeing 707 and 3 Boeing 747; 4 light transport squadrons with 18F-27, 6 C-54, 5 C-47, 7 Beaver, 3 Aero Commander 690, 4 Falcon 20, 30 F-33 A/C; 10 Huskie, 45 AB-205, 70 AB-206A, 5 AB-212, 5 CH-47C, and 16 Super Frelon helicopters; and over 60 trainers. On order: 65 F-14A, 36 F-4, 41 F-5E fighters; 12 RF-4E reconnaissance; 6 P-3 Orion MR; 12 Boeing 747, 19 Bonanza, 2 F-27 transports; 22 CH-47, 39 Bell 214C helicopters; and Blindfire SA, radar.	1 light bomber squadron with 10 Il-28; 11 FGA squadrons; 2 with 40 MiG-23, 3 with 50 Su-7B, 3 with 30 MiG-17, and 3 with 50 Hunter; 5 interceptor squadrons with 90 MiG-21, 20 MiG-19; 2 transport squadrons with 12 An-2, 6 An-12, 10 An-24, 2 Tu-124, 13 Il-14, and 2 Heron; 7 helicopter squadrons with 4 Mi-1, 35 Mi-4, 16 Mi-6, 30 Mi-8, 40 Alouette III and 9 Wessex; over 50 trainers; and SA-2, SA-3 and SA-6 SAM. On order: L-39 trainers and 20 Alouette III helicopters.	2 COIN/training squadrons with 30 BAC-167; 2 interceptor squadrons with 37 Lightning F52/3/4; 2 transport squadrons with 24 C-130 E/H; 2 helicopter squadrons with 16 AB-206 and 24 AB-205; 1 Boeing 707, 4 KC-130 tankers; 20 F-5B, 5 Lightning T55 trainers; 2 Falcon 20 light transport; 12 Alouette III, 1 AB-204 helicopters. On order: 100 F-5E/F, 38 Mirage VES/DS, 10 KC-130; Alouette III.
PARA-MILI- TARY FORCES: 70,000 Gendarmerie with helicopters and patrol boats.	4,800 security troops and 50,000 Peoples' Army.	20,000 National Guard and 6,500 Frontier Force

Source: The Military Balance, 1976-1977 (London: The International Institute for Strategic Studies, 1976), pp. 33-34, 37.

maintained. An early guiding principle to Iran's regional role is Tehran's determination to fill a presumed post-1971 power vacuum and play the role of a gulf "policeman" either by itself or, if possible, in collaboration with other gulf states. The catalysts of this particular conception—as well as of the spectacular military buildup—have been the strategic importance of the gulf in general and its economic and military vitality to Iran in particular, the British phaseout and the reluctance of the superpowers to assume Britain's former role, and the Iranian lack of confidence in the ability of most gulf regimes to maintain their own stability. This linkage between Iranian and regional security was expressed succinctly by the shah in 1973 when he stated, "All I am concerned about is the security of my country, and Iran's security is intimately related to the security and stability of the Persian Gulf region."[40]

The other side of the coin in Iran's astonishing military preparedness is the shah's own perception of Iranian (or if you will the present Iranian regime's) security in a hostile environment. After the Soviet-Iraqi friendship treaty of 1972 was concluded, the shah is reported to have voiced his fear that "Soviet friendship with Iraq, Afghanistan and India [was] meant to encircle Iran."[41] One year later, with nearly 80 percent of the Iranian ground forces deployed astride the Iraqi border, the shah again expressed his dismay that "Iran had nothing but enemies on [its] frontiers."[42] Iran's bitter experience with the great powers during and after World War II, coupled with the shah's lack of confidence in CENTO (formerly the Baghdad Pact) and the U.S.-Iranian bilateral agreement of 1959 as being of much help in the regional conflicts to which Iran is a party, has often been employed to justify what is occasionally described as Iran's military self-reliance. Indeed, the shah told an interviewer in 1973 that "what we are buying is a deterrent that will be credible to all our neighbors. . . . The Nixon Doctrine says the U.S. will help those who help themselves. That is what we are doing."[43]

It is precisely the shrewd and timely exploitation of the Nixon Doctrine that best helped Iran in achieving its military edge vis-à-vis other major gulf states. In armament, as in other strategically vital commodities, the presence of a financially able, willing, and friendly customer may not always mean automatic accessibility to conventional weapon systems of good quality. Political considerations can weigh heavily. Whereas Iraq's source of military hardware is primarily the Eastern bloc, the case of Saudi Arabia and Iran is interestingly different. Both countries rely heavily on Western sources for their armament; both have the financial capabilities to carry out military transactions of almost any size; and, above all, both are traditional allies of the West, particularly the United States. But similarities end here.

From the U.S. perspective, the British withdrawal from the gulf and the shah's readiness to fill the perceived ensuing power vacuum, thereby to act as a surrogate in the protection of Western interests in the region, coincided with the United States' policy of "reentrenchment" in the late 1960s as a result of its bitter experience in Vietnam. The image of the shah as a determined guardian of Western interests in the region[44] emerged at a time when his image as an intimate friend of Israel had already taken hold, especially in the U.S. Congress. Against this background, President Nixon, while on a visit to Tehran in 1972, is reported to have agreed that the shah "could buy anything he wants [from the United States] short of nuclear weapons."[45] And the then U.S. secretary of state, Henry Kissinger, later defended massive U.S. arms sales to the shah as "not a favor we do for Iran," but "in the national interest of the U.S."[46]

Saudi Arabia, on the other hand, has always been viewed in U.S. official circles as directly involved in the complex Arab-Israeli conflict. Hence, the Saudis' requests for military hardware from the United States have often been, qualitatively and quantitatively, considered in the light of a perceived enmity toward Israel or as part of an effort to maintain the military balance between Israel and the sum total of its Arab neighbors. Indeed, although Saudi Arabia obviously does not regret its involvement in countering what the Saudi policymakers perceive as Israeli expansionism and injustice to the Palestinians, such an image, often exaggerated in Washington, has created a stigma, particularly in the U.S. Congress, around this country's arms requisitions, at a time when Iran seems to have enjoyed exactly the opposite reputation.

Efforts at Concluding a Collective Security Pact

A formal collective security system in the gulf has the prospect of enhancing stability in an otherwise volatile region. It may also open new avenues for regional cooperation among all littoral states in a more relaxed and trust-filled atmosphere. To be sure, such a step is long overdue, but in light of the disparity in military capabilities, at least among the three principal powers, the realization of such a system on an equal footing may prove difficult. Iraq, until recently at odds with Iran over territorial and ideological matters, once called the shah's military buildup "chauvinistic, aggressive, and adventuristic."[47] Therefore, it appears that Baghdad's conception of collective security rules out "any form of Iranian hegemony" in the area.[48] From another viewpoint, Saudi Arabia's coolness toward security proposals put forward by either Iraq or Iran emanates from its determination to play nothing short of a leading role in gulf affairs. The shah's "self-appointed policeman's" role in the gulf, supported by Iran's offer to send military aid to Kuwait during the latter's clash with Iraq in 1973 and the Iranian military intervention in Oman later in the year, might be considered a contributing factor to Riyadh's apparent lack of enthusiasm toward this vital area of gulf politics.[49]

The idea of a gulf security arrangement of some sort was put into circulation immediately after Britain's momentous decision of 1968. The Iranian prime minister, Huveyda, declared on January 27 that "as the most powerful state in the entire Persian Gulf, naturally Iran [is] greatly interested in the stability and security of the Gulf area, and to that end, Iran [is] prepared to cooperate with any littoral state that desired cooperation."[50] But events in Iraq later in the year, when a Baathist regime came to power, along with the eruption of the Shatt al-Arab dispute in the spring of the following year (see above), seem to have led the Iranians to drop Iraq altogether as a potential partner in the hoped-for defense arrangement. In that year (1969), the shah expressed Iranian thinking about the matter in the following terms:

> We would be willing, in conjunction with Saudi Arabia, to provide protection for the Gulf states. Our paratroop and armored regiments at Shiraz can give them as much protection as the British forces in the area today. ... We would like to see a common defense policy established for the area.[51]

The Iranian call for a formal defense grouping of Iran, Saudi Arabia, and Kuwait in 1970 invoked an immediate reaction from Baghdad, which duly saw in the plan a deliberate attempt to isolate Iraq. The Iraqi regime thus counteracted by putting forward another proposal of its own to establish an "Arab Defense Organization" that could fill the British void. As expected, Iran immediately rejected the idea, and Saudi Arabia, on its part, declined both offers on the premise of their polarizing potential. The Saudis were inclined, instead, to enhancing regional cooperation on a nonformal basis pending resolution of regional problems that stood in the way of a formal pact.

But regional problems persisted. Iraq revived its territorial claim to Kuwait in 1973, and in 1974 Iraqi-Iranian relations reached their nadir in disputes over their land and water borders and the directly related problem of Iranian aid to the Kurdish rebellion in northern Iraq. A turning point on the security issue was reached, however, in the spring of 1975. At the OPEC (Organization of Petroleum Exporting Countries) summit in Algiers, thanks to the initiative of Algerian President Hawari

Boumedienne, an Irano-Iraqi accord resolved all outstanding major problems between the two countries. At the same time, the shah of Iran, the Saudi crown prince, and the deputy chairman of the Iraqi Revolutionary Command Council accepted the principle of a security pact in the gulf "including a mutual pledge on non-aggression by all three states."[52] In the summer of the same year, the foreign ministers of the gulf states took advantage of the occasion of an Islamic Foreign Ministers' Conference in Jeddah, Saudi Arabia, and managed to arrange for a gulf summit conference on regional security around the following issues:

1. How to keep foreign fleets and military bases out of the gulf region
2. How to secure military cooperation in order to maintain free navigation in the gulf
3. How to resolve outstanding territorial issues in the area
4. How to guarantee the territorial integrity of gulf states
5. Ways and means of finalizing the continental shelf divisions among littoral states[53]

But a conference of the gulf heads of state never materialized. Instead, in November 1976 the gulf foreign ministers met again for two days in Muscat, the Sultanate of Oman, but failed to reconcile their differences in regard to the collective security issue. One obstacle was the problem of navigation in the gulf. Iran and Oman, the two riparian states bordering on the highly strategic Strait of Hormuz,[54] seemed to prefer the principle of "innocent passage," whereby a measure of control could be exercised by the riparian states, particularly over warships in wartime if either of these states were a belligerent. Iraq, on the other hand, preferred the principle of "free navigation," which could apply any time with no restrictions.[55] Another stumbling block on the road to a collective security pact was the failure of the Muscat conferees to pinpoint the source of the threat that the security arrangement was supposed to forestall. Iraq adopted the position that any security link should be directed only against foreign intervention. This would leave home-grown subversive and revolutionary movements outside its perimeter. The Iraqi view was understandably not acceptable to the Iranians or the Saudis, who both tended to subscribe to the principle of inseparability between a threat posed by foreign aggression and one initiated by domestic opposition against the status quo.

Finally, the Muscat conference was faced with a narrower conception of security on the part of some small but significant states than the "big three" had anticipated. Both Kuwait and the UAE, the two states with outstanding territorial problems with larger neighbors, voiced the view that the principle of "national security first" should be emphasized before a collective effort were made. The position that bilateral problems should be settled first as a step toward a collective pact was bluntly voiced by the Kuwaiti minister of the interior when he declared that "Kuwait supports any measure that increases the security of the Gulf and any method of achieving this aim *provided* all existing problems between the states have been settled."[56] The relative lack of maneuvering space in this regard was underscored by Shaikh Zayed of the UAE in a recent interview. In response to a question on whether a collective security pact was impossible in light of the Muscat experience, the UAE president said:

> As long as there are those who are not in favor of the idea, any other arrangement will only contribute to discord. . . . Ours is a state that was established only a few years ago. It is the smallest in the region. So, we are not supposed to call for an idea that falls short of unanimity. If discord continues, our duty is to maintain silence and try to bridge the gap between opposing views.[57]

A collective security arrangement that includes all gulf states in a form of a defense alliance seems more difficult to realize today than ever. One major obstacle has been the conflicting conceptions as to who the potential culprit really is. The radical dimension of gulf politics lies at the heart of this security debate.

The Radical Dimension

Despite the long-standing isolation from Arab nationalist currents imposed by the colossus of British control, Arab radicalism has succeeded in establishing a limited foothold in the gulf since roughly the early 1950s. Whether sponsored by the Baath ("Arab Resurrection") or the Arab National Movement (both of Levantine origin), gulf revolutionaries originally restricted their activities to opposing the British presence in the area. When this was officially terminated, however, they turned their attention to the status quo, posing as either political dissidents critical of the ruling elites, or underground revolutionaries whose avowed aim was to topple traditional regimes throughout the gulf. It is precisely the latter variety that, taking South Arabia as a base, posed the most serious threat to the status quo, mostly during the period from 1968 to 1975. A brief exposé of this aspect of gulf politics will take us through the remainder of this section.

The overt threat of revolution that endangered traditional regimes in the gulf passed, in a matter of one decade, through three main stages depending on its scope, its foreign linkage and orientation, and its inner ideological and strategic shifts. The first stage dates back to 1964 when a movement by the name of the Dhufar Liberation Front (DLF) was established in the mountainous southwestern Omani province of Dhufar (see Figure 7-4). Formed jointly by the Dhufari chapter of the Arab Nationalist Movement (ANM) and the Dhufar Benevolence Society, the primarily parochial DLF's initial aim was limited to withdrawing Dhufar from the Sultanate of Muscat and Oman under the sterile, ultraconservative rule of Said bin Taimur. Because of an old rivalry between the sultan and the Saudis, the movement was able to enlist the limited support of Saudi Arabia, particularly during its early years.[58] Operating from sanctuaries in the mountains, its activities were limited to small-scale skirmishes with the British-led, largely foreign-manned security forces of the sultan.

The DLF's close linkage with Aden's anti-British revolutionaries, and the subsequent success of the latter in achieving independence from British colonialism in 1967 after a long history of domination,[59] introduced some profound changes in the ideological outlook of the front. Therefore, the second stage of this rebellion can be said to have been inaugurated during a conference at Himrin in South Yemen in September 1968. At that conference, the front decided to broaden its objective from "liberating" Dhufar to eliminating traditional rule by revolution not only in the Sultanate of Muscat and Oman but throughout the Arab side of the gulf. After the "imperialists and their lackeys—the feudal rulers" had been eliminated, according to the new program, an Arab gulf state extending from Kuwait to Dhufar would be established. To achieve this objective, the front adopted the principle of "prolonged people's war" guided by a Marxist-Leninist ideology. Furthermore, it changed its name to the Popular Front for the Liberation of the Occupied Arabian Gulf (PFLOAG).[60] One year later, the PFLOAG scored its first victory when its supporters, the radicals of the ruling National Liberation Front (NLF), overthrew the relatively moderate regime of Qahtan-al-Shaabi in South Yemen, thereby establishing an extremely radical Marxist government that immediately pledged its open and unqualified support for the PFLOAG.

The broadening of its objective and the adoption of a Marxist-Leninist ideology proved, in retrospect, to be the gravest error the front ever made. In fact its newly adopted program put it on a collision course not only with far more powerful forces in the gulf, but, in addition, with an essentially Islamic culture that repeatedly proved itself totally

FIGURE 7-4

THE DHUFARI REBELLION: A RADICAL

THREAT TO STATUS QUO IN THE GULF

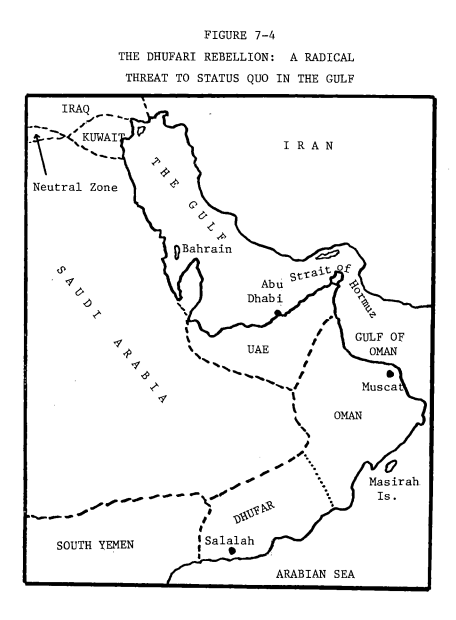

antipathetic to any form of communist dogma. To be sure, despite a narrow national base, the front was able with Chinese and, to a lesser extent, Russian and Iraqi help to score some successes. By the end of 1970 it nearly controlled all of Dhufar save for some coastal towns including Salalah, the sultan's seat, which was virtually under siege. It even consolidated its clandestine presence in the gulf, notably in Bahrain and Kuwait. But that was all it could achieve. As the present decade began, the front's fortunes began to decline.

The perception of the revolutionary struggle in Dhufar as a long-range, Communist-inspired threat to Western oil interests in the gulf naturally aroused fears in some official circles in the West. However, it was regional opposition to such a development that finally led to its demise. In 1970, King Faisal expressed his conviction as to where the real danger to the status quo in the gulf lay in the following terms: "Nobody ignores the fact that Communists are trying to interfere in the Gulf, but we don't think there will be any danger from outside the Gulf. The only danger may come from the area itself."[61] The deposition of Said bin Taimur by his son, Gabus, with British help in the summer of 1970, and the visit of the new sultan to Riyadh a year later seem to have laid the first foundation for the eventual Omani containment of the Dhufari rebellion. In return for Omani support of its policies in the gulf, Saudi Arabia recognized the new order in Muscat, extended substantial economic aid to Gabus, and agreed to block the PFLOAG's supply routes along the edge of al-Ruba al-Khali.[62]

The Iranian opposition to the spread of radicalism in the gulf has often been justified in strategic terms. Oman happens to be the peninsular riparian state on the strategic Strait of Hormuz. Hence, the security of this corridor, so vital to regional powers as well as the industrialized Western world, has been viewed by the shah as intimately linked to the ideological makeup and attitudes of regimes along its western side.[63] This Iranian conviction has also been bolstered by the recognition of a potential domino situation in the gulf, in that if Oman were taken over by the PFLOAG, the entire gulf would follow suit.[64] The direct linkage of such a state of affairs to the security of the shah's regime is that, as one analyst puts it, "in his [the shah's] mind, the most dangerous single foreign challenge to Iran's security comes from the threat of subversion on the Arab side, aimed at establishing a stranglehold on the Strait of Hormuz."[65]

Armed with a deep conviction of a potential danger to the security of his regime and the stability of the gulf region in general, the shah, upon an official request by the Omani sultan, decided to intervene in the Dhufari struggle. He sent troops in December 1973, which grew by mid-

1974 to a strength of 1,500 men with all necessary air and logistical support. No official Arab reaction to this Iranian presence on Arab soil was forthcoming,[66] and the Imperial Iranian Task Force in Oman (IITFO) totaled nearly 3,000 men by the end of 1976 with 15,000 to 18,000 rotations over a period of three years.[67] The shah told an interviewer late in 1975 that his unprecedented military buildup was in fact "spurred by tensions in the Gulf," and that his military support to Gabus was extended on the grounds that the Dhufari rebellion was "a Communist movement" to which Iran was opposed. However, the shah is reported to have added that "ideology is not the only issue here; security is the predominant factor."[68]

The direct military involvement of Iran, the support of a Jordanian contingent and the improved combat readiness of the sultan's security forces all combined by 1974 to tip the balance in favor of the Muscat government. This is when the third stage in the Dhufari drama actually started. The front was forced to reconsider its whole strategy as it began to lose appeal among the Dhufari tribesmen. In 1974, the front narrowed the scope of its objective back to the "liberation of Oman" instead of the whole gulf and, hence, was renamed the Popular Front for the Liberation of Oman (PFLO). But even the realization of this aim seemed at this time in grave doubt.

One contributing factor was that, in addition to the military campaign, the antirebellion camp launched another on the diplomatic front. Iranian diplomacy, active as it has always been, succeeded in mid-1973 in persuading Peking to phase out its support to the PFLOAG, thereby severing the front's most important linkage outside South Yemen.[69] On the Arab front, the Irano-Iraqi accord of March 1975 represented yet another step in the process of draining sources of support for the Dhufari revolutionaries. In fact, later that year, Iraqi diplomacy played a role along with that of Kuwait and Egypt in persuading South Yemen to reconsider its guerrilla connection in light of its economic interests and to end its relative isolation in the Arab world. These attempts paid off, for the South Yemenis came to realize the futility of a rebellion against all sorts of odds at a time when their own military and financial situation was at its worst.[70] The new change of heart on the part of South Yemen seems to have been bolstered by the 1976 rapprochement between their country and Saudi Arabia, as noted above, after nearly nine years of discord.[71]

By the end of 1976, the threat of a revolutionary sweep throughout the gulf seems to have abated. However, as recent political developments in some gulf states show,[72] radical elements of one orientation or another will always be a part of a clandestine presence in the gulf and may well surface on a small scale from time to time. The cosmopolitan nature of the gulf's population, the structure of its political systems, the linkage it has to other critical spots and issues in the Arab world, and the fact it is a theater of encounter between two rival nationalisms make total elimination of subversive radicalism an impossible task. Whether this justifies the continuing presence of Iranian troops on the peninsular side of the gulf is another matter.

The Two Superpowers and the Gulf

One of the most important considerations that guide a superpower's behavior vis-à-vis a certain region or a specific issue of contention is its policymakers' perception of the nature and extent of any threat posed by its powerful rivals. The rigid bipolarity of the international system in the postwar era and the perception by U.S. decision makers of a Soviet military threat to American interests in the Middle East in general and the gulf region in particular seem to have called for an extension of the policy of containment from the European theater, where it originated, to the Middle East region. The U.S. support of the Baghdad Pact in 1955, the Eisenhower Doctrine of 1957, and the bilateral agreements with Turkey, Iran, and Pakistan in 1959 attest to this essentially defensive posture.

The abatement of the cold war from roughly the mid-1960s on, following two decades of heightened inter-bloc tension, changed the American perception of the Soviet threat in the region as military to one as primarily political in nature. Thus it was support of radical subversive activities directed against Western interests and the instigation of leftist radicalism against pro-Western regimes that American foreign policymakers feared most.

The emergence of détente in Western Europe in the late 1960s has opened, so it would seem, a new era in East-West relations. However, its nonextension, at least officially, to other areas such as the gulf, especially after the official demise of Pax Britannica, seems at first glance to lend plausibility to the inevitable escalation of superpower competition in so vital a region as the gulf. Yet that has not quite been the case. The British withdrawal, and the resultant power vacuum, real or imagined, has instead signaled an era of regional gendarmerie, whereby predominant local powers have assumed guardian roles not only to maintain stability in the region but to protect vital interests of the superpowers and their allies where and when they appear compatible with their own. Since 1970 both the Soviet Union and the United States, by choice, to be sure, have opted to play officially limited self-assertive roles with limited presence, allowing regional powers to play the policeman's role. For the United States, this low-key, low-risk policy has been fully in line with the Nixon Doctrine of the late 1960s, which revolved essentially around the principle of allowing surrogates to guard American and Western interests in peripheral regions, instead of direct involvement as was the case in Vietnam. In the early 1970s, the Soviet Union, too, came to accept the principle of what we may label "regional autonomy" for the gulf. In the aftermath of the shah's visit to Moscow in October 1972, the two countries declared that "the Soviet Union and Iran expressed firm belief that questions relating to the Persian Gulf area should be settled in accordance with the principles of the UN Charter *by the states of the area themselves without any interference from outside.*"[73]

The United States and the Gulf Region

As noted in the opening of this chapter, the regional context of the UAE as a union of small territorial units has played, and continues to play, a far greater role in the emergence and development of the union than the global context. Regional political constraints can be said to have shaped the union's outlook on the outside world and have curbed, in some instances, the union's diplomatic initiatives. To be sure, the UAE weighs somewhat heavily in the world energy picture. In 1976, for instance, it ranked fourth among Arab oil-producing countries and ninth worldwide. In addition, the UAE's emergence as a federation did invoke reactions from the two superpowers. For the Soviet Union, reaction varied from initially negative to neutral to cautiously positive. The United States, on the other hand, viewed the new entity, as it emerged, as a positive step in fostering stability in the region. By the end of 1976, the union had also succeeded in establishing diplomatic relations with all member states of the Arab League in addition to many major Western and third-world countries. But it is the relative insignificance of the role it plays on the international political scene, compared to its more powerful neighbors, that makes its treatment as a unit by itself in the global context probably out of place. It is in all probability tantamount to an attempt to identify the role a country like, say, Luxembourg plays in East-West relations. That is primarily why, as far as the issue of relations with the superpowers is concerned, the emphasis here is on the gulf as a whole and those countries within it that assume recognizably greater international roles.

The initial American reaction to the putative British announcement in regard to British treaty obligations in the gulf was generally one of disappointment. American officials were concerned that the security of

Western interests in the region might be jeopardized in light of the
ensuing power vacuum, on the one hand, and of the Russian powerful
presence in Iraq, on the other. The U.S. undersecretary of state, Eugene
Rostow, spelled out the American conception of a post-British security
arrangement in the area when he stated that "some very strong and quite
active and stable states are interested in assuming responsibility for
regional security. . . . Iran, Turkey, Pakistan, Saudi Arabia and Kuwait
would certainly be a nucleus around which security arrangements could
hopefully be built."[74] This proposal, however, was never pursued for it
invoked a negative reaction not only from Moscow, which duly saw in
its acceptance a prospect for the renewal of cold-war encircling alliances,
but also from some of the states mentioned, which apparently wanted
no part in a security system so conceived. From a Western perspective,
however, one of the countries named in the statement, Iran, appeared the
most likely candidate for playing the role of a "gulf policeman." Both
the United States and Britain looked with tolerance as the shah occupied
the island of Abu Musa and the Tunbs, and by the time the British
withdrew their forces both countries seem to have agreed that "Iranian
diplomatic and military hegemony would remain a principal guarantor
of stability in the region."[75] In fact, it is reported that the principle of
Iranian regional hegemony was "fully supported"[76] during President
Nixon's visit to Tehran in mid-1972 when Iran seemed willing "to
defend parallel American interests in regions of immediate concern to
[itself] by reliance upon its own strength in situations short of nuclear
war."[77]

The strategy of security in the gulf without direct American
involvement was reiterated late in 1972 by Assistant Secretary of State for
Near Eastern and South Asian Affairs Joseph Sisco in the form of the
following five principles:

1. Noninterference in the internal affairs of other nations
2. Encouragement of regional cooperation for peace and progress
3. Support for friendly countries in their efforts to provide for their
   own security and development
4. Encouragement for the principles enunciated in the Moscow
   Summit of avoiding confrontations
5. Encouragement for international exchange of goods, services,
   and technology[78]

The U.S. experience in Southeast Asia in the 1960s and the principles of
the Nixon Doctrine thereafter allowed only a minimum American
military presence in distant but vital regions and more latitude in

improving the military readiness of local powers in order to defend the status quo against subversion instigated by rival powers. To this end, the United States relied heavily on the cooperation of the two most stable, pro-Western, politically conservative gulf states, Saudi Arabia and Iran. Because the latter, in particular, was not entangled in the complex Arab-Israeli conflict and, at the same time, bordered on the Soviet Union, it was able to exploit the Nixon Doctrine to its fullest, getting the latest in the Amercian military arsenal—surely far more than the doctrine's intended targets in Southeast Asia.

The 1973 Arab oil embargo and the energy crisis in general not only reinforced the linkage between the gulf region and the Arab-Israeli conflict, a complicating development for U.S. foreign policy planners, but, in addition, showed how vital the gulf region had really become to the industrialized economies of the West and Japan.[79] From that time on, economic factors have taken precedence over other considerations, and the question of guaranteeing the continued flow of oil at the lowest possible prices has become pivotal. It was indeed after the energy crisis had ensued that the United States found it consequentially prudent to upgrade its diplomatic missions to the smaller gulf states of Bahrain, Qatar, the UAE, and Oman to the rank of resident ambassadors.

U.S. policy toward the gulf region continues to rely heavily on cooperation between friendly regional powers, particularly Iran and Saudi Arabia, as the best means of fostering stability in the region and, hence, of guaranteeing the accessibility of the area's oil resources to the West, including the United States, which is becoming increasingly dependent on the region for satisfying a significant portion of its energy needs. Added to this, of course, is a limited U.S. naval presence, the so-called MIDEASTFOR of two flag ships that have made al-Jufair in Bahrain their home port since the late 1940s. However, the status of such a force has been uncertain since 1973 due to linkage of its presence with the American position vis-à-vis the Arab-Israeli conflict. As the question of the utility of maintaining such a presence resurfaced at the end of 1976, a senior U.S. naval officer stated that "Our presence . . . means more than just showing the U.S. flag in the Persian Gulf. It contributes to the stability of a highly volatile area. It would be a bad international signal to our many friends in these countries if we leave now."[80] Part of this limited presence, though involving the Indian Ocean as a whole, is the reported request by U.S. officials to Sultan Gabus of Oman, during a 1975 visit to Washington, that he grant permission for an "occasional" use of the Omani island of Masirah in the Arabian Sea (see map, p. 166) as a refueling station for U.S. air and sea reconnaissance in the Indian Ocean.[81]

The Soviet Union and the Gulf Region

Unlike the United States and its major allies, the Soviet Union has so far failed to establish a firm diplomatic presence in the gulf region despite repeated attempts that have extended over half a century. These attempts started in 1926 when the Soviet Union officially recognized the then nascent authority of King Abdul-Aziz Al Saud over most of the Arabian Peninsula and concluded a trade treaty with the imam of Yemen two years later.[82] But the great Saudi aversion to communist ideology in general has probably been the factor most likely responsible for frustrating Soviet diplomatic gestures. Even today, of the eight gulf states only Iran, Iraq, and Kuwait have proper diplomatic relations with Moscow.

In the heyday of the cold war—a time when considerations of Soviet security against perceived encircling Western military alliances ranked high—the Iraqi Revolution in 1958 and the subsequent defection of Iraq from the Baghdad Pact opened a new era of relations between Iraq and the Soviet Union that culminated in the Treaty of Friendship and Cooperation signed in 1972. Soviet naval facilities at Umm Qasr in the upper gulf now give the Soviets the type of limited military presence that the United States has in Bahrain.[83] It was also Soviet concern for security in its southern reaches that facilitated the onset of a diplomatic rapprochement with Iran in the early 1960s (see above) when the latter pledged not to allow foreign missile bases on its territory. The Soviet recognition of Kuwaiti independence in 1963 also cleared the way for commercial and, of late, even military cooperation between Moscow and Kuwait. The Kuwaitis apparently see in such a step an opportunity not only to balance their foreign relations and diversify their armament sources, but also a means of asserting their independence against the Iraqi threat to their territory in the north and against general regional pressure, though indirect, to pursue a certain foreign policy line.[84]

The more recent relaxation of tensions on the global stage in general, the Soviet rapprochement with Iran, the Kremlin's intimate relations with Iraq, and, above all, the Soviet naval buildup in the Indian Ocean[85] have all combined to enhance the Soviet sense of security and thereby lend less credibility to an American military threat to Russia proper from bases in the gulf. As a consequence, the Soviets have increasingly come to realize that in order to play the game of a superpower they must cautiously cooperate with existing regimes rather than attempt to subvert them. In the gulf, as in other regions where the Soviets have played a role, considerations of national interest have often outpaced those of ideology. And one aspect of national interest, to be sure, is to weaken, or if possible, dislodge Western influence from the area after many decades of predominance.[86]

The other aspect of this interest is mainly economic. The Soviet Union, too, will soon be importing oil, not for reexport to Eastern Europe as it now does, but for its own domestic consumption. Through a barter system, the Soviets have traded a steel mill for natural gas with Iran and along those lines concluded an agreement with Iraq for the exploitation of the Rumailah oil field. Short in high-level technology and capital in comparison to the West, Moscow finds the barter method with national oil companies in the gulf states the best approach it can pursue in this field.[87]

The Soviet quest for more influence in the region over the past fifteen years or so has been characterized by extreme caution and, in some cases, reluctance. In order to establish a position that will enable it to compete seriously with the West, however, the Kremlin must first succeed in building diplomatic bridges and trust with the most important country in the Arabian Peninsula—Saudi Arabia. If and when this is accomplished, other smaller gulf states will likely follow suit. In fact, following independence, Soviet diplomatic overtures were received positively in Abu Dhabi and al-Manama, and diplomatic relations between these two countries and Moscow could have been established had it not been for reported Saudi opposition to such a development.[88] Normalization of Saudi-Soviet relations would probably enhance Soviet influence in the region, give the Russians access to Saudi oil, and thereby lead to a greater Soviet stake in the stability of the gulf area. Such a step would also give Saudi Arabia more room in its dealings with the United States, particularly in the closely linked areas of armament and the Arab-Israeli conflict. It would also give Saudi Arabia more leverage as the spiritual leader of the sizable Islamic minority in the USSR and allow the Saudis more opportunity to check Soviet destabilizing ventures in the Middle East and, possibly, in East Africa. Until such normalization takes place, however, Moscow's position of influence in gulf affairs will continue to be inferior to that of the West.

Both the United States and the Soviet Union apparently have a stake in a stable, peaceful gulf region. Both have agreed that in the postcolonial era security in this vital but volatile part of the world can best be served not by a massive military involvement by either or both, but by keeping their military presences to a minimum and hence allowing local powers to work out a regional security system by themselves. The United States and its allies will probably continue their heavy reliance on the premise of close cooperation between the two principal monarchies of the gulf—Iran and Saudi Arabia—as the best guarantee against regional disruption. The Soviet Union, on the other hand, satisfied over the British withdrawal but lacking the diplomatic leverage to exploit it, will most likely continue its cautious, low-risk approach of awaiting better opportunities for the cultivation of influence in this largely diplomatic terra incognita and of undermining Western influence wherever and whenever possible. In addition, as the Soviet need for imported oil rises, Moscow will probably attempt to expand its oil dealings with gulf states on a purely commercial basis. The Kremlin's success or failure on either plane will largely depend, inter alia, on the perception of local leaders as to how much of a pro-status quo power the Soviet Union has really become.

Concluding Remarks

The evolution of the United Arab Emirates from a hazy idea to a solid reality is largely attributed to the receptivity of the larger political milieu within which this entity has emerged. The inevitability of interaction between this union, once realized, and its regional partners unavoidably thrusts upon it the type of constraints and lends it the same opportunities the region usually affords. Whether in the area of politics, territory, radical threat, or security, the UAE's reaction conforms largely to that of fellow states of a similar status, except that because of the union's federal nature, internal consensus on such issues is a bit harder to build.

The gulf may be the world's largest oil reservoir. But it is also a theater where two rival nationalisms meet. However, despite the deep-seated rivalry between Arab and Iranian nationalism, Iran, astride one side of the gulf, and at least six Arab states along the other have developed over the years a common interest in many areas affecting the gulf as a regional subsystem. Iran and the Arab gulf states agree on the overriding importance of preserving the status quo of a traditional, monarchical, and politically conservative brand of rule as the cornerstone for stability in the area. They also have a common interest in keeping the gulf region from the superpowers' competition; maintaining the free and unin-terrupted flow of trade, including oil, throughout the gulf; and establishing a security system that not only guards this vital region against foreign intrusion, but also guarantees the political and terri-torial integrity of the littoral states.

The question of security, however, inevitably brings up that of hegemony. In objective military terms, Iran is by far the most powerful state in the gulf. For a security pact to be realized, the likely source or sources of threat need to be spelled out, and anxieties of smaller gulf states about their national security and territorial integrity must first be allayed. But there is another facet of the question. In a situation as unique as that of the gulf's, parity in military terms, or if you will, balance, among the three principal powers is probably a prerequisite. Each of the three aspires to play a major role, if not the major role, and to be relegated to the status of a junior partner is obviously unacceptable. The intensity of nationalistic orientation on all sides makes a hegemonic situation untenable. Military superiority alone does not necessarily lead to a hegemonic relationship. For the latter to emerge, some form of politico-ideological association must also prevail. For example, while the U.S. hegemony within NATO is evident, it lost this advantage over Cuba, notwithstanding the latter's geographical proximity and military inferiority to the United States, once this small country shifted its ideological orientation by revolution. Iran does not subscribe to the same system of Soviet hegemony as that prevailing in East Europe. Within the gulf region itself, Saudi Arabia may be able to exercise more influence on smaller littoral states than Iran could possibly hope for. Apparently, hegemony flourishes most among friends.

The best guarantee for stability in the gulf is for all littoral states to realize that cooperation, rather than competition, is in their best respective national interests. Obstacles to cooperation are fortunately neither numerous nor profound. The Iranians, for instance, expect more appreciation from the Arabs of their special, intimate, historical attachment to the gulf, and of the role they can play in it. They also resent any step taken by the Arabs that might be construed as an attempt to isolate Iran by forming an Arab gulf bloc. On the Arab side, grievances include some apprehension about Iran's continued, unprecedented military buildup, the Iranian occupation of the islands, the repeated declarations of Iran's role as the gulf's guardian or protector, and, finally, the intimate Irano-Israeli relationship, despite Arab grievances over Palestinian rights as well as the continued Israeli occupation of Arab land.[89] Until these sensitive issues are settled, or at least approached in their proper perspective, Irano-Arab cooperation in the gulf will continue to be less than what is required for this region's stability.

8
Conclusion

The peaceful emergence of the United Arab Emirates represents a glaring contrast to the sad note included in the final chapter of many British colonial presences in the third world. Whether in the Indian subcontinent, Palestine, Cyprus, or South Arabia, strife and discord had immediately followed the departure of this colonial power. The UAE is in fact a successful attempt to cope with postcolonial realities. Its short experience as a federal entity leads one to the general conclusion that the attainment of a high level of socioeconomic and political development is not a necessary condition for the emergence of a federal structure among highly authoritarian and paternalistic political systems. Such development might help, however, in the growth process of a federal structure, particularly as political mobilization takes place and demand for wider political participation rises.

I have attempted in this study to trace the background, consummation, and development of the UAE as a federal entity in a primarily tribal culture. Tribalism, paternalism, territorial disputes, and immigration were approached as influences tending to hinder integration efforts, while the quest for survival, rising life standards, the existence of a core, gradualism, the sense of mission, geographical contiguity, and identity of culture were elaborated on as primarily integrative factors. Finally, I have tried to identify and discuss the political dynamics that have shaped the vital region in which the union has emerged, the role played by major regional actors in this emergence, and the significance of this part of the Middle East as perceived by the foreign policymakers of the two superpowers as they compete in pursuance of their respective global interests.

In consideration of the relatively short time since the union came into being, an observation of such a federal phenomenon can yield conclusions only on a very tentative basis. The propositions introduced

in Chapter 1 are neither exhaustive nor conclusive. Further studies of
this federal experiment, whether guided by the same set of propositions
or not, may well prove capable of challenging the conclusions reached
in this study as well as its assumptions. Nevertheless, it now seems
appropriate to reintroduce our earlier propositions with a brief
examination based upon the data presented in the preceding chapters.

> 1. The United Arab Emirates came into existence mainly as a result of the
> perception by pertinent political elites of an external military threat posed by
> the regional and/or global environments following the 1968 British decision
> to abrogate the protective treaties as of late 1971.

Plausible as it may sound, this conclusion is hardly supported by
available evidence. As was pointed out in Chapter 6, and as the UAE's
reaction to the Iranian occupation of the islands of Abu Musa and the
two Tunbs has shown, it is highly unrealistic for such an entity to
challenge militarily any of the three principal regional powers,
provided any of these powers exhibit a determination to violate the
territorial integrity of the nascent union. The pooling of military forces
for the purpose of a stronger defense (or as a successor to the British
protective shield) was only a secondary, long-term motivation behind
the evolving coalition of political elites that finally brought the idea of a
union to fruition. Hence, our conclusion will probably be more correct
if made to read:

> The UAE came into existence mainly as a result of the perception by
> pertinent political elites of the inability of the emirates taken individually to
> assume the responsibilities of statehood in a highly complicated world and in
> light of the meager material and human resources each commanded after over
> a century of dependence on a foreign power.
>
> 2. The smaller the number of the member units of a prospective federation,
> the better the chances for its realization and growth.

This is probably a truism. As was indicated in Chapter 2, the federal
venture started as a bilateral endeavor between Abu Dhabi and Dubai
following the British announcement of 1968. The federation of nine that
followed did not fare well mainly due to difficulties in reconciling the
disparate, and often conflicting, views as each state sought to embody in
the new entity its own vision of a postcolonial era according to its
perceived national interests. The question "who does what and where"
proved a bit easier to deal with when six of the original nine agreed on a
provisional constitution in mid-1971. The relatively larger number of
federating units (some twenty-odd shaikhdoms) was probably one factor

in the failure in 1967 of the earlier federating attempt in South Arabia.

> 3. The more capabilities a core unit in a federation has, the greater the acceleration of integration among these units.
>
> 3-1. Given the various constraints of the environment in which the UAE emerged, economic rewards at the disposal of the core unit are more likely to contribute to integration of the federating units than that core's military capabilities.

We pointed out in Chapter 4 the magnitude of the wealth of Abu Dhabi, the union's core unit. Chapter 6, on the other hand, dealt with the question of how this wealth is being utilized to build a federal structure around this core. The flow of material rewards across state boundaries in generally one direction is probably the strongest and most obvious incentive in keeping the emirates together and, hence, in leading to what we have already labeled "integration by dependence." In addition, although Abu Dhabi is by far the most powerful state in the federation militarily, this prowess may not be easily utilized to effect a federal orientation. Such an effort is likely to be inhibited not only by the many simmering rivalries, personal and tribal, but also by regional linkages in the form of preunion solid alignments and connections of some member units with one or the other of the principal gulf states.

> 4. The more varied and developed the means of communication among member states in a federation, the greater are the chances for integration to develop among the same states.

The UAE's geographical contiguity and relatively small size have made it easier for a communication network to develop. As a result, not only socioeconomic exchange among the emirates has intensified, but, in addition, federal authorities have utilized this means for the assertion of control and the management of the wide-ranging developmental programs undertaken by the central government. As noted in Chapter 4, the 1976 opening of the first hard-surface road ever to link Fujairah and Sharigah's enclaves on the Gulf of Oman with the rest of the union on the other side of the rugged Hajjar Mountains has represented a significant step along the path to more federal consolidation. Earlier, Saudi Arabia financed the construction of a highway linking the four emirates of Sharigah, Ajman, Umm al-Guiwain, and Ras al-Khaimah astride the coast of the gulf. Improvement and proliferation of telecommunications, too, will in the future help undermine parochial attitudes—a prerequisite for the emergence of a federal culture.

5. The UAE as a federation of ministates will hold, and hence be categorized as successful, as long as major regional powers perceive such an amalgamative venture to be in their respective national interests or, at least, not incompatible with those interests.

One way to approach the UAE's regional relations is to visualize it as a small and fragile entity in a zone of regional rivalry. We have discussed in Chapter 2 and again in Chapter 7 the crucial role played by regional powers such as Iran, Iraq, Saudi Arabia, and Kuwait (particularly, the latter two states) in the emergence and development of the union. Iran's support, for instance, emanates mainly from the shah's perception of the union as a step in the consolidation of the status quo on the opposite side of the gulf—an Iranian strategic interest in the region. Saudi Arabia and Kuwait, on the other hand, have consistently viewed the union as a stabilizing factor in the lower gulf. Saudi Arabia, in particular, sees it as an essential link in a sort of *cordon sanitaire*, extending astride its eastern frontiers from Kuwait in the north to Oman in the south, against the future possibility of an extremely radicalized Iraq or an ultranationalistic Iran. Iraq, in turn, has viewed the union as a step in the preservation of the Arab character of the peninsular side of the gulf and, since 1975, as a stabilizer of the status quo.

6. Major Western industrialized nations, including Britain, the former protecting power, perceive that the need for stability in the gulf region is greatly enhanced by the fact that this region supplies a highly significant portion of the West's petroleum demand and controls the world's largest known reserves of this vital energy resource.

Again, as has been noted in Chapters 2 and 7, Britain's relentless support throughout the negotiations that finally led to the union; the acquiescence by both Britain and the United States to the Iranian occupation of the three islands; Washington's unprecedented role in the Iranian military buildup and its "two-pillar" strategy of relying on the cooperation between Iran and Saudi Arabia; the upgrading of American diplomatic missions to the smaller gulf states after the 1973 energy crisis; and the more recent American request to utilize the Omani island of Masirah in the Arabian Sea for reconnaissance purposes in the Indian Ocean all combine to underscore the importance to Western interests of a stable and friendly gulf region.

From another perspective, the previous inaccessibility of the gulf's mineral resources to the Soviet Union, except in a limited sense, along with the area's strategic value for Soviet defense, are obviously significant factors in explaining Moscow's intimate relationship with Baghdad (which culminated in the 1972 friendship treaty), the augmentation of the Soviet naval presence in the gulf, the Russian naval buildup in the Indian Ocean, and the Kremlin's repeated diplomatic signals to the otherwise less receptive regimes of the Arab gulf littoral.

In an area as volatile as the Middle East, the best prediction is probably the one made in retrospect. This, in turn, means no prediction at all. Nevertheless, it is perhaps safe at this juncture to conclude that as a federation the UAE has already reached the point of difficult if not impossible return. Federal authorities have demonstrated some remarkable abilities, thanks to the continued cooperation between Abu Dhabi and Dubai, in coping with earlier challenges such as the Sharigan succession crisis of 1972, the Fujairah-Sharigah clash over territory in the same year, and the problem of extending the life of the Provisional Constitution at the end of 1976.

The survival of the union will probably continue to be as much a regional concern as it is domestic. The present regimes of Iran and Saudi Arabia will likely continue to view the union in their respective interests and in the interest of stability in the region as a whole. Hence, the two regimes will probably exert whatever pressure is necessary to keep the union on the track toward further consolidation.

In the domestic arena, however, the salience of personal considerations in such highly paternalistic political systems (where the institutionalization of political authority is not widely recognized) tends to complicate any attempt to identify trends. It is fairly well established that it was largely the coalition of local leadership initiatives that brought the idea of a union to realization. Will such coalitional leadership be able to cope with increasing popular demands for wider political participation? More specifically, will elites be flexible enough to relax their virtual monopoly of political authority at the highest level? As rulers come and go in such a highly personalistic brand of politics, will their perceptions of their individual authorities as well as the roles their emirates should play in the union structure be changed? If so, how, positively or negatively, will this affect the union?

The UAE Provisional Constitution expires in 1981. Integrative achievements so far point in the direction of a unitary system. When and if a permanent constitution is promulgated, it will likely reflect this trend. In the meantime, it remains for a determined federal authority to multiply its efforts in order to create a sense of political community in a federal setup. A federal structure has already been built, but a federal culture has yet to take root. The emirates are presently undergoing extremely rapid change with wide-ranging socioeconomic implications. Social dislocations on a large scale are characteristic of this modernizing stage. As the gradual erosion of parochial attitudes and traditional loyalties takes place, a more solid popular foundation for this partnership will evolve. Only then will there emerge a more profound expression of *e pluribus unum* along the Coast of Oman in the lower gulf.

Notes

Chapter 1

1. The literature on small states' proliferation, power, status, and utility as a tool for analysis, etc., is an impressive one. For example, see Annette B. Fox, *The Power of Small States: Diplomacy in World War II* (Chicago: University of Chicago Press, 1959); David Vital, *The Inequality of States: A Study of the Small Power in International Relations* (Oxford: Clarendon Press, 1967) and his *The Survival of Small States: Studies in Small Power/Great Power Conflict* (London: Oxford University Press, 1971); Robert L. Rothstein, *Alliances and Small Powers* (New York and London: Columbia University Press, 1968); Jacques Rapaport et al., *Small States and Territories: Status and Problems* (New York: Arno Press, 1971); Trygve Mathisen, *The Functions of Small States in the Strategies of Great Powers* (Oslo: Scandinavian University Books, 1971); Marshall R. Singer, *Weak States in a World of Powers: The Dynamics of International Relations* (New York: Free Press, 1972); and Robert O. Keohane, "Lilliputians' Dilemmas: Small States in International Politics," *International Organization* 23, no. 2 (1969):291-310 and "The Big Influence of Small Allies," *Foreign Policy*, no. 2 (Spring 1971), pp. 161-82. The works by Fox and Vital (1971) both deal with specific cases. The former points out the remarkably successful diplomacy of wartime leaderships primarily in Turkey, Sweden, and Spain in keeping these countries reasonably out of the Second World War; the latter discusses the relations of three small states vis-à-vis three major ones: Czechoslovakia versus Germany (1938); Israel versus the Soviet Union after 1967; and Finland versus the Soviet Union through varying historical periods. For a fairly recent criticism of the use of the small state as an analytical concept, see Peter R. Baehr, "Small States: A Tool for Analysis?", *World Politics* 27, no. 3 (1975):456-66.

2. Theoretical efforts in this area, especially after the EEC came into being, are impressive. See, for example, Karl W. Deutsch, *Political Community at the International Level* (Garden City, N.Y.: Doubleday and Co., 1954); Karl W. Deutsch et al., *Political Community and the North Atlantic Area: International*

Organization in the Light of Historical Experience (Princeton, N.J.: Princeton University Press, 1957); Ernest B. Haas, *The Uniting of Europe: Political, Economic and Social Forces, 1950-1957* (Stanford, Calif.: Stanford University Press, 1958); Ernest B. Haas, "The Challenge of Regionalism," *International Organization* 12, no. 4 (Autumn 1958):440-58; Bela Balassa, *The Theory of Economic Integration* (Homewood, Ill.: Richard D. Irwin, 1961); Joseph S. Nye, "Comparative Regional Integration: Concept and Measurement," *International Organization* 22, no. 4 (Autumn 1968):855-80; Amitai Etzioni, "The Epigenesis of Political Communities at the International Level," in James N. Rosenau, ed., *International Politics and Foreign Policy* (New York: Free Press, 1969), pp. 346-58; and Roger D. Hansen, "Regional Integration: Reflections on a Decade of Theoretical Efforts," *World Politics* 21, no. 2 (January 1969):242-71. The following discussion of the concept of integration draws heavily on these works.

3. Deutsch et al., *Political Community and North Atlantic Area*, p. 5.

4. Haas, *Uniting of Europe*, p. 16.

5. The ten cases are (1) the emergence of the United States in 1789 and their reunion after the Civil War; (2) the England-Scotland union of 1707; (3) the 1921 breakup of the union between Ireland and the United Kingdom; (4) the German unification of 1871; (5) the Italian unification of 1859-1860; (6) the dissolution of the Hapsburg Empire in 1918; (7) the Norway-Sweden union of 1814 and its breakup in 1905; (8) the gradual Swiss integration that culminated in the federation of 1848; (9) the England-Wales union after 1485; and (10) the formation of England in the Middle Ages.

6. See Deutsch et al., *Political Community and North Atlantic Area*, p. 6.

7. Ibid., p. 29.

8. Ibid., p. 138.

9. However, a celebrated example of a community of equal, or nearly equal, partners is the Scandinavian case. For analyses that generally stress the pluralistic, egalitarian, and cooperative, rather than integrative, nature of this region, see, for example, Norman J. Padelford, "Regional Cooperation in Scandinavia," *International Organization* 11, no. 4 (Autumn 1957):597-614; Frantz Wendt, *The Nordic Council and Cooperation in Scandinavia* (Copenhagen: Mumsgaard, 1959), pp. 98-100 ff.; Stanley V. Anderson, *The Nordic Council: A Study of Scandinavian Regionalism* (Seattle: University of Washington Press, 1967); and Nils Orvik, "Nordic Cooperation and High Politics," *International Organization* 28, no. 1 (Winter 1974):61-88.

10. In addition to Haas's works cited above, see Ernest B. Haas and Philippe C. Schmitter, "Economics and Differential Patterns of Political Integration: Projections about Unity in Latin America," *International Organization* 18, no. 4 (Autumn 1964):705-37.

11. See, for example, Hansen, "Regional Integration," p. 242. Indeed, the most salient concepts of neofunctionalism such as spillover, takeoff, "corism," and elitism are also those of the so-called traditional approach of Deutsch and others.

12. Haas and Schmitter, "Political Integration," p. 707. Along these lines,

also see Ernest B. Haas, *The Obsolescence of Regional Integration Theory* (Berkeley: University of California, Institute of International Studies, 1975).

13. This framework is elaborated in Haas and Schmitter, "Political Integration," to ten cases of economic integration in Europe, Central and South America, and Africa.

14. Ibid., p. 726. However, the authors do not find in the Latin American cultural setting enough functional equivalents to put into action the automaticity in the transformation of the Latin American Free Trade Area into a political union. Only a crisis, they assert, might bring this about.

15. Nye, "Comparative Regional Integration," pp. 858 ff.

16. Ibid., p. 858.

17. Ibid., pp. 865 ff.

18. Ibid., pp. 868 ff.

19. Ibid., p. 868. The author points to the difficulties involved in determining public policy sectors in different systems and their loci of power. He further suggests the utility of Leon Lindberg's scale in measuring this component. For an early version of the Lindberg model, see his "The European Community as a Political System: Notes toward the Construction of a Model," *Journal of Common Market Studies* 5, no. 4 (June 1967):344-87.

20. In fact, the Deutsch et al. approach is based initially on the concept of historical security communities.

21. On regional integration in Africa, see, for instance, Immanuel Wallerstein, *Africa* (New York: Random House, 1962), Chapter 7; Joseph S. Nye, Jr., "East African Economic Integration," *Journal of Modern African Studies* 1, no. 4 (December 1963):475-502; Joseph S. Nye, Jr., *Pan-Africanism and East African Integration* (Cambridge, Mass.: Harvard University Press, 1965); Donald Rothchild, "The Limits of Federalism: An Examination of Political Institutional Transfer in Africa," *Journal of Modern African Studies* 4, no. 3 (November 1966):275-93; Aaron Segal, "The Integration of Developing Countries: Some Thoughts on East Africa and Central America," *Journal of Common Market Studies* 5, no. 3 (March 1967):252-82; and Donn M. Kurtz, "Political Integration in Africa: The Mali Federation," *Journal of Modern African Studies* 8, no. 3 (1970):405-24. Wallerstein highlights consolidation of independence as an additional function of unions in Africa; Rothchild points to the dilemma of "reconciling the requirements of central leadership with the demands of regional autonomy"; Segal asks whether coalitions of elites suffice to sustain integration or whether there is a need for a "regional nationalism" to evolve, and Kurtz applies the Haas-Schmitter framework to the short-lived Federation of Mali, pointing to the differences in political culture and style of politics.

On Central and Latin America, see, for example, "The Emerging Common Markets in Latin America," *Monthly Review* (Federal Reserve Bank of New York), September 1960, pp. 154 ff.; Philippe C. Schmitter and Ernest Haas, *Mexico and Latin American Economic Integration* (Berkeley: University of California, Institute of International Studies, 1964); Ernest Haas and Philippe C. Schmitter, *The Politics of Economics in Latin American Regionalism*

(Denver: University of Denver Monograph, 1965); Joseph S. Nye, Jr., "Central American Regional Integration," *International Conciliation*, no. 562 (March 1967); James D. Cochrane, *The Politics of Regional Integration: The Central American Case* (New Orleans: Tulane University Press, 1969); Philippe C. Schmitter, "Central American Integration: Spill-Over, Spill-Around or Encapsulation?," *Journal of Common Market Studies* 9, no. 1 (September 1970):1-48 and his *Autonomy on Dependence as Regional Integration Outcomes: Central America* (Berkeley: University of California, Institute of International Studies, 1972).

Some authors have approached regionalism from a systemic perspective. Examples are Leonard Binder, "The Middle East as a Subordinate International System," *World Politics* 10, no. 3 (April 1958):408-29; George Modelski, "International Relations and Area Studies: The Case of South East Asia," *International Relations* 2 (April 1961):148 ff.; Thomas Hodgkin, "The New West African State System," *University of Toronto Quarterly* 31, no. 1 (October 1961):74-82; and Michael Brecher, "International Relations and Asian Studies: The Subordinate State System of Southern Asia," *World Politics* 15, no. 2 (January 1963):213-35.

22. Schmitter and Haas, *Mexico and Latin American Integration*, p. 4, emphasis added.

23. For the purposes of this study, mainly because of the still fluid nature of this integrative case, the terms *union* and *federation* will be used interchangeably. The same can be said in the case of *shaikh* and *amir* and *shaikhdom* and *emirate*.

24. For a discussion of the sociopolitical structure in this part of the world, see, for example, P. W. Harrison, "Economic and Social Conditions in East Arabia," *Muslim World* 14 (1924):163 ff.; Reuben Levy, *The Social Structure of Islam* (Cambridge, England: University Press, 1965), pp. 242 ff.; Frauke Heard-Bey, "The Gulf States and Oman in Transition," *Asian Affairs* 59, pt. 1 (1972):14-22 and her "Social Changes in the Gulf States and Oman," *Asian Affairs* 59, pt. 3 (1972):309-16.

25. Heard-Bey, "Gulf States," p. 16.

26. James A. Bill and Carl Leiden, *The Middle East: Politics and Power* (Boston: Allyn and Bacon, 1974), pp. 105-06. Bill and Leiden embrace the definition of patrimonial rule provided by Reihard Bendix as "an extension of the ruler's household in which the relation between the ruler and his officials remains on the basis of paternal authority and filial dependence." For an interesting discussion of Middle Eastern patrimonialism, see Chapter 4, et passim, of this work.

27. These figures were taken from the UAE census of 1975. Area (square miles) and population for each of the smaller six emirates were given, respectively, as follows: Dubai, 1,500 and 206,861; Sharigah, 1,000 and 88,188; Ras al-Khaimah, 650 and 57,282; Fujairah, 450 and 26,498; Umm al-Guiwain, 300 and 16,879; and Ajman, 100 and 21,566.

28. Elitism is used here in the same conception elaborated in Etzioni, "Epigenesis of Political Communities," pp. 348 ff.

29. See Deutsch et al., *Political Community and North Atlantic Area*, p. 44.

30. Haas and Schmitter, "Political Integration," p. 737.

31. The shared heritage of all Arabs has frequently been emphasized as a catalyst for unity by Arab unionists. However, as a perceptive observer of the Nordic integrative experience puts it: "History demonstrates that common heritage is neither a necessary condition (Canada, Switzerland, Yugoslavia) nor a sufficient condition (Scandinavia, the Arab World, Latin America) for amalgamation." See Anderson, *Scandinavian Regionalism*, p. 143.

32. For the nine historical conditions, see Deutsch et al., *Political Community and North Atlantic Area*, p. 58.

33. A more or less similar view is expressed in Aristide R. Zolberg, "Patterns of National Integration," *Journal of Modern African Studies* 5, no. 4 (1967):449-67. Other interesting definitions of integration on the national level can be found, for example, in Clifford Geertz, "The Integrative Revolution: Primordial Sentiments and Civil Politics in the New States," in Clifford Geertz, ed., *Old Societies and New States* (London: Free Press of Glencoe, 1963), p. 163; and Myron Weiner, "Political Integration and Political Development," *Annals of the American Academy of Political and Social Science* 358 (March 1965):53.

Chapter 2

1. For the history of the gulf littoral and British relations with that part of the Middle East, four works for the English-speaking reader generally stand unchallenged. First, there is J. G. Lorimer's *Gazetteer of the Persian Gulf, Oman and Central Arabia*. This work was issued by the British government of India in two volumes dealing with the two areas of geography (1908) and history (1915). Despite its early publication, this work has been available for public readership only since the early 1950s. The second major work is S. B. Miles's *Countries and Tribes of the Persian Gulf;* it first appeared in two volumes (London: Harrison, 1919) but a later edition (London: Frank Cass and Co., 1966) combined the two. This work deals mainly with the history, ethnography, and geography of Oman. The third work is that of Sir Arnold Wilson, entitled *The Persian Gulf* (London: George Allen and Unwin, 1959). It was first published in 1928 and a second edition appeared in 1954. Finally, there is the more recent work by Donald Hawley entitled *The Trucial States* (London: George Allen and Unwin, 1970). These four authors have one thing in common: they all were British officials who served at one time or another in the gulf region. Hence, their interpretations of events have generally affected and/or seldom deviated from official British policy toward the area.

Other works in this area also include Ahmad Abu Hakima, *History of Eastern Arabia, 1750-1800* (Beirut: Khayats, 1965); Husain M. Albaharna, *The Legal Status of the Arabian Gulf States: A Study of Their Treaty Relations and Their International Problems* (Manchester, England: Manchester University Press, 1968); Abdul Amir Amin, *British Interests in the Persian Gulf* (Leiden, Netherlands: E. J. Brill, 1967); and J. B. Kelly, *The Legal and Historical Basis of the British Position in the Persian Gulf* (London: Chatto and Windus, 1958) and his *Britain and the Persian Gulf 1795-1880* (Oxford: Clarendon Press, 1968).

2. See Hawley, *Trucial States*, p. 17; and also Robert G. Landen, "The Modernization of the Persian Gulf," in T. C. Young, ed., *Middle East Focus: The Persian Gulf* (Princeton, N.J.: Princeton University, 1968), pp. 6 ff.

3. For the text of this treaty, see Government of India Foreign Department, *A Collection of Treaties, Engagements and Sanads Relating to India and Neighboring Countries,* 5th ed., vol. 11 (New Delhi, 1933), pp. 289-90. This treaty was the first to be concluded with a gulf Arabian state.

4. By the beginning of the century, al-Gawasim had built an impressive sea fleet of 63 large vessels and over 800 small ships, manned by 19,000 men. For this and other details about the wars with this formidable tribe during the first two decades of the eighteenth century, see, for instance, Hawley, *Trucial States,* Chapter 5.

5. For the full text of this treaty, see ibid., pp. 314-16.

6. For the full text of the treaty, see ibid., pp. 317-18.

7. Germany sought to extend its influence in the gulf region through the proposed extension of the Berlin-Baghdad railroad to Basrah and by attempts to mine iron oxide from the island of Abu Musa. The Russians, on the other hand, have always entertained the idea of reaching the warm waters of the Indian Ocean via the gulf.

8. See Hawley, *Trucial States*, pp. 320, 321.

9. Quoted in J. F. Standish, "Britain in the Persian Gulf," *Contemporary Review* 211, no. 1222 (November 1967):238.

10. Ibid., pp. 238-39. For the full text of the speech, see Hawley, *Trucial States,* pp. 323-25.

11. Other major powers had recognized British supremacy in the gulf region during the decade before the outbreak of the First World War. See Landen, "Modernization of Persian Gulf," p. 14.

12. Quoted in Hawley, *Trucial States,* p. 322. Other agreements were those of 1902 regarding "the Prohibition of Traffic in Arms," and 1911 by which the rulers bound themselves not to grant concessions for fishing for pearls or sponges to foreigners "without first consulting the Residency through the Residency Agent." For the texts of these two agreements, see ibid., pp. 321f.

13. The British had also introduced into the gulf an instrument of indirect control known as "the adviser system." According to this system, which was originally proposed before World War I but only implemented in the 1920s, a ruler was advised to hire a British subject, who was not considered a British official, to advise him on a wide range of issues, mainly administrative.

14. Hawley, *Trucial States,* p. 171.

15. In a less than conventional view, Fred Halliday portrays a model of British involvement in that part of the world as follows:

> Local tribal leaders were patronized by the supply of money and weapons; if they resisted, these gifts were withheld and they were attacked. As a consequence, the policy of formally preserving the existing system became one of arresting certain changes and of encouraging others. None of the more conventional indices of

colonial economic exploitation were found; there was no extraction of raw materials or growing of commercial crops, no settling of significant numbers of European settlers, no opening of lucrative but weak markets. Political and economic influences from outside were excluded. On the other hand, certain leaders became stronger, and divisions between tribes and between different regions were strengthened.

See his *Arabia without Sultans* (Middlesex, England: Penguin Books, 1974), pp. 56-57.

16. Behind these persisting skirmishes were, inter alia, tribal rivalries, family feuds, and, later, territorial disputes. However, considering the fact that we are here dealing with a shattered tribal society with meager natural resources and harsh climate, one probably finds at the base of all this disorder, in the words of one analyst, a genuine effort "to rise above a bare subsistence level of life." See Landen, "Modernization of Persian Gulf," p. 3.

17. The British had reinforced their military units in Bahrain and Sharigah following their withdrawal from Aden in 1967 to compensate for the strategic loss of the latter. This move may have contributed to the bewilderment of local rulers who were duly taken by surprise as a result of the British announcement. For a discussion of the circumstances surrounding that announcement, see, for example, *The Gulf: Implication of British Withdrawal* (Washington, D.C.: The Center for Strategic and International Studies, Georgetown University, SRS: no. 8, 1969), Chapters 5 and 6; Neville Brown, "Britain and the Gulf—The Wisdom of Withdrawal Reconsidered," *New Middle East*, no. 24 (September 1970), pp. 14-21; David Holden, "The Persian Gulf: After the British Raj," *Foreign Affairs* 49, no. 4 (1971):721-35; J. C. Hurewitz, "The Persian Gulf: British Withdrawal and Western Security," *Annals* 401 (May 1972):106-15; Sir William Luce, "Britain's Withdrawal," *Survival* 11, no. 6 (June 1969):186-92; Jan Nasmyth, "If the British Leave the Gulf...," *World Today* 28, no. 2 (February 1972):75-81; and D. C. Watt, "The Decision to Withdraw from the Gulf," *Political Quarterly* 39, no. 3 (July-September 1968):310-21.

18. The assertion that Britain had maintained a total aloofness vis-à-vis matters of domestic concern during the earlier period may be misleading. British authorities had often made sure that domestic behavior on the part of a local ruler was not incompatible with British perceived interests. Accordingly, gunboat diplomacy, an important feature of nineteenth-century international politics, had not been an unfamiliar practice in gulf waters and on its shores. In fact, those who emphasize the "foreign-affairs-only" aspect of British control seem to have in mind the absence of a colonial government in the gulf and the fact that the British Colonial Office at no time took charge of the emirates.

19. The latest wars in this long chain of violence, which the British political resident tried unsuccessfully to mediate, were those between Dubai and Sharigah in 1940 and Abu Dhabi and Dubai between 1945 and 1948.

20. See K. G. Fenelon, *The United Arab Emirates: An Economic and Social Survey* (London: Longman, 1976), p. 21.

21. Hawley, *Trucial States*, p. 175. From its inception, the TOL had been

dependent on the British government for its finances.

22. Ibid., n. 10, p. 184.

23. See Chapter 7.

24. The first chairman to be elected by the rulers was Sagr bin Muhammed al-Gasimi, ruler of Ras al-Khaimah, who chaired the council from May 1966 to October 1968 when he was succeeded by his fellow Gasimi, Khalid bin Muhammed, ruler of Sharigah.

25. Up to that date, council meetings were held at the British Political Agency, first in Sharigah and later, after 1954, in Dubai.

26. These figures were quoted in M. T. Sadik and W. P. Snavely, *Bahrain, Qatar, and the United Arab Emirates* (Lexington, Mass.: D. C. Heath & Co., 1972), pp. 188, 189.

27. Literature on the three-year efforts to federate, especially in Arabic, is not lacking. For a journalistic, and often impressionistic, analysis of this whole question of union, see, for example, Saleem al-Lawzi, *Rasasatan fi al-Khalij* [Two Bullets in the Gulf] (Beirut, Lebanon: Manshurat al-Hawadith, 1971); Riyadh al-Rayyis, *Siraal-Wahat wa al-Naft* [Struggle of Oases and Oil] (Beirut, Lebanon: al-Nahar, 1973); and Zakariyya Neel, *Burat al-Khatar fi al-Khalij al-Arabi* [Center of Danger in the Arabian Gulf] (Cairo, Egypt: Matabi al-Ahram al-Tijariyyah, 1974), especially pp. 105-267. Other works also include W. Rifat, "Hawl Ittihad al-Imarat al-Arabiyyah fi al-Khalij" [On the Union of Arab Emirates in the Gulf], *Egyptian Journal of International Law* 26 (1970):1-158 and his "Hawl Inhiyar al-Ittihad al-Tusa'i lil-Imarat al-Arabiyyah fi al-Khalij wa Guiyam Ittihad Subaee Badil" [On the Collapse of the Union of the Nine Arab Emirates in the Gulf, and the Emergence of a Union of Seven Instead], *Egyptian Journal of International Law* 28 (1972):234-56; H. M. al-Baharna, "Al-Tatawurat al-Ganuniyyah wa-al-Dusturiyyah fi Duwal al-Khalij [Legal and Constitutional Developments in the Gulf States], *Egyptian Journal of International Law* 28 (1972):257-88; Ralph Izzard, "The Fight for Federation," *Middle East International* 1 (April 1971), pp. 33-35; J. D. Anthony, "The Union of Arab Emirates," *Middle East Journal* 26, no. 3 (Summer 1972):271-87; Sadik and Snavely, *Bahrain, Qatar, and United Arab Emirates*, Chapters 6-8; and Khalida Qureshi, "The United Arab Emirates," *Pakistan Horizon* 26, no. 4 (1973):3-27.

28. For the full text of this agreement, see "Wathaiq Ittihad al-Khalij al-Arabi" [Documents of Arabian Gulf Union], *Egyptian Journal of International Law* 26 (1970):242.

29. For the text of this agreement, see ibid., pp. 254-56. The agreement also fell short of designating the permanent seat of the federal government, i.e., the capital of the federation.

30. I am truly indebted to Khalid al-Safarini, legal adviser to the ruler of Ras al-Khaimah, for allowing me to look into the full minutes (who said what to whom) of the Supreme Council's four rounds of negotiations. Thumbing through these minutes, one could not help but observe that the representatives of the "big four" (Qatar, Bahrain, Abu Dhabi, and Dubai) were the ones who did most of the talking while the others listened.

31. For the texts of these decrees, see "Wathaiq Ittihad al-Khalij al-Arabi," pp. 265-74.

32. Ibid., p. 283.

33. Izzard, "Fight for Federation," p. 34.

34. However, Shaikh Muhammed bin Mubarak, director of the Bahraini Foreign Department, at that time had suggested that beyond these obvious points of contention there were more fundamental issues. Among these were (1) that the union should be based on an economic foundation by which a more equitable distribution of wealth could be realized; (2) that the constitution should bind the different entities more fundamentally than just on the official level; and (3) that a central government, with wider authorities than those enjoyed by local government, was necessary for the union to be durable. See al-Lawzi, *Rasasatan fi al-Khalij*, p. 124.

35. Quoted in Izzard, "Fight for Federation," p. 33.

36. This came about when Iran accepted the conclusion of the UN secretary-general's special representative to Bahrain, V. W. Guicciardi. The latter found that the overwhelming majority of Bahrainis wanted self-determination. For a discussion of this whole question, see, for example, Edward Gordon, "Resolution of the Bahrain Dispute," *American Journal of International Law* 65, no. 3 (July 1971):560-68; and Hooshang Moghtader, "The Settlement of the Bahrain Question: A Study in Anglo-Iranian-United Nations Diplomacy," *Pakistan Horizon* 26, no. 2 (1973):16-29.

37. Some analysts even go as far as to assert that in order to avoid antagonizing Iran, most of the rulers were reluctant to include Bahrain in the federation. Their objection to holding the third Supreme Council's meeting in Bahrain was part of a "teasing" process. See, for instance, al-Lawzi, *Rasasatan fi al-Khalij*, pp. 67-76.

38. This unanimity of the larger regional states was apparently not shared by all smaller ones. Some of the emirates were fearful of a future without a British formal presence. It has even been suggested that Shaikh Zayed, ruler of Abu Dhabi, offered in 1968 to reimburse the British treasury for the cost of British troops in the area on a yearly basis should their stay be extended. The British, however, declined. See Anthony, "Union of Arab Emirates," p. 137.

39. Qatar maintains a claim to the island of al-Huwar, currently occupied by Bahrain. And the latter, in turn, has some historical claims to al-Zubarah on the west coast of the Qatari peninsula.

40. Some Arab analysts contend that Britain did not desire from the very beginning to include Qatar and Bahrain in a gulf union. In such a case, the assertion goes, Saudi Arabia would be forced to protect Bahrain against the Iranian claim and, hence, a state of tension would exist between the two powers most allied to the United States in the area. In addition, by keeping Qatar away, Saudi Arabia would lose a voice for influence within the proposed union. See al-Lawzi, *Rasasatan fi al-Khalij*, pp.14-15.

Both Bahrain and Qatar introduced rather extensive reforms in their respective governmental structures in 1970. Bahrain even went so far as to establish foreign and defense departments even though it was officially a member of a federation whose authority had included foreign and defense affairs. In 1971, Bahrain and Qatar both acquired their independence; the former on August 15 and the latter on September 1.

41. Rifat, "Hawl Inhiyar al-Ittihad al-Tusa'i," p. 242.

42. Ras al-Khaimah was not an original member of the UAE. Among other things, it objected to the veto power reserved for Abu Dhabi and Dubai in the Supreme Council, the distribution of seats in the Federal Council, and the allocation of ministerial portfolios. Ras al-Khaimah, however, joined the UAE on February 10, 1972.

43. Upon the abrogation of the exclusive agreements, a Treaty of Friendship was concluded with the UAE. An overriding concern of this treaty, it seems, was the question of security. According to this treaty, Britain would (1) hand over to the UAE the Trucial Oman Scouts; (2) provide the union with British military personnel for training and supply; (3) station in the area, with the union's permission, British military units adequate for liaison and training; (4) hold joint exercises in the area involving land and air military elements; (5) send Royal Navy ships on regular visits to the area; and (6) assist the union in other fields as needed. See Qureshi, "United Arab Emirates," p. 18.

44. Shortly after independence, the UAE became the 132d member of the United Nations and the eighteenth member state of the Arab League.

Chapter 3

1. For a discussion of these concepts and the evolution of tribalism into ministatism in nineteenth-century Eastern Arabia, see, in addition to the two articles by Frauke Heard-Bey, "The Gulf States and Oman in Transition," *Asian Affairs* 59, pt. 1 (1972) and "Social Changes in the Gulf States and Oman," *Asian Affairs* 59, pt. 3 (1972), J. E. Peterson, "Tribes and Politics in Eastern Arabia," *Middle East Journal* 31, no. 3 (Summer 1977):297-312.

2. UAE, *Provisional Constitution*, Arts. 14-22, 25-44.

3. None of the seven member emirates has so far attempted to frame a constitution of its own. This state of affairs might encourage the trend toward the evolution of a unitary system of government on the national level in the long run.

4. The Second Amendment to the constitution extends its provisional term of five years, as stipulated in Article 144, for another of equal duration as of December 2, 1976. See *al-Jaridah al-Rasmiyyah* [Official Gazette] 43 (December 1976):7.

5. As noted above, Ras al-Khaimah is not a founding member of the union, for it did not join until February 1972.

6. Constitution, Arts. 1-3, 6-9. I have utilized the translation provided by *Middle East Journal* 26 (1972):307-25. Comparing this translation with the original Arabic text, however, points out a few inaccuracies in the translation that I have tried to avoid.

7. Ibid., Art. 11.

8. Ibid., the Preamble.

9. Ibid., Art. 10.

10. Ibid., Art. 12.

11. Ibid., Arts. 12, 47 (1), 120 (1).

12. Ibid., Art. 47 (4).

13. Ibid., Art. 54 (6) (7).

14. Ibid., Arts. 140, 8, respectively.

15. Ibid., Art. 121.

16. Ibid., Art. 120. The constitution (Art. 146) also charges federal authorities with the declaration and lifting of martial law if and when needed as regulated by law.

17. Ibid., Arts. 116, 122.

18. Ibid., Art. 151.

19. Ibid., Arts. 3, 23, 5, 118, 142, respectively. See also pp. 82, 92.

20. Ibid., Art. 123. Should the Supreme Council of the Union object to the conclusion of any such administrative agreements, then the matter shall be suspended pending decision by the Federal Supreme Court.

21. Ibid., Art. 124. The high court is presumably the one to decide in case of a dispute over whether an international agreement or treaty does indeed affect the status of an emirate.

22. Ibid., Art. 149.

23. At the time the federation was forged, the seven rulers, along with the dates of their accession, were Zayed bin Sultan al-Nuhayyan (Abu Dhabi, 1966); Rashid bin Said al-Maktum (Dubai, 1958); Khalid bin Muhammad al-Gasimi (Sharigah, 1965); Rashid bin Humaid al-Nuaimi (Ajman, 1928); Ahmad bin Rashid al-Mualla (Umm al-Guiwain, 1929); Sagr bin Muhammad al-Gasimi (Ras al-Khaimah, 1948); and Muhammad bin Hamad al-Shargui (Fujairah, 1952). In 1972, the ruler of Sharigah was murdered and was succeeded by a younger brother, and two years later, the ruler of Fujairah died and was succeeded by his son, Shaikh Hamad.

24. Constitution, Art. 45.

25. For a particularly good, albeit slightly repetitive, analysis of the foundations, constitutional bases, and organization of the UAE federation, see al-Sayyid Muhammad Ibrahim, *Asas al-Tanthim al-Siyasi wa al-Dusturi li Dawlat al-Imarat al-Arabiyyah al-Muttahidah* [Foundations of the Constitutional and Political Organization for the UAE] (Abu Dhabi: Center for Documentation and Research, 1975).

26. See Article 46 of the constitution and Arts. 5-9 of the bylaws, the Supreme Council of the Union.

27. Constitution, Art. 47.

28. Ibid., Art. 51 and the SCU's bylaws.

29. Constitution, Art. 1.

30. Ibid., Art. 47.

31. Ibid., Arts. 47, 146, 140, respectively.

32. Ibid., Art. 47.

33. Ibid., Arts. 47, 64.

34. Ibid., Arts. 143, 118, 123, respectively.

35. Ibid., Art. 115.

36. Ibid., Arts. 51-53. In the latter case, either an SCU member or the federal prime minister may summon the council for an immediate session.

37. Ibid., Art. 141. The latter title was assigned the president later in accordance with Federal Law 19 (1972). Members of the council include the vice-president; the prime minister; ministers of foreign affairs, defense, finance, and interior; general commander of the armed forces; and chief of the general staff.

38. Ibid., Art. 54.

39. Ibid., Arts. 47, 140, 146, 96, 115.

40. Ibid., Arts. 54, 60, 64-65.

41. Ibid., Arts. 55-57.

42. Ibid., Art. 58.

43. Ibid., Arts. 59-61, 64.

44. Ibid., Arts. 60, 65.

45. Ibid., Art. 66.

46. Ibid., Art. 68 and the First Amendment; and the SCU's Decisions 2 and 3 (1972) to the effect of, first, admitting Ras al-Khaimah as the seventh member emirate of the union and, second, increasing the number of seats in the FNC from thirty-four to forty, with the extra seats being assigned to the new member emirate.

47. Constitution, Arts. 69-70. There is apparently a contradiction between the first condition here and another provision of the constitution, i.e., Article 8, insofar as the latter stipulates that all nationals of the union are to enjoy one citizenship, and, hence, no particular citizenships for the individual emirates, at least by implication, are allowed.

48. Ibid., Arts. 71-72, 77. The prohibition of assuming other federal posts for FNC members is presumably to insure their independence. The constitution does not prohibit council members from holding positions at the emirate level.

49. Ibid., Arts. 81-83. According to Article 28 of the council's bylaws, this body's premises also have immunity against assault by any law-enforcement authority except with the permission of the president of the council.

50. Ibid., Arts. 75, 78, 86-88, 145. According to Article 73 of the constitution, each council member has to be sworn in before the council in an open session before assuming his duties.

51. Ibid., Arts. 79-80. The president may, if he so wishes, delegate his authority to deliver the opening speech to the vice-president or the prime minister.

52. Ibid., Arts. 84-85, 76, respectively. The FNC's bylaws detail the prerogatives of the council's officers, the procedure of voting and debate, the designation of committees, and the like. These bylaws were issued by Federal Decree 44 (1972).

53. Ibid., Art. 89.

54. Ibid., Arts. 133-34, 90, respectively.

55. Ibid., Arts. 92-93. The FNC's role in treaty making is limited to its being notified of such by the federal government. This, in effect, means no role whatsoever. See Article 91 of the constitution.

56. Ibid., Arts. 25, 28, 41.

57. Ibid., Arts. 95-96. The SCU's authority to ratify the appointment of federal

judges under no circumstance can be delegated. See above.

58. Ibid., Art. 94.

59. Ibid., Arts. 97-98. Article 97 further stipulates the cases whereby federal judges are relieved from their positions as (1) death; (2) resignation; (3) end of contract or secondment for those on either; (4) reaching mandatory retirement age; (5) inability to perform duties due to ill health; (6) disciplinary reasons as stipulated by law; and (7) appointment to other offices with their approval.

60. Ibid., Art. 99.

61. Ibid., Art. 102.

62. Ibid., Art. 106.

63. Ibid., Art. 101.

64. Ibid., Arts. 104-05.

65. Ibid., Arts. 110-11.

66. Ibid., Art. 113.

67. Ibid., Art. 114. Federal decrees are required to be published in the official gazette. Ibid.

68. Ibid., Arts. 47, 91.

69. Ibid., Art. 144.

70. Despite all this, having attended two consecutive FNC meetings during the month of April 1977, this writer was impressed by the appearance of a lively parliamentary debate during which attending cabinet ministers were vigorously questioned by deputies over matters relating to the performance of their ministries. During those two sessions, deputies discussed matters such as agricultural development, prices of petroleum exports in local markets, Islamic affairs, public housing, quality of electrical services, and government policies, or lack of them, in the areas of health and telecommunications. The FNC also issued recommendations on some of these topics.

Chapter 4

1. UAE, *UAE Laws and Decrees* (in Arabic), vol. 1 (1974), p. 71.

2. In support of this assertion, Anthony observes that the dissolution of Abu Dhabi's cabinet in December 1973 was "bitterly opposed by the incumbent ministers, particularly those among the Ruler's relatives." See J. D. Anthony, *Arab States of the Lower Gulf: People, Politics, Petroleum* (Washington, D.C.: Middle East Institute, 1975), p. 125.

3. On January 3, 1977, a new Council of Ministers was announced. Headed by the same prime minister, but deputized by Abu Dhabi's Hamdan bin Muhammad al-Nuhayyan (head of the Khalifa branch of the Abu Dhabi ruling family), replacing Shaikh Khalifa bin Zayed, this twenty-three-member body had four less posts than its predecessor. This was accomplished by merging public works and housing, education and youth, Islamic affairs and justice, and labor and social affairs. See *Al-Jaridah* [Official Gazette] 44 (January 1977):36-37.

4. These percentages were given during an interview with a union official directly connected with civil service affairs.

5. See Ministry of Planning, UAE, *Annual Statistical Group, 1972-1975* (1976) (in Arabic), pp. 57, 189, 233, 369, 393, 437, respectively.

6. At the time of its establishment, the board was chaired by the UAE finance minister, Hamdan bin Rashid al-Maktum, and included in its membership four cabinet ministers, one ambassador and three expatriate advisers. With 54 banks and 376 branches in all, the UAE stood at the end of 1976 as one of the most overbanked countries in the world. Despite a two-year moratorium on the incorporation of new banks, imposed by the board in May 1976, two additional banks were since chartered in Dubai, bringing this emirate's share to 40 with 102 branches.

7. Figures for this table and throughout this chapter have been obtained from various sources. The reader is therefore cautioned that due to occasional discrepancies, the accuracy and hence the reliability of some of these figures may be in doubt.

8. As has been pointed out in Chapter 2, Abu Dhabi, starting from the time its present ruler, Shaikh Zayed, came to power in 1966, made a steady contribution of over 70 percent of the Trucial States Development Fund's budget.

9. According to Anthony McDermott (*Financial Times*, 4 April 1977, p. 14), Dubai had contributed a relatively symbolic Dh 150 million to the federal budget of 1976. Concomitant with the circumstances surrounding the extension of the union's provisional constitutional period for another five years, a high-level committee was formed under the chairmanship of Shaikh Sultan bin Muhammad al-Gasimi, ruler of Sharigah, in order to come up with an acceptable formula for sharing the federal financial burden by all member emirates. Although no official figures have been disclosed as yet, a federal official suggested to this writer at the close of the committee meetings in the spring of 1977 that the new arrangement has thrown the burden on the three financially capable oil-producing emirates of Abu Dhabi, Dubai, and Sharigah in the proximity of 70, 20, and 10 percent, respectively.

10. For details of Arab oil production, see, for instance, Ministry of Petroleum and Mineral Resources, UAE, *Oil Statistical Review* (1977), p. 13.

11. Ibid., p. 60.

12. This example is based on an interview with a federal (expatriate) oil official. According to this source, however, Dubai was more willing to cooperate in the areas of oil data and coordination than was Sharigah. This is somewhat ironic in light of the latter's well-known enthusiasm for the federation.

13. The National Planning Board is chaired by the prime minister or his deputy with the ministers of planning, finance and industry, public works, health, education, communications, and housing as members. The board meets at least once a month and considers development priorities originating in the Ministry of Planning.

14. Ministry of Planning, UAE, *Federal Investment Plan for Socioeconomic Development, 1976* (in Arabic), p. 46.

15. For an item-by-item listing of such projects and the federal ministries and agencies sponsoring them, see ibid., pp. 90-100.

16. Dubai's oil revenues rose from Dh 386 million in 1971 to over Dh 3.7 billion in 1974 to nearly Dh 5.2 billion in 1976. See Anthony McDermott,

Financial Times, p. 18.

17. The 1976 budget of Dubai Municipality was more than Dh 635 million for social services and infrastructural improvements. However, this figure represents only 5 percent of total allocations for industrial development over several years.

18. As shown in Tables 4-3 and 4-5 (pp. 66, 69), Sharigah has been an oil producer and exporter since 1974. Its relatively modest oil revenues ranged from approximately Dh 350 million in 1974 to an estimated half a billion dirhams in 1976.

19. For an emirate-by-emirate detailed list of the hundreds of development projects and their sponsoring federal ministries, see UAE, *Federal Investment Plan,* pp. 121-205.

20. Ministry of Economy and Commerce, UAE, *Economy and Commerce* (in Arabic) (March 1977):11.

21. Ibid., pp. 13, 19.

22. Ibid., p. 32.

23. Actual federal expenditure on housing for previous years was Dh 0.3; 15.9; 17.0; and 36.4 million for the years 1972-1975 inclusively. This reflects a rapid growth in this sector that is not uncommon in others as well. See Ministry of Information and Culture, UAE, *UAE Yearbook, 1976* (in Arabic), p. 24; and Emirate of Abu Dhabi, *Statistical Yearbook, 1975,* p. 85.

24. Corresponding actual figures for earlier years were (in millions of dirhams) 81.2, 102.2, 144.0, and 359.6 for the years 1972, 1973, 1974, and 1975, respectively. See ibid.

25. The federal Ministry of Education also sponsors students in colleges and universities abroad. In 1976, for instance, there were over 2,000 of such students—two-thirds of whom were citizens of the UAE—receiving higher education in various countries at UAE expense. A law was enacted in 1976 to establish the first university in the country. This institution of higher learning will be located in al-Ain in the eastern part of Abu Dhabi. Classes were scheduled to open in the fall of 1977 in initially four colleges: education for women, science, literature, and commerce and public administration.

26. The new curriculum, in the words of Dr. Omar al-Shaikh, the chairman of this committee, "is warranted by the need to create a new national consciousness compatible with the phase of sociopolitical development which the area is now passing."

27. *Al-Jaridah al-Rasmiyyah* [Official Gazette] 42 (November 1976):7, 8. As early as 1972, Abu Dhabi's media facilities, despite being under an Abu Dhabian Ministry of Information and Tourism, were utilized by the federal government. They became federal, however, when this emirate abolished its Council of Ministers in 1973. The broadcasting stations of Sharigah and Ras al-Khaimah were transferred to federal jurisdiction in 1975, and Dubai's radio and television stations came under federal control in 1976.

28. There are several privately owned newspapers that also receive governmental subsidies.

29. Ministry of Planning, *Annual Statistical Group, 1972-1975,* p. 363.

30. In November of the same year, a constitutional amendment deleted Article 142 of the Provisional Constitution altogether, thereby reserving the right of maintaining armed forces solely to the federal government. See *al-Jaridah al-Rasmiyyah* 42 (November 1976):13.

31. From another perspective, the inordinate influence of Abu Dhabi in the unified armed forces is emphasized by the postunification appointment of the heir apparent of Abu Dhabi, Shaikh Khalifa bin Zayed, as the deputy supreme commander of the armed forces after his father who, ex officio, holds this title.

32. For the texts of the three laws, the amendment, and the SCU's decision, see *al-Jaridah al-Rasmiyyah* 7 (November 1972), 12 (August 1973), 19 (June 1974), and 42 (November 1976). Another SCU decision of the same date approved the establishment of a directorate for civil defense manned by uniformed personnel based on the recommendations of a Saudi Arabian mission that also advised on matters of traffic, police, and coast guard.

33. Decrees relating to the appointment, transfer, promotion, demotion, or dismissal of federal officials are not included in this table. The transient nature of such decisions undermines their usefulness in either weighing performance or identifying trends.

Chapter 5

1. For Shaikh Zayed's acknowledgment of sending such letters, see Saleim al-Lawzi, "An Interview with Shaikh Zayed," *al-Hawadith*, no. 1061 (March 11, 1977), p. 24.

2. Quoted in D. L. Price, *Oil and Middle East Security* (Washington, D.C.: Georgetown University, Center for Strategic and International Studies, 1976), p. 81.

3. These observations are mostly based on informal interviews conducted in the emirates by this writer with a limited number of individuals of varying social and political status and background.

4. For a now outdated but useful work on the tribes in this part of the Arab world, see S. B. Miles, *The Countries and Tribes of the Persian Gulf*, 2d ed., especially Chapter 8. On al-Gawasim tribal confederation, see, for instance, Donald Hawley, *The Trucial States* (London: George Allen and Unwin, 1970), Chapter 5. On the more recent history of tribalism in Abu Dhabi, especially the Bani Yas tribal confederation, see C. Mann, *Abu Dhabi: Birth of an Oil Sheikhdom* (Beirut: Khayats, 1964). On the evolution of the lower gulf small states and Oman from tribal origins, see J. E. Peterson, "Tribes and Politics in Eastern Arabia," *Middle East Journal* 31, no. 3 (Summer 1977), especially pp. 299-304; and Frauke Heard-Bey, "The Gulf States and Oman in Transition," *Asian Studies* 59, pt. 1 (1972). The concept of "urban tribalism" as a synthesis of modernity and tradition along the Arab gulf littoral is formulated by Emile A. Nakhleh in his *Bahrain: Political Development in a Modernizing Society* (Lexington, Mass.: D. C. Heath and Company, 1976), pp. 165-68.

5. Frank Stoakes, "Social and Political Change in the Third World: Some Peculiarities of Oil-Producing Principalities of the Persian Gulf," in D.

Hopwood, ed., *The Arabian Peninsula: Society and Politics* (London: George Allen and Unwin, 1972), p. 199.

6. For more details on this tribal "walkout," see Mann, *Abu Dhabi*, pp. 40-41, 59-62, et passim.

7. J. B. Kelly, *Eastern Arabian Frontiers* (New York: Praeger, 1964), p. 18.

8. This piece of information was relayed to this writer by a former official of the Trucial States Council, now a federal cabinet minister. For a discussion of the territorial issue from a largely British point of view, see Sir Rupert Hay, "The Persian Gulf States and Their Boundary Problems," *Geographical Journal* 120 (1954):433-45.

9. For many years, the Abu Dhabi–Dubai border was a source of friction between the two emirates. However, the issue was finally settled in 1968 by the creation of a neutral zone.

10. See J. D. Anthony, *Arab States of the Lower Gulf: People, Politics, Petroleum* (Washington, D.C.: Middle East Institute, 1975), pp. 214-15.

11. Quoted in M. R. al-Fil, "Mushkilat al-Hudud Baina Imarat al-Khalij al-Arabi" [Boundary Problems among Emirates of the Arabian Gulf], *Journal of the Gulf and Arabian Peninsula Studies* 2, no. 8 (October 1976):36.

12. M. T. Sadik and W. P. Snavely, *Bahrain, Qatar, and the United Arab Emirates* (Lexington, Mass.: D. C. Heath & Co., 1972), p. 123.

13. The two most obvious examples of individuals who rose to positions of influence in local and union politics from nonruling families are Ahmad al-Suwaidi, the foreign minister, and Mahdi al-Tajir, the UAE ambassador to the United Kingdom and France. As unofficial advisors to Shaikh Zayed and Shaikh Rashid, respectively, they have played far greater roles than their official positions suggest, particularly in shaping the political thinking of the top two men in the union.

14. Anthony, *Arab States*, p. 220.

15. One important factor behind the interruption of this cycle of dynastic violence may be the oath that Shakhbut's brothers took, thanks to their mother's behest, to support and not to revolt against him. For more details on this turbulent period of Abu Dhabi's political history, see Mann, *Abu Dhabi*, p. 77-83, et passim.

16. For more details on this incident, see Michael Tomkinson, *The United Arab Emirates* (London: Michael Tomkinson Publishing, 1975), p. 150; and Anthony, *Arab States*, pp. 117-19, 174-76.

17. After spending several years under house arrest on an Abu Dhabian island, Sagr is reported to be now on the mainland.

18. Anthony, *Arab States*, p. 25.

19. A brief personality exposé of the two Bani Yas rulers can be found in Dana Schmidt, "A Larger Role for Three Persian Gulf Rulers," *New York Times*, (11 October 1971), p. 12.

20. "Rashid Yatahaddath Bisarahah" [Rashid Speaks Frankly], *Majallat Akhbar Dubai* [Dubai News Magazine] 49 (December 1975):26. In this same interview, which was originally published two weeks earlier by the Kuwaiti *al-Rai al-Am* [Public Opinion], Rashid expressed his confidence in Shaikh Zayed

personally but blamed what he called "the invisible hands . . . with their negative attitudes and tactics" for hurting the union by their "emotional" thrusts that tend to disregard the realities of the situation as far as integration is concerned.

21. Viewing some of the incumbent ruling shaikhs as the most serious obstacle along the path of further integration, a federal deputy minister suggested to this writer that the best way to cope with these shaikhs is to engage them in high administrative posts in the federal government. This, he added, would serve the union in two ways: (1) it would keep them busy so they would be less of an impediment to the union; and (2) more positively, it might provide them with a feeling of having more stake in the federal experiment.

22. Ministry of Labor and Social Affairs, UAE, *Annual Statistical Report* (in Arabic), 1976, p. 4.

23. Work permits issued to Arabs in 1976 were distributed as follows: Egypt, 37.1 percent; Lebanon, 23.7 percent; Syria, 12.9 percent; Jordan, 9.2 percent; Palestine, 6.8 percent; the two Yemens, 5.1 percent; and the rest of the Arab world, 5.2 percent. The overall figure is 106 percent more than that of the preceding year. See ibid., pp. 5, 18.

24. For more details, see Anthony, *Arab States*, pp. 14-21.

25. This, in effect, means that the Arab population, indigenous and foreign, is in the minority. The seriousness of the impact that this might have on the Arabic character of the area was recently underscored by Abu Dhabi's attempt to rectify this imbalance by the granting of mass citizenship to several thousand South Yemenites.

Chapter 6

1. Joseph Nye and Ernest Haas, "The Uniting of Europe and the Uniting of Latin America," *Journal of Common Market Studies* 5, no. 4 (June 1967):315.

2. Of the 30,000 square-mile area of Trucial Oman, less than half of 1 percent was considered cultivable in 1967. See M. T. Sadik and W. P. Snavely, *Bahrain, Qatar, and the United Arab Emirates* (Lexington, Mass.: D. C. Heath & Co., 1972), p. 46.

3. For more details on the material aspects of the Trucial States in the late 1960s, see ibid., Chapters 7-8.

4. This comment was made to this writer by an influential Abu Dhabian businessman who was also a member of the Federal National Council (FNC).

5. Leading union officials have repeatedly stressed the regional nature of the federation, especially the hope that the other small gulf states join in. Along these lines, see, for instance, Shaikh Zayed's statement in *al-Ittihad* (Abu Dhabi), no. 1703, p. 1. The same theme was stressed by Ahmad al-Suwaidi, the UAE foreign minister, during an interview with this writer.

6. Literature on dependence as a parameter in the relations between regions in a global context is voluminous. For the conception of this variable as an end result of the interaction between an economically developed center and a less-developed periphery, see, for example, S. Bodenheimer, "Dependency and Imperialism: The Roots of Latin American Underdevelopment," in K. T. Fann

and D. Hodges, eds., *Readings in U.S. Imperialism* (Boston, Mass.: Porter Sargent, 1971), pp. 155-82; J. Esseks, "Economic Dependency and Political Development in New States of Africa," *Journal of Politics* 33 (November 1971):1052-75; B. Stallings, *Economic Dependency in Africa and Latin America* (Beverly Hills, Calif.: Sage Publications, 1972); Osvaldo Sunkel, "Transnational Capitalism and National Disintegration in Latin America," *Social and Economic Studies* 22, no. 1 (March 1973):132-76; and W. Levi, "Third World States: Objects of Colonialism or Neglect?" *International Studies Quarterly* 17, no. 2 (June 1973):227-48.

7. This is one of Ernest B. Haas's neofunctionalist hypotheses. See his *The Uniting of Europe: Political, Economic and Social Forces, 1950-1957* (Stanford, Calif.: Stanford University Press, 1958), especially Chapter 8.

8. While touring the area in the spring of 1977, this writer was impressed by the response of a newly settled bedouin in a remote Fujairan village. When asked as to how he could obtain his new house, his swift answer was: *Hathi afdhal Zayed tal umruh* [These are the blessings of Zayed, may he be long-lived]. This acknowledgment of the union distributive function as a personal favor by its president and wealthiest member is not an isolated case. It is rather part of the traditional conception of established authority in personalistic terms.

9. One factor behind the collapse of the union between Egypt and Syria in 1961 is probably the haste that accompanied its establishment three years earlier. In other contexts, the failure of the British-inhabited federations in East Africa, Malaysia, and South Arabia one observer largely attributes to the fact that all these federal ventures sprang to life as the British were withdrawing. Hence, the gradual development of an organizational structure that could take their place was generally lacking. See John S. Badeau, "Inter-Arab Social and Political Relationships," in *Middle East Focus: The Persian Gulf* (Princeton, N.J.: Princeton University Conference, 1968), p. 197.

10. This particular view of the role of defense forces, no less than the shakiness of integration in this sector, was dramatically demonstrated by a sudden rise in tension between Abu Dhabi and Dubai to such a degree that Shaikh Rashid placed the 4000-man Central Command on the alert. Although details are still incomplete, this crisis apparently arose over a decree issued by Shaikh Zayed, the president of the union, while on vacation in Pakistan. According to this decree, Shaikh Sultan, Zayed's second son, was promoted to the rank of brigadier general and then appointed as the commander-in-chief of the UAE armed forces. Rashid's objection here was said to be based on three grounds: (1) he was not consulted; (2) such a decree should have been issued by him in his capacity as acting president; and (3) such a development would undermine the authority of his son, the UAE defense minister, and hence tip the political balance in Abu Dhabi's favor. See *Arab Report and Memo* (Beirut: An-Nahar) 2, no. 7 (February 1978):6.

11. The question came up during an interview with the president by Yasir Hawari, editor-in-chief of *al-Diyar*, a Lebanese newsmagazine, whether the union would continue should one or more member states decide to secede, quoted in Jamal Badawi, ed., *Support of the Union: An Issue before the People*

and the State (in Arabic), Information Studies Series no. 13 (Abu Dhabi: Ministry of Information and Tourism, 1975), pp. 42, 45, 46.

12. According to Article 9 of the Provisional Constitution, Abu Dhabi Town was to be adopted as the temporary seat of the federal government pending the construction of a permanent capital city (al-Karamah) in an area astride the Abu Dhabi–Dubai border. This feat was supposed to be completed within seven years from independence. However, nothing of the sort was done, and the idea seems to have been set aside at least for the time being.

13. See, for example, Richard Johns, "The Emergence of the United Arab Emirates," *Middle East International,* no. 21 (March 1973), p. 10; and J. D. Anthony, *Arab States of the Lower Gulf: People, Politics, Petroleum* (Washington, D.C.: Middle East Institute, 1975), p. 102.

14. For a multifaceted discussion of this unitarian experiment between Egypt and Syria, including the most likely factors behind its failure, see M. H. Haykal, *Ma Allathi Jara fi Suriyya* [What Happened in Syria] (Cairo: Dar al-Qawmiyyah, 1962); Michael Aflaq, *Maarakat al-Masir al Wahid* [Struggle of the Common Destiny] (Damascus: Dar al-Adab, 1963); Monte Palmer, "The United Arab Republic: An Assessment of its Failure," *The Middle East Journal* 20, no. 1 (Winter 1966):50-67; and Malcolm H. Kerr, *The Arab Cold War: Gamal Abdul al-Nasir and Rivals, 1958-1970* (London: Oxford University Press, 1971), especially Chapter 1.

15. For the conception of interstate relations in the gulf littoral extending from Bahrain to Oman in a "leapfrog" pattern of good and bad, see Anthony, *Arab States,* p. 109. According to this conception, a state tends to have bad relations with its immediate neighbors and good relations with the states immediately beyond. This pattern would put Bahrain, Abu Dhabi, Sharigah, Umm al-Guiwain, and Fujairah in one bloc and Qatar, Dubai, Ajman, and Ras al-Khaimah in another. As territorial disputes are resolved, however, this pattern of relations tends to fade.

16. Literature on Arab nationalism and the intellectual turmoil surrounding it is voluminous. In English, see, for example, G. Antonius, *The Arab Awakening* (New York: Capricorn Books, 1965); D. E. Ashford, "Contradiction of Nationalism and Nation-Building in the Muslim World," *Middle East Journal* 18, no. 4 (Autumn 1964):421-30; Sylvia G. Haim, ed., *Arab Nationalism: An Anthology* (Berkeley and Los Angeles: University of California Press, 1962), especially the editor's introduction; Albert Hourani, *Arabic Thought in the Liberal Age, 1798-1939* (London: Oxford University Press, 1962); Hisham Sharabi, *Nationalism and Revolution in the Arab World: The Middle East and North Africa* (Princeton, N.J.: D. Van Nostrand, 1965) and his "The Transformation of Ideology in the Arab World," *Middle East Journal* 19, no. 4 (Autumn 1965):471-86; and H. E. Tutsch, *Facets of Arab Nationalism* (Detroit, Mich.: Wayne State University Press, 1965).

Chapter 7

1. R. Ramazani, *The Persian Gulf: Iran's Role* (Charlottesville: University

Press of Virginia, 1972), pp. 26-27. For other excellent, though slightly apologetic, studies of Iran's foreign policy toward the gulf region, see S. Chubin and S. Zabih, *The Foreign Relations of Iran: A Developing State in a Zone of Great-Power Conflict* (Berkeley: University of California Press, 1974), especially Chapters 4-7; and R. Ramazani, *Iran's Foreign Policy, 1941-1973: A Study of Foreign Policy in Modernizing Nations* (Charlottesville: University Press of Virginia, 1975), Chapter 16.

2. Ramazani, *Persian Gulf*, p. 33.

3. Chubin and Zabih, *Foreign Relations*, p. 196.

4. An earlier attempt to relax tensions between the two countries failed primarily because of Iranian reluctance to give such a pledge. According to one explanation, the deployment of the strategic Polaris missiles by the United States in 1961 had reduced the significance of land bases for the less sophisticated Jupiter rockets. Polaris missiles can easily reach the Soviet heartland if launched from submarines in the Indian Ocean or the eastern Mediterranean. See Ramazani, *Iran's Foreign Policy*, p. 318.

5. D. L. Price, *Oil and Middle East Security* (Washington, D.C.: Georgetown University, CSIS, 1976), p. 57. For a thorough account of the conflict in Yemen, see, for example, D. A. Schmidt, *Yemen: The Unknown War* (New York: Holt, Rinehart, and Winston, 1968).

6. Irano-Egyptian relations were ruptured in July 1960 and were not restored until a decade later. The shah's obsession with a Nasserite threat to his rule in the 1960s can be ascertained from his description of Nasser's policy as "aggressive and imperialistic" (1964) and as "dangerous and inhuman" (1967). See Ramazani, *Iran's Foreign Policy*, pp. 405, 421. For more details on Irano-Egyptian relations during the sixties, see Chubin and Zabih, *Foreign Relations*, Chapter 3.

7. *Manchester Guardian*, 25 May 1968. Quoted in Chubin and Zabih, *Foreign Relations*, p. 217.

8. Quoted in Ramazani, *Persian Gulf*, p. 48.

9. It is further reported that an "understanding" was reached by the two heads of state to the effect of "taking over the British role in the area." See Mordechai Abir, *Oil, Power and Politics: Conflict in Arabia, the Red Sea and the Gulf* (London: Frank Cass, 1974), p. 19.

10. Quoted in Peter Harvey, "Shah's Aims in the Gulf," *Manchester Guardian*, 9 October 1971, p. 7.

11. More recent studies on Saudi Arabia have primarily centered on oil and its wealth, politics, and impact upon this sparsely populated conservative country. See, for example, Ramon Knauerhase, *The Saudi Arabian Economy* (New York: Praeger, 1975); Sheikh Rustum Ali, *Saudi Arabia and Oil Diplomacy* (New York: Praeger, 1976); and David E. Long, *Saudi Arabia* (Beverly Hills, Calif.: Sage Publications, 1976). The latter work is particularly concise and useful. Other shorter studies along these lines include Malcolm Peck, "Saudi Arabia's Wealth: A Two-Edged Sword," *New Middle East* 40 (January 1972), pp. 5-7; William Rugh, "Emergence of a New Middle Class in Saudi Arabia," *Middle East Journal* 27, 1 (Winter 1973):7-20; "Saudi Arabia: A Nation We'd

Better Get to Know," *Forbes*, 15 February 1973, pp. 28-42; Faris Glubb, "Saudi Arabia: The Challenge of Power," *Middle East International* 44 (February 1975), pp. 14-16; and Peter Snow, "Saudi Arabia: Keeping Change under Control," ibid., pp. 17-18.

12. It was reported that Saudi Arabia at the same time extended economic aid to South Yemen in the vicinity of $400 million and later proposed to finance the construction of an oil-tanker terminal on the coast of the Arabian Sea to be linked by pipelines to oil fields along the peninsular gulf littoral. See John Cooley, "Saudi-Yemen Détente Irritates Iran," *Christian Science Monitor*, 4 May 1976, p. 6.

13. From a *New York Times* interview, quoted in Chubin and Zabih, *Foreign Relations*, p. 216.

14. Since 1958, Iraq has undergone four successful coups and two attempted ones. For more details on the Iraqi republican regime, see Majid Khadduri, *Republican Iraq* (London: Oxford University Press, 1969); Phebe Ann Marr, "Iraq's Leadership Dilemma: A Study in Leadership Trends, 1948-1968," *Middle East Journal* 24, no. 3 (Summer 1970):283-301; L. K. Kimball, *The Changing Pattern of Political Power in Iraq, 1958-1971* (New York: Robert Speller and Sons, 1972); Roy E. Thoman, "Iraq under Baathist Rule," *Current History* 62 (January 1972):31-37, 41; and A. Kelidar, *Iraq: The Search for Stability* (London: Institute for the Study of Conflict, 1975).

15. See Wycliffe D. Toole, Jr., "Soviet Interest in Arabia," *Military Review* 48, no. 5 (May 1968):91-97.

16. From a Beirut interview in 1973, quoted in R. M. Burrell, "The Gulf Pot Begins to Boil Once More," *New Middle East*, no. 56 (May 1973), p. 37.

17. See Faris Glubb, "New Spirit in the Gulf," *Middle East International*, no. 48 (June 1975), p. 15. Shortly afterwards, however, the two countries clashed over oil policies within OPEC. In the words of the Iraqi minister of information to the *Washington Post* in July 1975, "We wanted to build good close relations with Saudi Arabia but, unfortunately, the Saudi Government is following an oil policy which Iraq cannot accept." See Price, *Oil and Middle East Security*, p. 65.

18. Enver M. Koury, *Oil and Geopolitics in the Persian Gulf Area: A Center of Power* (Beirut, Lebanon: Catholic Press, 1973), p. 17.

19. On the latter incident, see *Christian Science Monitor*, 15 December 1976, p. 4.

20. A high UAE official has confided to this writer the following exchange between King Faisal and Shaikh Zayed during the negotiations:

> Faisal: The whole thing to us is a matter of dignity and honor. The British evicted us by force and we won't forget that. Our 1970 proposal for Saudi Arabia's eastern border is quite reasonable.

> Zayed: No, your Majesty. Your eastern boundary should be like this (taking a pencil and drawing a line in the middle of the gulf from Shatt al-Arab to the Strait of Hormuz).

> Faisal: Now we have a solution!

This exercise in wit by Shaikh Zayed may well be credited, more than anything else, with breaking the deadlock over this issue.

21. For more details on the background and events of this territorial dispute, see Alexander Melamid, "The Buraimi Oasis Dispute," *Middle Eastern Affairs* 7, no. 1 (February 1956):56-63; George Lenczowski, *Oil and State in the Middle East* (Ithaca, N.Y.: Cornell University Press, 1960), pp. 141-52; J. B. Kelly, *Eastern Arabian Frontiers* (New York: Praeger, 1964); and Husain M. Alba-harna, *The Legal Status of the Arabian Gulf States* (Manchester, England: Manchester University Press, 1968), Chapter 13.

22. On the latter point, see Chubin and Zabih, *Foreign Relations*, p. 180.

23. For the treaty and the three accompanying protocols, see "Iran-Iraq: Treaty on International Borders and Good Neighborly Relations," *International Legal Materials* 14, no. 5 (September 1975):1133-38. For more details on the background and development of this controversy, see, for example, Alexander Melamid, "The Shatt al-Arab Boundary Dispute," *Middle East Journal* 22, no. 3 (1968):351-57; and Shameen Akhtar, "The Iraqi-Iranian Dispute over the Shatt-el-Arab," *Pakistan Horizon* 22, no. 3 (1969):213-20.

24. In most of these cases, median lines were demarcated on the principle of equidistance from the two shores with close-to-shore islands generally being a complicating factor. For the division of the continental shelf on an economic rather than a geographic basis, see Richard Young, "Equitable Solutions for Offshore Boundaries: The 1968 Saudi Arabia–Iran Agreement," *American Journal of International Law* 64, no. 1 (January 1970):152-57.

25. Joseph Churba, *Conflict and Tension among the States of the Persian Gulf, Oman and South Arabia* (Alabama: Maxwell Air Force Base, Air University Documentary Research Study [AU-204-71-IPD], 1971), p. 68.

26. Chubin and Zabih, *Foreign Relations*, p. 222; Emile A. Nakhleh, *Arab-American Relations in the Persian Gulf* (Washington, D.C.: American Enterprise Institute for Public Policy Research, 1975), p. 31; and R. K. Ramazani, "Emerging Patterns of Regional .Relations in Iranian Foreign Policy," *Orbis* 18, no. 4 (Winter 1975):1053. On the settlement of the Bahraini dispute, see Edward Gordon, "Resolution of the Bahrain Dispute," *American Journal of International Law* 65, no. 3 (July 1971):560-68; and Hooshang Moghtader, "The Settlement of the Bahrain Question: A Study in Anglo-Iranian-United Nations Diplomacy," *Pakistan Horizon* 26, no. 2 (1973):16-29.

27. Ramazani, *Persian Gulf*, p. 57.

28. Ibid.

29. Ibid,. p. 59.

30. Quoted in Koury, *Oil and Geopolitics*, p. 21.

31. For the text of this agreement, see Ramazani, *Persian Gulf*, p. 140. For other pertinent documents, see "Documents on the Abu Musa Affair," *Middle East Economic Survey* 15, no. 28 (5 May 1972):1-7.

32. Quoted in Roy E. Thoman, "Iraq and the Persian Gulf," *Current History* 64 (January 1973):25.

33. See entire text of this interview, in Ramazani, *Persian Gulf*, pp. 143-48.

34. For more details on the islands affair, including the background, the circumstances, and the various arguments surrounding the issue, see, for example, ibid., pp. 56-68; Chubin and Zabih, *Foreign Relations,* pp. 222-34; Rosemary Said, "Al-Nizaa Haul al-Juzur al-Arabiyyah fi al-Khalij, 1928-1971" [Dispute over Arab Islands in the Gulf, 1928-1971), *Journal of the Gulf and Arabian Peninsula Studies* 2, no. 6 (April 1976):9-32; and M. A. Shukri, *Masaalat al-Juzur fi al-Khalij al-Arabi; wa al-Ganun al Dawli* [The Question of Islands in the Arabian Gulf and International Law] (n.p., 1972).

35. For more details on this clash, see R. M. Burrell, "The Gulf Pot Begins to Boil Once More," *New Middle East,* no. 56 (May 1973), pp. 37-38.

36. Quoted in J. K. Cooley, "Iraq-Kuwait Border Friction Stirs Persian Gulf Concern," *Christian Science Monitor,* 18 January 1977, p. 3. According to one source, in 1975 Saudi Arabia agreed in principle on the necessity for Iraq to establish naval defense facilities on these islands (Warbah and Bubiyan), which will be extremely important to the Umm Qasr naval base and the projected deepwater terminal in the area. See Glubb, "New Spirit," p. 15.

37. For an illuminating study of the arms race among the three regional states, along with the potential danger it entails, see Dale R. Tahtinen, *Arms in the Persian Gulf* (Washington, D.C.: American Enterprise Institute for Public Policy Research, 1974).

38. See Ramazani, *Persian Gulf,* p. 101.

39. See Arnaud de Borchgrave's interview with the shah of Iran, *Newsweek,* 14 November 1977, p. 70.

40. Quoted in Alvin J. Cottrell, "Iran, the Arabs and the Persian Gulf," *Orbis* 17, no. 3 (Fall 1973):988.

41. See R. M. Burrell, "Iranian Foreign Policy: Strategic Location, Economic Ambition, and Dynastic Determination," *Journal of International Affairs* 29, no. 2 (Fall 1975):137.

42. See Frances FitzGerald, "Giving the Shah Everything He Wants," *Harper's Magazine* 249, no. 1494 (November 1974):80. This particular piece is highly critical of the shah's domestic policies.

43. See Arnaud de Borchgrave, "Colossus of the Oil Lanes," *Newsweek,* 21 May 1973, p. 44.

44. The shah told de Borchgrave (ibid.) that "Western Europe, the United States and Japan see the Gulf as an integral part of their security, yet they are not in a position to ensure that security. *That is why we are doing it for them.*" (Emphasis added).

45. *Newsweek,* 23 August 1976, p. 51. For a critique of American military involvement in building up Iran's armed forces, a venture that is projected to cost $10 billion for the period 1975-1980, see Michael T. Klare, "Hoist with Our Own Pahlavi," *Nation* 222 (January 1976):110-14.

46. Quoted in *Christian Science Monitor,* 9 August 1976, p. 1. A few months later, the secretary, in a press conference, described Iran as "a country . . . that did not join the [oil] embargo; that is selling oil to Israel; that has declared that it will not join any other embargo; and that has been a great friend and supporter

of the United States on almost all objectives of foreign policy." See U.S., Department of State, *Bulletin* (Washington, D.C.: U.S. Government Printing Office) 75, no. 1943 (20 September 1976), p. 372.

47. See *Time*, 6 August 1973, p. 30.

48. Nakhleh, *Arab-American Relations*, p. 28.

49. According to one observer, the shah's dispatch of troops to Oman was accomplished with no prior consultation with Riyadh. See David E. Long, "U.S. Strategic Interests in the Persian Gulf: Problems and Policy Analysis," mimeographed (Washington, D.C.: National War College, 1975), p. 54.

50. Quoted in R. K. Ramazani, "Iran's Search for Regional Cooperation," *Middle East Journal* 30, no. 2 (1976):174.

51. Quoted in Chubin and Zabih, *Foreign Relations,* p. 238.

52. Glubb, "New Spirit," p. 16. Shortly after, however, King Khalid is reported to have told Jim Hoagland of the *Washington Post* that Saudi Arabia "was not in agreement with efforts made by Iraq and Iran to arrange a security pact for the Persian Gulf." See Ramazani, "Iran's Search," p. 184.

53. See Price, *Oil and Middle East Security*, p. 80; and Abdul Lateef, "A Security Pact in the Gulf?" *Middle East International*, no. 55 (January 1976), p. 23.

54. Approximately 20 million barrels of crude oil, loaded on 200 tankers, pass through this twenty-six-mile corridor every day. This strait's importance in the world energy picture is beyond measure. For more details on this strategic sea lane, see Charles Heller, "The Strait of Hormuz—Critical in Oil's Future," *World Petroleum* 40, no. 11 (October 1969):24-26.

55. See J. K. Cooley, "Soviets Make Presence Visible on Arab Seas," *Christian Science Monitor*, 30 December 1976, p. 4.

56. See Lateef, *Security Pact*, p. 23. Emphasis added.

57. *Al-Hawadith* (Beirut), 11 March 1977, p. 25.

58. See Abir, *Oil, Power and Politics*, p. 15.

59. For a discussion of Aden's relations with Britain and this colony's place in Britain's colonial strategy, see Gillian King, *Imperial Outpost—Aden: Its Place in British Strategic Policy* (Chatham House: Oxford University Press, 1964).

60. See Churba, *Conflict and Tension*, p. 59.

61. Quoted in Tom Dammann, "Saudi Arabia's Dilemma: An Interview with King Faisal," *Interplay* 3, no. 12 (September 1970):19.

62. Abir, *Oil, Power and Politics*, p. 26.

63. See Ramazani, *Persian Gulf*, p. 46.

64. See the shah's interview with al-Siyasah (Kuwait) of December 28, 1974, quoted in *Journal of Gulf and Arabian Peninsula Studies* 1, no. 2 (April 1975):164.

65. David Holden, "Iran's View of the Gulf," *Middle East International*, no. 36 (June 1974), p. 8.

66. See Nakhleh, *Arab-American Relations*, p. 37. However, it is reported that the Arab League tried later, apparently with little success, to effect a mediation between the PDRY (South Yemen) and Oman in an attempt to replace the

Iranian presence with an Arab force. See Ramazani, "Emerging Patterns," p. 1055.

67. Price, *Oil and Middle East Security*, p. 42.

68. See the shah's interview with the well-known Egyptian journalist, Muhammed H. Heikel, as quoted by Lateef, *Security Pact*, p. 22.

69. The shah extended diplomatic recognition to China in mid-1971 and the latter subsequently established diplomatic relations with Iran, Turkey, Bahrain, and Qatar. This might have contributed to a change in Chinese foreign policy orientation from a heavy emphasis on ideology to one on national interest. In fact, in mid-1973, the Chinese gave their explicit support to the shah's policy in the gulf at the same time that this policy aimed at the eradication of liberation movements in the area. See Tareq Y. Ismael, "The People's Republic of China and the Middle East," in Ismael, ed., *The Middle East in World Politics: A Study in Comparative International Relations* (Syracuse, New York: Syracuse University Press, 1974), pp. 160-61; and Chubin and Zabih, *Foreign Relations*, p. 310. For greater details on the Chinese shift toward gradually becoming a pro-status quo power in the Middle East, see W.A.C. Adie, "Peking's Revised Line," *Problems of Communism* (September-October, 1972), pp. 54-68.

70. The PDRY's loss of interest in the guerrillas of Dhufar and its grave consequences bring to mind an interestingly similar case that took place earlier. As a result of the Irano-Iraqi accord reached in the spring of 1975, the shah severed his relations with the Kurds, thereby leading to the overnight collapse of their rebellion against the Iraqi government.

71. For further details on the origins, development, and decline of the Dhufari revolution, see, for example, Barbo Karabuda, "Red Guerrillas of Arabian Gulf," *Eastern Horizon* (Hong Kong) 9, no. 5 (1970):48-54; Ray L. Cleveland, "Revolution in Dhofar," *Middle East Forum* 47, nos. 3-4 (Winter 1971):92-102; R. M. Burrell, "Rebellion in Dhofar: The Spectre of Vietnam," *New Middle East*, no. 4243 (March/April, 1972), pp. 55-58; R. P. Owen, "The Rebellion in Dhofar—A Threat to Western Interests in the Gulf," *World Today* 29, no. 6 (June 1973):266-73; Charles Wakebridge, "Dhofar: The Achilles Heel," *Middle East International*, no. 33 (March 1974), pp. 8-10; D. L. Price, *Oman: Insurgency and Development* (London: Institute for the Study of Conflict, 1975); and J. B. Kelly, "Hadramut, Oman, Dhufar: The Experience of Revolution," *Middle Eastern Studies* 12, no. 2 (May 1976):213-30.

72. In September 1976, the Kuwaiti constitution was suspended and the National Assembly dissolved. Bahrain went through a similar experience the year before.

73. Quoted in Chubin and Zabih, *Foreign Relations*, p. 265. Emphasis added.

74. Quoted in Stephen Page, "Moscow and the Persian Gulf Countries, 1967-1970," *Mizan* 13, no. 2 (October 1971):81.

75. Nakhleh, *Arab-American Relations*, p. 41.

76. Abir, *Oil, Power and Politics*, p. 32.

77. R. K. Ramazani, "Iran and the U.S.: An Experiment in Enduring Friendship," *Middle East Journal* 30, no. 3 (1976):333.

78. Quoted in David E. Long, *The Persian Gulf* (Boulder, Colorado: Westview Press, 1976), p. 139.

79. On the 1973 war, the Arab oil embargo and the energy crisis, see, for example, Ibrahim F. Shihata, "Destination Embargo of Arab Oil: Its Legality under International Law," *American Journal of International Law* 68, no. 4 (October 1974):591-627; and William E. Griffith, "The Fourth Middle East War, the Energy Crisis and U.S. Policy," *Orbis* 17, no. 4 (Winter 1974):1161-88.

80. Quoted in J. K. Cooley, "Anchors Aweigh in Bahrain?" *Christian Science Monitor*, 29 December 1976, p. 3.

81. See F. Glubb, "Back Door to Arabia," *Middle East International*, no. 45 (March 1975), p. 11; and Alvin Z. Rubinstein, "Soviet Persian Gulf Policy," *Middle East Review* 10, no. 2 (Winter 1977-78), p. 54.

82. On the evolution of the Soviet interest in the Arabian Peninsula, see, for example, Stephen Page, *The USSR and Arabia* (London: Central Asian Research Centre, 1971); and Walid al-Sharif, "al-Ittihad al-Sufiati wa Mantagat al-Khalij al-Arabi" [The Soviet Union and the Arabian Gulf Region], *Journal of the Gulf and Arabian Peninsula Studies* (in Arabic) 2, no. 5 (January 1976):87-104.

83. Articles 8 and 9 of the treaty call for bilateral cooperation in the military security area. For the text of the treaty, as well as an analysis of Soviet short-, intermediate-, and long-term aims, see A. Yodfat and M. Abir, *In the Direction of the Gulf: The Soviet Union and the Persian Gulf* (London: Frank Cass and Co., 1977).

84. The Kuwaitis are reported to have recently concluded a deal for an arms purchase with the Soviet Union. If this deal goes through, the importation of highly sophisticated weapons will probably be accompanied by military experts—a new development of wider regional implications. See Rubinstein, "Soviet Persian Gulf Policy," p. 50.

85. On the superpowers, the littoral states, and the Indian Ocean, see Sheldon W. Simon, "A Systems Approach to Security in the Indian Ocean Arc," *Orbis* 14, no. 2 (Summer 1970):401-42; G. Jukes, "The Soviet Union and the Indian Ocean," *Survival* 13, no. 11 (November 1971):370-405 and his *The Indian Ocean in Soviet Naval Policy* (London: International Institute for Strategic Studies, Adelphi Papers no. 87, 1972); K. P. Misra, "International Politics in the Indian Ocean," *Orbis* 18, no. 4 (Winter 1975):1088-128; J. Saksena, "La Penetration américano-soviétique dans l'Océan Indien," *Politique Etrangère*, no. 1 (1976), pp. 57-72; Ferenc A. Vali, *Politics of the Indian Ocean Region: The Balances of Power* (New York: Free Press, 1976); and D. Tahtinen, *Arms in the Indian Ocean: Interests and Challenges* (Washington, D.C.: American Enterprise Institute for Public Policy Research, 1977).

86. On this particular aspect of Soviet foreign policy, see O. M. Smolansky, "Moscow and the Persian Gulf: An Analysis of Soviet Ambitions and Potentials," in T. Gayler Young, ed., *Middle East Focus: The Persian Gulf* (Princeton, N.J.: Princeton University Conference, 1968), pp. 150-56.

87. See al-Sharif, "al-Ittihad al-Sufiati," pp. 95ff. For an evaluation of the Soviet interest in Middle East oil from the economic, strategic, and commercial points of view, see R. E. Hunter, *The Soviet Dilemma in the Middle East: Oil and the Persian Gulf* (London: International Institute for Strategic Studies, Adelphi Papers no. 60, 1969); J. H. Berry, "Oil and Soviet Policy in the Middle

East," *Middle East International* 26, no. 2 (Spring 1972):149-60; M. I. Goldman, "Red Black Gold," *Foreign Policy,* no. 8 (Fall 1972):138-48; L. Landis, *Politics and Oil: Moscow in the Middle East* (New York: Dunellen Publishing, 1973); and Yodfat and Abir, *In Direction of Gulf,* Chapter 1.

88. See Rubinstein, "Soviet Persian Gulf Policy," p. 49.

89. Irano-Israeli cooperation goes beyond the area of trade and economics to the more sensitive plane of security and defense. According to Arnaud de Borchgrave, for instance, "Hundreds of Iranian officers have been to Israel for advanced training and Washington, Tehran and Jerusalem have set up an active three-way exchange of intelligence on military developments throughout the Middle East." See his "Colossus of the Oil Lanes," *Newsweek,* 21 May 1973, p. 44. On Irano-Israeli relations, see, for example, Chubin and Zabih, *Foreign Relations,* pp. 156-62; R. B. Reppa, *Israel and Iran: Bilateral Relationships and Effect on the Indian Ocean Basin* (New York: Praeger, 1974); and M. G. Weinbaum, "Iran and Israel: The Discreet Entente," *Orbis* 18, no. 4 (Winter 1975):1070-87.

The Irano-Israeli axis is viewed by the United States in light of yet another "two-pillar" defense strategy not only against Soviet advances in the area but also as a countervailing force against emerging, pro-Soviet, Arab radicalism. However, Washington has always found it difficult to reconcile its deep moral commitment to the so-called survival of Israel, on the one hand, and its extensive economic interests in the Arab world, on the other, particularly since 1967 when the concept of Israeli security was openly broadened to mean the acquisition of more Arab lands. The use of oil by the Arabs as a political weapon in 1973 and the 1977 Sadat peace initiative have ostensibly contributed to the evolution of a more "even-handed" American foreign policy in the Middle East. The latest pointer in this direction is the failure of the extremely powerful Israeli lobby in the U.S. Congress to block the sale of advanced military aircraft to Saudi Arabia.

Bibliography

(Sources listed here are in addition to those cited and/or recommended in the text.)

1. Official Documents

"Complaint against Iranian Occupation of Arabian Gulf Islands: Security Council Begins Consultation." *UN Monthly Chronicle* 9, no. 1 (1972):46-50.

Government of the United Arab Emirates, Abu Dhabi. *al-Jaridah al-Rasmiyyah* [Official Gazette]. 45 vols. 1971-77.

Government of the United Arab Emirates, Foreign Ministry: *United Arab Emirates: An Outline*. London, 1972.

Great Britain. *Exchange of Notes concerning the Termination of Special Treaty Relations between the United Kingdom and the Trucial States*. Treaty Series, no. 34 (1972), Cmnd. 4941.

———. *Memorial of the Government of the United Kingdom of Great Britain and Northern Ireland in Arbitration concerning Buraimi and the Common Frontier between Abu Dhabi and Saudi Arabia*. 2 vols. London, 1955.

"Iran: Iraq: Documents on Abrogation of the 1937 Treaty concerning Shatt al-Arab Waterway." *International Legal Materials* 8, no. 3 (1969):492-96.

"Iran: Saudi Arabia: Agreement concerning Sovereignty over al-Arabiyah and Farsi Islands and Delimitation of Sub-Marine Boundaries." *International Legal Materials* 8, no. 3 (1969):492-496.

"The Provisional Constitution of the United Arab Amirates." *Middle East Journal* 26, no. 3 (1972):307-25.

Saudi Arabia. *Memorial of the Government of Saudi Arabia in the Arbitration for the Settlement of the Territorial Dispute between Muscat and Abu Dhabi on One Side and Saudi Arabia on the Other*. Cairo, 1955.

United States, Congress, House of Representatives. *U.S. Interests in and Policy toward the Persian Gulf*. Hearings before the Subcommittee on the Near East and South Asia. Washington, D.C.: USGPO, 1972.

———. *New Perspectives on the Persian Gulf*. 93d Cong., 1st sess., 6 June, 17,

23, 24 July, and 28 November 1973. Washington, D.C.: USGPO, 1973.

————. *The Persian Gulf, 1974: Money, Politics, Arms and Power.* 93d Cong.,
2d sess., 30 July, 5, 7, 12 August 1974. Washington, D.C.: USGPO, 1975.

————. *United States Arms Sales to the Persian Gulf: Report of a Study Mission to Iran, Kuwait, and Saudi Arabia, May 22-31, 1975.* 94th Cong., 1st sess.
Washington, D.C.:USGPO, 1975.

————. *Proposed Foreign Military Sales to Middle Eastern Countries—1976.*
Hearings before the Subcommittee on International Political and Military
Affairs. 94th Cong., 2d sess., 23 February, 1 March, and 21 September 1976.
Washington, D.C.: USGPO, 1976.

2. Books, Pamphlets, Monographs, Proceedings

Abd al-Karim, Ibrahim. *al-Bahrain Wa Ahamiyyatuha Bayna al-Imarat al-
Arabiyyah* [Bahrain and Its Importance among the Arab Emirates]. Beirut:
Dar al-Ilm lil-Malayin, 1970.

Abir, Mordechai. *Oil, Power and Politics: Conflict in Arabia, the Red Sea, and
the Gulf.* London: Frank Cass, 1974.

Abu Hakima, Ahmed. *Muhadharat fi Tarikh, Shargi al Jazirah al-Arabiyyah fi
al-Usur al-Hadithah* [Lectures on the History of the Eastern Arabian Peninsula in the Modern Ages]. Cairo: n.p., 1967.

Adamiyat, Fereydoun. *Bahrein Island: A Legal and Diplomatic Study of the
British-Iranian Controversy.* New York: Praeger, 1955.

al-Aggad, Salah. *al-Istimar fi al-Khalij al-Farisi* [Imperialism in the Persian
Gulf]. Cairo: Maktabat al-Anjilu al-Misriyyah, 1956.

————. *al-Tayyarat al-Sirasiyyah fi al-Khalij al-Arabi* [Political Currents in the
Arabian Gulf]. Cairo: Maktabat al-Anjilu al-Misriyyah, 1965.

Ahmad, Magbul S. *Indo-Arab Relations: An Account of India's Relations with
the Arab World from Ancient up to Modern Times.* New Delhi: Indian
Council for Cultural Relations, 1969.

Amirie, Abbas, ed. *The Persian Gulf and Indian Ocean in International Politics.*
Tehran: Institute for International Political and Economic Studies, 1976.

al-Ansari, Muhammed J. *Lamahat min al-Khalij al-Arabi* [Glimpses from the
Arabian Gulf]. Manama, Bahrain: al Sharikah al-Arabiyyah lil-Wikalat wa
al-Tawzi, 1970.

Anthony, John D. *Arab States of the Lower Gulf: People, Politics, Petroleum.*
Washington, D.C.: Middle East Institute, 1975.

Anthony, John D., et al. "The Great Powers, the Indian Ocean and the Gulf."
Panel Series Resume no. 4. Washington, D.C.: Middle East Institute, 1972.

————, ed. *The Middle East: Oil, Politics and Development.* Washington,
D.C.: American Enterprise Institute for Public Policy Research, 1975.

The Arab States of the Persian Gulf and Southeast Arabia. London: Central
Office of Information, 1962.

The Arabian Peninsula, Iran and the Gulf States: New Wealth, New Power.
Summary Record of the 27th Annual Conference of the Middle East Institute.
Washington, D.C.: Middle East Institute, 1973.

The Arabian Peninsula States Today. Washington, D.C.: K. Key Publications, 1976.

Azar, Edward E. *Probe for Peace: Small-State Hostilities.* Minneapolis, Minn.: Burgess Publishing Co., 1973.

Bayne, E. A. *Persian Kingship in Transition.* American Universities Field Staff, 1968.

Bill, James A. *The Politics of Iran: Groups, Classes and Modernization.* Columbus, Ohio: Charles E. Merrill Publishing Co., 1972.

Binder, Leonard. *Factors Influencing Iran's International Role.* RM-5968. Santa Monica, Calif.: Rand, 1969.

Blair, P. W. *The Ministate Dilemma.* Occasional Paper no. 6. Carnegie Endowment for International Peace, 1967.

Burrell, R. M. *The Persian Gulf.* The Washington Papers, no. 1. Washington, D.C.: Center for Strategic and International Studies, 1972.

Burrell, R. M., and Cottrell, A. *Iran, Afghanistan and Pakistan: Tensions and Dilemmas.* The Washington Papers, no. 20. Beverly Hills, Calif.: Sage Publications, 1974.

————. *Iran, the Arabian Peninsula, and the Indian Ocean.* New York: National Strategy Information Center, 1972.

al-Buruni, Ahmad Q. *al-Imarat al-Sabala al-Sahil al-Akhdhar* [The Seven Emirates on the Green Coast]. Beirut: Dar al-Hukmah, 1957.

Busch, Briton C. *Britain and the Persian Gulf, 1894-1914.* Berkeley: University of California Press, 1967.

————. *Britain, India and the Arabs, 1914-1921.* Berkeley: University of California Press, 1969.

Caroe, O. *Wells of Power: The Oilfields of Southwestern Asia.* Westport, Conn.: Hyperion Press, 1976 (first published in 1951).

The Changing Balance of Power in the Persian Gulf. Rome: Center for Mediterranean Studies, American Universities Field Staff, 1972.

Chubin, S., and Fard-Saidi, M. *Recent Trends in Middle East Politics and Iran's Foreign Policy Options.* Tehran: Institute for International Political and Economic Studies, 1975.

Churba, Joseph. *Conflict and Tension Among the States of the Persian Gulf, Oman and South Arabia.* Montgomery, Ala.: Air University, 1971.

Cottam, Richard. *Nationalism in Iran.* University of Pittsburgh Press, 1964.

Daniels, John. *Abu Dhabi: A Portrait.* London: Longman, 1974.

DeGaury, Gerald. *Faisal: King of Saudi Arabia.* London: Arthur Barker, 1966.

Demir, Soliman. *The Kuwait Fund and the Political Economy of Arab Regional Development.* New York: Praeger, 1976.

El Mallakh, Ragaei. *Economic Development and Regional Cooperation: Kuwait.* Chicago: University of Chicago Press, 1968.

Fabian Research Bureau. *Arabia: When Britain Goes.* Fabian Research Series, no. 259. London: Fabian Society, 1967.

Faroughy, Abbas. *The Bahrain Islands, 1750-1951: A Contribution to the Study of Power Politics in the Persian Gulf.* New York: Verry, Fisher, 1951.

Fiennes, Ranulph. *Where Soldiers Fear to Tread.* London: Hodder and

Stoughton, 1975.

Freedman, Robert L. *Soviet Policy toward the Middle East since 1970.* New York: Praeger, 1975.

Freeman, S. D. *Energy: The New Era.* New York: Vintage Books, 1974.

Freeth, Zahra. *A New Look at Kuwait.* London: George Allen and Unwin, 1972.

Gerard, Bernard. *Le Qatar.* Paris: Editions Delroisse, 1974.

————. *Les emirats arabes unis.* Paris: Editions Delroisse, 1973.

Hay, Sir Rupert. *The Persian Gulf States.* Washington, D.C.: Middle East Institute, 1959.

Hirst, David. *Oil and Public Opinion in the Middle East.* New York: Praeger, 1966.

Holden, David. *Farewell to Arabia.* New York: Walker and Co., 1966.

Hopwood, Derek. *The Arabian Peninsula: Society and Politics.* London: George Allen and Unwin, 1972.

Humeidan, Ali. *Les princes de l'or noir, evolution politique de Golfe persique.* Paris: SEDEIS, 1968.

Hurewitz, J. C. *The Persian Gulf: Prospects for Stability.* Headline Series, no. 220. New York: Foreign Policy Association, 1974.

al-Ibrahim, Hassan A. *al-Kuwayt: Dirasah Siyasiyyah, 1972* [Kuwait: A Political Study, 1972]. Kuwait: Dar al-Bayan, 1972.

Imperialism in the Arab-Persian Gulf. Research Report no. 2, Washington, D.C.: Middle East Research and Information Project, 1971.

Kaushak, Devendra. *The Indian Ocean: Towards a Peace Zone.* New Delhi: Vikas Publications, 1972.

Key, Kerim K. *The State of Qatar: An Economic and Commercial Survey.* Washington, D.C.: K. Key Publications, 1976.

Khadduri, Majid, ed. *Major Middle Eastern Problems in International Law.* Washington, D.C.: American Enterprise Institute of Public Policy Research, 1972.

Koury, Enver M. *Oil and Geopolitics in the Persian Gulf Area: A Center of Power.* Beirut: Catholic Press, 1973.

Landen, Robert G. *Oman since 1856: Disruptive Modernization in a Traditional Arab Society.* Princeton, N.J.: Princeton University Press, 1967.

Leipold, L. E. *Come Along to Saudi Arabia.* Minneapolis: Denison, 1974.

Lenczowski, George, ed. *United States Interests in the Middle East.* Washington, D.C.: American Enterprise Institute, 1973.

Long, David E. *Confrontation and Cooperation in the Gulf.* Middle East Problem Paper no. 10. Washington, D.C.: Middle East Institute, 1974.

————. *The Persian Gulf: An Introduction to Its Peoples, Politics, and Economics.* Boulder, Colorado: Westview Press, 1976.

Longrigg, S. H. *Oil in the Middle East: Its Discovery and Development.* London: Oxford University Press, 1968.

Marlowe, John. *The Persian Gulf in the Twentieth Century.* London: Crescent Press, 1962.

Mertz, R. A. *Education and Manpower in the Arabian Gulf.* Washington, D.C.: American Friends of the Middle East, 1972.

Mikdashi, Zuhayr M. *The Community of Oil Exporting Countries.* Ithaca, N.Y.: Cornell University Press, 1972.

Millar, T. B. *Soviet Policies in the Indian Ocean Area.* Canberra: Australian National University Press, n.d.

Monroe, Elizabeth. *Britain's Moment in the Middle East.* London: Chatto and Windus, 1964.

———. *The Changing Balance of Power in the Persian Gulf.* New York: American Universities Field Staff, 1972.

Moser, R. *Welcome to Sharjah.* Paris: Editions Delroisse, 1974.

Mosley, L. *Power Play: Oil in the Middle East.* New York: Random House, 1973.

Mutawalli, Muhammed. *Hawdhal-Khalij al-Arabi* [The Arabian Gulf Basin]. Cairo: Maktabat al-Anjilu al-Misriyah, 1970.

Nakhleh, Emile. *Arab-American Relations in the Persian Gulf.* Washington, D.C.: American Enterprise Institute for Public Policy Research, 1975.

———. *Bahrain: Political Development in a Modernizing Society.* Lexington, Mass.: D. C. Heath and Co., 1976.

———. *The United States and Saudi Arabia: A Policy Analysis.* Washington, D.C.: American Enterprise Institute for Public Policy Research, 1975.

Nawfal, al-Sayyid, M. A. *al-Awda al-Siyasiyyah li Imarat al-Khalij al-Arabi wa Janub al-Jazirah* [The Political Conditions of the Amirates of the Arabian Gulf and South Arabia]. Cairo: Dar al-Maarif, 1961.

———. *al-Khalij al-Arabi wa al-Hudud al-Sharqiyyah lil-Watan al-Arabi* [The Arabian Gulf and the Eastern Boundaries of the Arab Nation]. Beirut: Dar al-Taliah, 1969.   '

Nirumand, Bahman. *Iran: The New Imperialism in Action.* New York: Monthly Review Press, 1969.

Owen, Roderic. *The Golden Bubble: Arabian Gulf Documentary.* London: Collins, 1957.

Pachachi, Nadim. *The Role of OPEC in the Emergence of New Patterns in Government-Company Relations.* London: Royal Institute of International Affairs, 1972.

Pahlevi, H.I.M. Muhammad R. S. *Mission for My Country.* New York: McGraw-Hill, 1961.

Qalaji, Qadri. *al-Khalij al-Arabi* [The Arabian Gulf]. Beirut: Dar al-Katib al-Arabi, 1965.

al-Rayyis, R. N. *Ittihad al-Imarat al-Arabiyyah* [The Union of Arab Emirates]. Beirut: Dar al-Nahar, 1972.

Reppa, Robert B. *Israel and Iran: Bilateral Relationships and Effect on the Indian Ocean Basin.* New York: Praeger, 1974.

Rida, Adel. *Uman wa al-Khalij, Qadaya wa Munaqashat* [Oman and the Gulf: Legal Problems and Disputes]. Cairo: Dar al-Katib al-Arabi, 1969.

Rouhani, Fuad. *A History of O.P.E.C.* New York: Praeger, 1971.

al-Rumayhi, M. G. *Petroleum and Social Change in the Arabian Gulf.* Cairo: Arab League, 1975.

Said, Amin. *al-Khalij al-Arabi fi Tarikhihi al-Siyasi: wa Nahdhatihi al-*

Hadithah [The Arabian Gulf in Its Political History and Its New Awakening]. Beirut: Dar al-Katib al-Arabi, 1965.

Sanghvi, Ramesh. *Shatt al-Arab: The Facts behind the Issue.* London: Transorient Books, 1969.

Shaker, Amin. *Mustaqbal al-Khalij al-Arabi* [The Future of the Arabian Gulf]. Cairo, 1971.

Sheean, Vincent. *Faisal: The King and His Kingdom.* Tavistock, England: University Press of Arabia, 1975.

Shwadran, Benjamin. *The Middle East, Oil and the Great Powers.* New York: John Wiley and Sons, 1973.

Skeet, Ian. *Muscat and Oman: End of an Era.* London: Faber and Faber, 1974.

Smith, Harvey, et al. *Area Handbook for Iran.* Foreign Area Studies, American University. Washington, D.C.: USGPO, 1971.

————. *Area Handbook for Iraq.* Foreign Area Studies, American University. Washington, D.C.: USGPO, 1971.

Stanford Research Institute, *Area Handbook for the Peripheral States of the Arabian Peninsula.* Foreign Area Studies, American University. Washington, D.C.: USGPO, 1971.

Stephens, Robert. *The Arabs' New Frontiers.* London: Temple Smith, 1973.

Stocking, George W. *Middle East Oil: A Study in Political and Economic Controversy.* Nashville, Tenn.: Vanderbilt University Press, 1970.

Stork, Joe. *Middle East Oil and the Energy Crisis.* New York: Monthly Review Press, 1975.

Tahtinen, Dale R. *National Security Challenges to Saudi Arabia.* Washington, D.C.: American Enterprise Institute, 1978.

Takriti, Salim. *al-Sira ala al-Khalij al-Arabi* [The Struggle on the Arabian Gulf]. Baghdad: Wizarat al-Thaqafah Wa al-Irshad, 1966.

Van Ess, D. *Pioneers in the Arab World.* Grand Rapids, Mich.: Eerdmans, 1975.

Vicker, Ray. *The Kingdom of Oil.* New York: Scribner, 1974.

Walpole, Norman D., et al. *Area Handbook for Saudi Arabia.* 2d ed. Foreign Area Studies, American University. Washington, D.C.: USGPO, 1971.

Wilson, Arnold T. *The Persian Gulf: An Historical Sketch from the Earliest Times to the Beginning of the Twentieth Century.* London: George Allen and Unwin, 1959.

Wilson, Harold. *A Personal Record: The Labor Government, 1964-1970.* New York: Little, Brown, 1971.

Winston, Harry, and Freeth, Zahra. *Kuwait: Prospect and Reality.* New York: Crane, Russak and Co., 1972.

World Energy Demands and the Middle East. Summary Record of the 26th Annual Conference, 2 parts. Washington, D.C.: Middle East Institute, 1972.

Yar-Shater, E., ed. *Iran Faces the Seventies.* New York: Praeger, 1971.

Young, T. C., ed. *Middle East Focus: The Persian Gulf.* Proceedings of the Twentieth Annual Near East Conference. Princeton, N.J.: Princeton University Press, 1969.

Zonis, Marvin. *The Political Elite of Iran.* Princeton, N.J.: Princeton University Press, 1971.

3. Periodical Literature and Parts of Books

Abourezk, James. "New War in the Offing." *The Nation* 218 (16 February 1974): 203-04.

Abu Hakima, A. M. "Kuwait and the Eastern Arabian Protectorates." In Tareg Y. Ismael, ed., *Governments and Politics of the Contemporary Middle East.* Homewood, Ill.: Dorsey Press, 1970.

Adelman, M. A. "Is the Oil Shortage Real? Oil Companies as OPEC Tax Collectors." *Foreign Policy* 9 (Winter 1972-73), pp. 69-107.

Akins, James. "The Oil Crisis: This Time the Wolf Is Here." *Foreign Affairs* 51, no. 3 (April 1973):462-90.

"Aladdin's Troubled Dream." *Forbes*, 15 February 1976, pp. 28-36.

Ali, Mehrunnisa. "Iran's Relations with the U.S. and U.S.S.R." *Pakistan Horizon* 26, no. 4 (1973):45-68.

Amuzegar, Jahangir. "The Oil Story: Facts, Fiction and Fair Play." *Foreign Affairs* 51, no. 4 (July 1973):676-89.

"The Arabian/Persian Gulf: Oil on Troubled Waters." *MERIP Reports* 1, no. 2 (August 1971):1-8.

"The Arabs' New Oil Squeeze." *Time*, 19 November 1973, pp. 88-95.

Aruri, Naseer H. "Kuwait: A Political Study." *Muslim World* 60, no. 3 (July 1970):321-43.

Aruri, Naseer H. and Hevener, N. K. "France and the Middle East." In Tareg Y. Ismael, *The Middle East in World Politics*, pp. 59-93. Syracuse, N.Y.: Syracuse University Press, 1974.

Atherton, Alfred L., Jr. "Department Discusses Arms Sales and U.S.-Saudi Arabia Relations." *Department of State Bulletin* 75, no. 1947 (18 October 1976):475-78.

_____. "Department Discusses U.S.-Saudi Arabia Defense Relationship." *Department of State Bulletin* 74, no. 1917 (22 March 1976):377-81.

_____. "Department Reviews U.S. Relations with the Countries of the Arabian Peninsula-Persian Gulf Region." *Department of State Bulletin* 71, no. 1836 (2 September 1974):335-42.

_____. "Department Testifies on Human Rights in Iran." *Department of State Bulletin* 75, no. 1945 (4 October 1976):429-37.

_____. "U.S.-Iran Relations: Cooperation and Shared Interests." *Department of State Bulletin* 73, no. 1903 (15 December 1975):862-64.

Avery, Peter. "The Many Faces of Iran's Foreign Policy." *New Middle East*, no. 47 (August 1972), pp. 17-19.

Azadeh, Behrouze. "L'Iran aujourd'hui." *Les Temps Modernes*, no. 298 (May 1971):2031-45.

Baehr, Peter R. "Small States: A Tool for Analysis?" *World Politics* 27, no. 3 (1975):456-66.

"Bahrain: Foundations Are Laid for an Oil-less Future." *Middle East Economic Digest* 17, no. 11 (16 March 1973):289-91.

"Bahrein: From Dhow to Discoteque." *Mid East* 8, no. 3 (May/June 1968): 32-37.

Baldwin, H. "The Indian Ocean Contest and the U.S. Presence." *New York Times,* 22 March 1971.

Balfour-Paul, H. G. "Recent Developments in the Persian Gulf." *Royal Central Asian Journal* 56, pt. I (1969):12-19.

Beasley, R. "The Vacuum That Must Be Filled." *New Middle East,* no. 32 (May 1971):38-39.

de Beauce, T. "Trois fonds arabes de cooperation." *Politique Etrangère,* no. 1 (1976):43-56.

Becker, A. "Oil and the Persian Gulf in Soviet Policy in the 1970's." In M. Confino and S. Shamir, eds., *The U.S.S.R. and the Middle East,* pp. 173-214. New York: John Wiley, 1973.

Beedham, B. "Out of the Fire: Oil, the Gulf and the West." *Economist,* May 1975, pp. 7-85.

Belgrave, Sir Charles. "Persian Gulf—Past and Present." *Royal Central Asian Journal* 55, pt. 1 (1968):28-34.

Belgrave, James. "The Changing Social Scene in Bahrain." *Middle East Forum* 38, no. 7 (1962):62-66.

Bell, J. B. "Southern Yemen: Two Years of Independence." *World Today* 26, no. 2 (February 1970):76-82.

Ben-dak, J. D. "China in the Arab World." *Current History* 59, no. 349 (September 1970):147-52 ff.

Berreby, Jean Jacques. "La situation politique des emirats du Golfe persique." *Politique Etrangère* 27, no. 6 (1962):567-80.

Berry, A.S.I. "A Gulf Journey." *Middle East International,* no. 63 (September 1976), pp. 29-30.

Best, Geoffrey. "Middle East Oil and the U.S. Energy Crisis: Prospects for New Ventures in a Changed Market." *Law and Policy in International Business 5,* no. 1 (1973):215-73.

Bill, James A. "The Plasticity of Informal Politics: The Case of Iran." *Middle East Journal* 27, no. 2 (Spring 1973):131-50.

Bird, T. C. "British East of Suez Policy: A Victim of Economic Necessity." *Naval War College Review* 22, no. 8 (April 1970):54-71.

Bondarevsky, G. "The Continuing Western Interest in Oman—As Seen from Moscow." *New Middle East,* no. 35 (August 1971), pp. 11-15.

de Borchgrave, A. "Colossus of the Oil Lanes." *Newsweek,* 21 May 1973, pp. 40-44.

———. "Sadat's Shift." *Newsweek,* 10 September 1973, pp. 34-36.

Brewer, W. "Yesterday and Tomorrow in the Persian Gulf." *Middle East Journal* 23, no. 2 (1969):149-58.

Burrell, Richard. "Canal, Pipeline or Cape?" *New Middle East,* no. 41 (February 1972), pp. 29-32.

———. "The Gulf Pot Begins to Boil Once More." *New Middle East,* no. 56 (May 1973), pp. 37-38.

———. "Iran in Search of Greater Responsibilities." *New Middle East,* no. 49 (October 1972), pp. 27-28.

———. "Iranian Foreign Policy during the Last Decade." *Asian Affairs* 61, pt. 1 (1974):7-15.

———. "Iranian Foreign Policy: Strategic Location, Economic Ambition, and Dynastic Determination." *Journal of International Affairs* 29, no. 2 (Fall 1975):129-38.

———. "Politics and Participation Where Britannica Once Ruled." *New Middle East*, no. 51 (December 1972), pp. 32-36.

"Can the Oil Cartel Be Broken?" *Newsweek*, 14 October 1974, pp. 53-56.

De Cardi, B. "Trucial Oman in the Sixteenth and Seventeenth Centuries." *Antiquity* 44, no. 176 (1970):288-95.

Carey, Jane P. C. "Iran and Control of Its Oil Resources." *Political Science Quarterly* 89, no. 1 (1974):147-74.

Collard, Elizabeth. "Economic Prospects for the U.A.E." *Middle East International*, no. 21 (April 1973), pp. 11-13.

Cottrell, Alvin J. "British Withdrawal from the Persian Gulf." *Military Review* 50, no. 6 (June 1970):14-21.

———. "Concern over Saudi Arabia's Viability: An Exclusive Interview with the Shah of Iran." *New Middle East*, April 1971, pp. 21-23.

———. "Conflict in the Persian Gulf." *Military Review* 51, no. 2 (February 1971):33-41.

———. "Iran, the Arabs and the Persian Gulf." *Orbis* 17, no. 3 (Fall 1973):978-88.

———. "A New Persian Hegemony?" *Interplay* 3, no. 12 (September 1970):9-15.

———. "The U.S. and the Future of the Gulf after the Bahrain Agreement." *New Middle East*, no. 22 (1970), pp. 18-21.

Croizat, J. "Stability in the Persian Gulf." *U.S. Naval Institute Proceedings* 99, no. 7 (June 1973):48-59.

Dallaporta, C. "Les transferts institutionnels et politiques dans l'emirat d'abou dhabi." *Politique Etrangère*, no. 6 (1974), pp. 689-717.

Dammann, Tom. "Saudi Arabia's Dilemma: An Interview with King Faisal." *Interplay* 3, no. 12 (September 1970):16-19.

Darby, P. "Beyond East of Suez." *International Affairs* (London) 46, no. 4 (1970):655-69.

Davies, R. P. "U.S. Commercial Interests and Policy in the Persian Gulf Area." *Department of State Bulletin* 69, no. 1798 (17 December 1973):725-30.

Defarge, Claudi, and Troeller, Gordian. "Secret War Number Eleven." *Atlas* 18, no. 5 (1969):32-37.

Deutsch, Karl W. "The Growth of Nations: Some Recurrent Patterns of Political and Social Integration." *World Politics* 5, no. 2 (January 1953):168-94.

Djalili, M. R. "Le rapprochement irano-irakien et ses consequences." *Politique Etrangère*, no. 3 (1975), pp. 273-91.

Drambyantz, G. "The Persian Gulf: Twixt the Past and the Future." *International Affairs* (Moscow), no. 10 (October 1970), pp. 66-72.

———. "The Thorny Path of Federation: Persian Gulf." *International Affairs* (Moscow), no. 8 (May 1971), pp. 66-68.

Duchene, Francois. "The Arms Trade and the Middle East." *Political Quarterly* 44, no. 4 (October-December 1973):453-65.

Dymos, G. "Persian Gulf Countries at the Crossroads." *International Affairs* (Moscow), no. 3 (March 1973), pp. 53-59.

East, Maurice A. "Size and Foreign Policy Behavior: A Test of Two Models." *World Politics* 25, no. 4 (July 1973):556-76.

"Economic Report: U.A.E." *Arab Economist* 6, no. 60 (January 1974):63-66.

"Faisal and Oil: Driving toward a New World Order." *Time*, 6 January 1975, pp. 8-13 ff.

Fallaci, Oriana. "The Shah of Iran: An Interview." *New Republic*, 1 December 1973, pp. 16-21.

Fenelon, Kevin G. "Banking in the Gulf." *The Banker* 120, no. 537 (November 1970):1198-210.

FitzGerald, Frances. "Giving the Shah Everything He Wants." *Harper's Magazine* 249, no. 1494 (November 1974):55-82.

Foltz, C. S., Jr. "Why Should We Cut the Price of Oil to U.S.?: An Exclusive Interview with the Shah of Iran." *U.S. News and World Report* 76 (6 May 1974), pp. 34-36.

Gannon, E. J. "Military Considerations in the Indian Ocean." *Current History* 64, no. 375 (November 1972):218-21 ff.

Gaspard, J. "Faisal's Arabian Alternative." *New Middle East*, no. 6 (March 1969), pp. 15-19.

Glubb, Faris. "New Spirit in the Gulf." *Middle East International*, no. 48 (June 1975), pp. 15-16.

Graham, R. "Iraq and Iran: Gulf Power Struggle Sharpens." *New Middle East*, no. 45 (June 1972), pp. 14-16.

Guillain, R. "China in the Middle East." *Survival* 13, no. 1 (January 1971):22-24.

Habib, Philip C. "Department Testifies on Proposed Military Sales to Foreign Government." *Department of State Bulletin* 75, no. 1946 (11 October 1976): 447-49.

Haley, P. Edward. "Britain and the Middle East." In Tareg Y. Ismael, ed., *The Middle East in World Politics*, pp. 18-58. Syracuse: Syracuse University Press, 1974.

Halliday, Fred. "Class Struggle in the Arab Gulf." *New Left Review*, no. 58 (November-December, 1969), pp. 31-37.

Hay, Sir Rupert. "The Impact of the Oil Industry on the Persian Gulf Shaykh-doms." *Middle East Journal* 9, no. 4 (Autumn 1955):361-70.

Heard-Bey, Frauke. "Development Anomalies in the Beduin Oases of al-Liwa." *Asian Affairs* 61, pt. 3 (October 1974):272-86.

Holden, David. "Iran's View of the Gulf." *Middle East International*, no. 36 (June 1974), pp. 7-9.

Hoskins, H. L. "Background of the British Position in Arabia." *Middle East Journal* 1, no. 2 (1947):137-47.

Housego, David. "Iran in the Ascendant: Economic Strengths, Political Weaknesses." *Round Table*, no. 248 (October 1972), pp. 497-507.

"How Iran Spends Its New-found Riches." *Business Week*, 22 June 1974, pp. 44, 49, 52.

Howard, H. "The United States and the Middle East." In Tareg Y. Ismael, ed.,

The Middle East in World Politics, pp. 115-37. Syracuse, N.Y.: Syracuse University Press, 1974.

Howe, Marvine. "Britain Still Dominant in Persian Gulf Area." *New York Times*, 12 January 1972, p. 120.

"Independent Qatar." *Middle East Economic Digest* 15, no. 50 (10 December 1971):1429-436.

"Iran Rethinks Its Grandiose Goals." *Business Week*, 17 November 1975, pp. 58, 63.

"Iran: The White Revolution." *Current Notes on International Affairs* 42, no. 7 (July 1971):353-61.

"Iran's Shah: Key to U.S. Aims in Mideast." *U.S. News and World Report* 75 (6 August 1976):44.

"Iraq: An End to Isolation." *Time*, 19 May 1975, pp. 32, 35.

Ismael, T. Y. "The People's Republic of China and the Middle East." In Tareg Y. Ismael, ed., *The Middle East in World Politics*, pp. 138-61. Syracuse, N.Y.: Syracuse University Press, 1974.

————. "The Soviet Union and the Middle East." In Tareg Y. Ismael, ed., *The Middle East in World Politics*, pp. 94-114. Syracuse, N.Y.: Syracuse University Press, 1974.

Ivanov, K. "The U.S.S.R. and the Persian Gulf." *Mizan* 10, no. 2 (1968):51-59.

Izzard, Ralph. "Qatar Pledges Support for a Gulf Federation." *Middle East International*, no. 3 (June 1971), pp. 18-19.

Johns, R. "The Emergence of the United Arab Emirates." *Middle East International*, no. 21 (March 1973), pp. 8-13.

"A Jump of Centuries: A Survey of the Arabian Peninsula." *Economist*, 6 June 1970, pp. xi-xxxvi.

Kelly, J. B. "The Future in Arabia." *International Affairs* 42, no. 4 (October 1966):619-40.

————. "Sovereignty and Jurisdiction in Eastern Arabia." *International Affairs* 34, no. 1 (January 1958):16-24.

Keohane, Robert O. "The Big Influence of Small Allies." *Foreign Policy*, no. 2 (Spring 1971), pp. 161-82.

Khadduri, M. "Iran's Claim to the Sovereignty of Bahrain." *American Journal of International Law*, no. 45 (1951), Supplements, pp. 631-47.

Kimche, Jon. "Selling Out the Kurds." *New Republic*, 19 April 1975, pp. 19-21.

Klare, M. T. "Hoist with Our Own Pahlavi." *Nation* 222 (31 January 1976): 110-14.

Kraar, L. "The Shah Drives to Build a New Persian Empire." *Fortune*, October 1974, pp. 145-49 ff.

Kudryavtsev, V. "Abu Dhabi Enters the 20th Century." *New Times*, no. 51 (December 1972), pp. 30-31.

"Kuwait: A Special Report." *Middle East Economic Digest* 17, no. 13 (30 March 1973):353-68.

"Kuwait Continues to Expand Aid Operations." *Middle East Economic Digest* 17, no. 16 (20 April 1973):439-43.

Lake, Michael. "New Direction in Oman." *Venture* 22, no. 9 (October

1970):20-24.

Landen, R. G. "Gulf States." In Abid al-Marayati, ed., *The Middle East: Its Governments and Politics*, pp. 295-316. Belmont, Calif.: Duxbury Press, 1972.

—————. "State of Kuwait." In Abid al-Marayati, ed., *The Middle East: Its Governments and Politics*, pp. 275-94. Belmont, Calif.: Duxbury Press, 1972.

Lanterpacht, E. "River Boundaries: Legal Aspects of the Shatt al Arab Frontier." *International and Comparative Law Quarterly*, no. 9 (1960), pp. 208-36.

Lateef, Abdul. "Bahrain: Emerging Gulf State." *Pakistan Horizon* 26, no. 1 (1973):10-15.

—————. "A Security Pact in the Gulf?" *Middle East International*, no. 55 (January 1976), pp. 21-22.

Law, John. "The Persian Gulf: U.S. Role in a Struggle Over Oil." *U.S. News and World Report* 74 (21 May 1973):90-94.

Ledger, David. "Gulf Union." *Middle East International*, no. 9 (December 1971), pp. 6-7.

Lee, C. "Soviet and Chinese Interest in Southern Arabia." *Mizan* 13, no. 1 (August 1971):35-47.

Liebesny, Herbert. "Administration and Legal Development in Arabia: The Persian Gulf Principalities." *Middle East Journal* 10, no. 1 (Winter 1956): 33-42.

—————. "International Relations of Arabia: The Dependent Areas." *Middle East Journal* 1, no. 2 (April 1947):148-68.

Lindt, A. R. "Politics in the Persian Gulf." *Royal Central Asian Society Journal* 26, pt. 4 (October 1939):619-33.

Long, David. "Kingdom of Saudi Arabia." In Abid al-Marayeti, ed., *The Middle East: Its Governments and Politics*, pp. 255-74. Belmont, Calif.: Duxbury Press, 1972.

—————. "The Politics of OPEC." Paper delivered to the Council on Foreign Relations, New York, 22 April 1975.

—————. "U.S. Strategic Interests in the Persian Gulf: Problems and Policy Analysis." Paper delivered to the Second Annual National Security Affairs Conference, National War College, Fort McNair, Washington, D.C., 14-15 July 1975.

—————. "United States Policy toward the Persian Gulf." *Current History* 68, no. 402 (February 1975):69-73 ff.

Luce, Sir William. "Britain in the Persian Gulf." *Round Table*, no. 227 (July 1967), pp. 277-83.

—————. "A Naval Force for the Gulf: Balancing Inevitable Russian Penetration." *Round Table*, no. 236 (October 1969), pp. 347-56.

Magnus, Ralph. "Middle East Oil." *Current History* 68, no. 402 (February 1975):49-53 ff.

—————. "Middle East Oil and the OPEC Nations." *Current History* 70, no. 412 (January 1976):22-26 ff.

El Mallakh, R. "Abu Dhabi: The Challenge of Affluence." *Middle East Journal* 24, no. 2 (1970):135-46.

—————. "Economic Requirements for Development, Oman." *Middle East*

Journal 26, no. 4 (1972):415-28.

———. "Kuwait's Economic Development and Her Foreign Aid Programmes." *World Today* 22, no. 1 (January 1966):13-22.

Malone, Joseph J. "America and the Arabian Peninsula: The First Two Hundred Years." *Middle East Journal* 30, no. 3 (1976):406-24.

———. "The Arabian Peninsula." In Joseph J. Malone, ed., *The Arab Lands of Western Asia*, pp. 211-45. Englewood Cliffs, N.J.: Prentice-Hall, 1973.

Mangold, Peter. "Force and Middle East Oil: The Post-War Record." *Round Table*, no. 261 (January 1976), pp. 93-101.

Mansfield, Peter. "Oman Emerges." *Middle East International*, no. 19 (January 1973), pp. 12-14.

al-Marayati, Abid. "The Problem of Oman." *Foreign Affairs Reports* (New Delhi) 15, no. 8 (August 1966):99-109.

———. "Republic of Iraq." In Abid al-Marayata, ed., *The Middle East: Its Government and Politics*, pp. 169-89. Belmont, Calif.: Duxbury Press, 1972.

Marbo, R., and Monroe, E. "Arab Wealth from Oil: Problems of Its Investment." *International Affairs* 50, no. 1 (January 1974): 15-27.

Melamid, Alexander. "Oil and the Evolution of Boundaries in Eastern Arabia." *Geographical Review* 44, no. 2 (April 1954):295-96.

———. "Political Geography of Trucial Oman and Qatar." *Geographical Review* 43, no. 2 (April 1953):194-206.

Middle East Institute. "The United States and the Middle East: Changing Relationships." Proceedings of the 29th Annual Conference of the Middle East Institute, Washington, D.C., 3-4 October 1975.

Mozafari, M. "Les nouvelles dimensions de la politique étrangère de l'iran." *Politique Etrangère*, no. 2 (1975), pp. 141-59.

Mullin, Dennis. "Behind Shah's Quest to Restore Glories of Persian Empire." *U.S. News and World Report* 80 (22 March 1976):55-58.

———. "Iraq Turns Sour on Russia." *U.S. News and World Report* 79 (25 August 1975):53-55.

Nath, V. "Economic Development and Regional Cooperation: Kuwait." *Economic Development and Cultural Change* 20, no. 2 (January 1972):342-49.

"Oil-for-Weapons Barter Spurned." *Aviation Week*, 17 May 1976, p. 14.

"Oman: A Special Report." *Middle East Economic Digest* 17, no. 29 (20 July 1973):818-44.

Owen, R. P. "Bahrain's Widening Horizon." *Middle East International*, no. 41 (November 1974), pp. 30-31.

———. "Developments in the Sultanate of Muscat and Oman." *World Today* 26, no. 9 (September 1970):379-83.

Page, Stephen. "Moscow and the Persian Gulf Countries, 1967-1970." *Mizan* 13, no. 2 (1971):72-88.

Paul, Balfour H. G. "Recent Developments in the Persian Gulf." *Journal of the Royal Central Asian Society* 56 (1969):12-19.

Pigasse, J. P. "Geopolitique des petroles et strategie des grandes puissances dans le golfe persique." *Strategie*, no. 19 (1969), pp. 47-91.

"Policeman of the Persian Gulf." *Time*, 6 August 1973, pp. 30-31.

"The Power of Defense [in Abu Dhabi]: Nucleus for the Federation Army and Support for Arabism and Islam" (in Arabic). *al-Ittihad* (Abu Dhabi), 6 August 1970, pp. 45-52.

Prager, Karsten. "The Shah: Thoughts of a Royal Decision Maker." *Time,* 4 November 1974, pp. 34-38.

Price, D. L. "Building Bridges in the Gulf." *Middle East International,* no. 59 (May 1976), pp. 24-25.

Ramazani, Rouhollah K. "Emerging Patterns of Regional Relations in Iranian Foreign Policy." *Orbis* 18, no. 4 (Winter 1975):1043-069.

————. "Iran and the United States: An Experiment in Enduring Friendship." *Middle East Journal* 30, no. 3 (1976):322-34.

————. "Iran's Changing Foreign Policy: A Preliminary Discussion." *Middle East Journal* 24, no. 3 (Summer 1970):421-37.

————. "Iran's Search for Regional Cooperation." *Middle East Journal* 30, no. 2 (1976):173-86.

————. "The Settlement of the Bahrain Question." *Indian Journal of International Law* 12, no. 1 (January 1972):1-14.

Reich, Bernard. "United States Policy in the Middle East." *Current History* 70, no. 412 (January 1976):1-4 ff.

Rentz, George. "Saudi Arabia: The Islamic Island." *Journal of International Affairs* 19, no. 1 (1965):77-86.

"Resolution of the Bahrain Dispute." *American Journal of International Law* 65, no. 3 (July 1971):560-63.

Rifaat, Wahid. "Study on the Union of Arabian Gulf Amirates" (in Arabic). *Revue égyptienne de droit international* 26 (1970):1-11.

Rodolfo, Claudine. "Le Golfe persique: Situation actuelle et perspectives d'avenir." *Politique Etrangère* 34, nos. 5-6 (1969):631-66.

Rondot, Pierre. "L'Iran face à l'arabisme sur le Golfe Persique." *Revue de defense national* 24 (June-July 1968):1047-061.

El-Rufaie, A. A. "The Kuwait Development Fund: Arab Bank for Arabs." *Mid East* 9, no. 6 (1969):35-40.

Rumney, LTC Mason. "The View from Iran." *Military Review* 52, no. 1 (January 1972):68-77.

Ruszkiewicz, Maj. John. "The Power Vacuum in the Persian Gulf." *Military Review* 53, no. 10 (October 1973):84-92.

Said, Rosemari. "The 1938 Reform Movement in Dubai." *al-Abhath* 23, nos. 1-4 (December 1970):247-318.

"Saudi Arabia: Next in Line for Revolution." *Atlas* 19, no. 9 (September 1970): 30-34.

"Saudi Arabia: What Happens after Faisal?" *Foreign Report,* no. 1225 (2 December 1971), pp. 4-5.

Sayigh, Yusif. "Problems and Prospects of Development in the Arabian Peninsula." *International Journal of Middle East Studies* 2, no. 1 (1971):40-58.

Schmidt, Dana Adams. "A Larger Role for Three Persian Gulf Rulers." *New York Times,* 1 October 1972, p. 120.

_____. "The Persian Gulf—Profitable and Strategic." *Near East Report* 16, no. 2 (1972):6-8.

Schulz, Ann T. "A Leadership Role for Iran in the Persian Gulf?" *Current History* 62, no. 365 (January 1972):25-30 ff.

_____. "United States Policy in the Middle East." *Current History* 68, no. 402 (February 1975):54-57 ff.

Searby, Daniel M. "Doing Business in the Mideast: The Game Is Rigged." *Harvard Business Review*, no. 54 (January-February 1976), pp. 56-64.

"Secretary Kissinger Attends Session of U.S.-Iran Joint Commission . . ." *Department of State Bulletin* 75, no. 1941 (6 September 1976):305-14.

"Shaikhdoms of the Persian Gulf." *Petroleum Press Service* 28 (August 1961): 294-97.

Sheehan, E.R.F. "Unradical Sheiks Who Shake the World." *New York Times Magazine*, 24 March 1974, pp. 13-16 ff.

Shwadran, B. "Middle East Oil." *Current History* 66, no. 390 (February 1974): 79-82.

Sisco, J. J. "Department Discusses the Arab-Israeli Conflict and the Arabian Peninsula–Persian Gulf Area." *Department of State Bulletin* 69, no. 1775 (2 July 1973):29-33.

_____. "U.S. Policy in the Area of the Persian Gulf and Arabian Peninsula." *Department of State Bulletin* 73, no. 1881 (14 July 1975):73-81.

_____. "United States Policy toward the Persian Gulf Region." *Department of State Bulletin* 67, no. 1731 (28 August 1972):241-45.

Smart, I. "Future Political Patterns in the Middle East." *World Today* 32, no. 7 (July 1976):243-50.

Smolansky, O. M. "Moscow and the Persian Gulf: An Analysis of Soviet Ambitions and Potential." *Orbis* 14, no. 1 (Spring 1970):92-108.

_____. "Soviet Policy in the Middle East." *Current History* 65, no. 386 (October 1973):155-57 ff.

Sober, Sidney. "Department Discusses Military Exports to Kuwait and Other Persian Gulf Nations." *Department of State Bulletin* 73, no. 1899 (17 November 1975):702-07.

Spiers, R. I. "U.S. National Security Policy and the Indian Ocean Area." *Department of State Bulletin* 65, no. 1678 (23 August 1971):199-203.

Standish, J. F. "British Maritime Policy in the Persian Gulf." *Middle East Studies* 3, no. 4 (1967):324-54.

_____. "Pursuit of Peace in the Persian Gulf." *World Affairs* 132, no. 3 (December 1969):234-43.

Stevens, W. "L'Iran et Le Monde arabe." *Chronique de politique étrangère* 20, no. 2 (1967):119-31.

Sullivan, Robert R. "The Architecture of Western Security in the Persian Gulf." *Orbis* 14, no. 1 (Spring 1970):71-91.

Sweet, Louise. "Pirates or Politics?" *Ethnohistory* 11, no. 3 (1972):262-80.

Szulc, Tad. "Battle over the Persian Gulf: Oil and Arms." *New Republic*, 23 June 1973, pp. 21-23.

Taggiasco, R. J. "Recession's Impact on Iran: Interview with Shah Mohammad Reza Pahlavi." *Business Week,* 17 November 1975, pp. 56-57.

"A Talk with the Shah of Iran." *Time,* 1 April 1974, p. 41.

Tarabulski, F. "Rebellion in Dhofar." *MERIP Reports* 1, no. 3 (1972):1, 3ff.

Tarokh, A. "Iran and the Arab States." *New Outlook* 9, no. 1 (1966):23-28.

"Technical Education and Training in the Arabian Gulf States." *Labor Developments Abroad* 16, no. 3 (March 1971):1-8.

"Tensions in the Gulf." *Petroleum Press Service* 35, no. 3 (March 1968):83-87.

Teplinsky, B. "The Persian Gulf in Imperialist Plans." *New Times,* no. 36 (September 1972), pp. 23-24.

Thoman, Roy. "Iraq and the Persian Gulf Region." *Current History* 64, no. 333 (January 1973):21-25 ff.

———. "The Persian Gulf Region." *Current History* 60, no. 353 (January 1971):38-45 ff.

Toole, W. D. "Soviet Interest in Arabia." *Military Review* 48, no. 5 (May 1968): 91-97.

"The Trucial States Development Office." *Orient* (Hamburg) 11, nos. 3-4 (1970): 75-81.

"The Trucial States—Nations in Building." *Oil Progress* 21, no. 4 (1971):2-9.

"The United Arab Emirates: A Special Report." *Middle East Economic Digest* 17, no. 26 (29 June 1973):i-xxvii.

"U.S. Arms Sales Abroad." *Department of State Bulletin* 75, no. 1943 (20 September 1976):371-72.

"The U.S.S.R. and the Persian Gulf." *Mizan* 10, no. 1 (January-February 1968): 51-57.

Vasilyev, Alexei. "Persian Gulf: Where Epochs Meet." *New Times,* no. 4 (January 1974), pp. 26-29.

Vianney, J. J. "Aspects of Hadramaut and the Trucial States." *Levante* 14, nos. 3-4 (1967):28-36.

Viennot, Jean-Cyrille. "Arabistan—a Second Palestine." *Flash,* no. 6 (January 1972), pp. 9-12.

Wall, Michael. "Saudi Arabia: Riches and Responsibility." *Middle East International,* no. 28 (October 1973), pp. 6-9.

Watt, D. C. "The Arabs, the Heath Government and the Future of the Gulf." *New Middle East,* no. 30 (March 1971), pp. 25-27.

———. "Can the Union of Arab Emirates Survive?" *World Today* 27, no. 4 (April 1971):144-47.

———. "The Decision to Withdraw from the Gulf." *Political Quarterly* 39, no. 3 (July-September 1968):310-20.

———. "The Persian Gulf: Cradle of Conflict?" *Problems of Communism* 21, no. 3 (May-June 1972):32-40.

Weinbaum, M. G. "Iran Finds a Party System: The Institutionalization of Iran Novin." *Middle East Journal* 27, no. 4 (1973):439-55.

———. "Iran and Israel: The Discreet Entente." *Orbis* 18, no. 4 (Winter 1975): 1070-087.

Weiss, Seymour. "U.S. Interests and Activities in the Indian Ocean Area."

Department of State Bulletin 70, no. 1815 (8 April 1974):371-75.

Wilkinson, John C. "The Oman Question: The Background to the Political Geography of South East Arabia." *Geographical Journal* 137, pt. 3 (September 1971):361-71.

"Will the Indian Ocean Become a Soviet Pond?" *Atlas* 19, no. 11 (November 1970):20-21.

Wissa-Wassef, C. "L'arabie seoudite et le conflit israelo-arabe du mois d'octobre 1973." *Politique Etrangère*, no. 2 (1974), pp. 185-98.

Wright, D. "The Changed Balance of Power in the Persian Gulf." *Asian Affairs* 60, pt. 3 (October 1973):255-62.

Yakubov, N. "The Soviet Union and the Arab East." *International Affairs* (Moscow), no. 9 (September 1974), pp. 26-36.

Yodfat, Aryeh. "Iraq: Russia's Other Middle East Pasture." *New Middle East,* no. 38 (November 1971), pp. 26-29.

Zabih, Sepehr. "Iran's International Posture: DeFacto Nonalignment within a Pro-Western Alliance." *Middle East Journal* 24, no. 4 (Autumn 1970):302-18.

———. "Iran Today." *Current History* 66, no. 390 (February 1974):66-69.

Index